Restoring the Laity's Balance to an Unsteady Church

Balancing Tradition with Traditions

By

John Vincent Broadbent

ISBN: 0-7596-9396-X (e-book)
ISBN: 0-7596-9397-8 (Paperback)
ISBN: 1-4033-4013-7 (Hard Cover)

This book is printed on acid-free paper.

1stBooks – rev. 10/11/03

"History was no longer the domain of scholars, ferreting in dusty libraries. It was relived every day, in fiction or in documentary form on television screens. It was invoked in panel discussions as a paradigm of the present, a warning for the future. It stirred in the dark pools of tribal memory, raising old ghosts and the stink of ancient battlefields.

It was no longer possible to rewrite history - the facts showed through the overwritten fiction. It was not possible to plaster over the graffiti scratched into ancient stone. The plaster flaked off or fell away under the tapping hammers of the archaeologists."

Morris West "Lazarus"

CONTENTS

FORWARD

In 1859 John Henry Newman provoked a storm in the catholic theological world with his article 'Consulting the Faithful on matters of Doctrine.' Newman was drawing on his expert knowledge of the early Church and theology to point out that the laity had as of right the duty to be consulted on theological matters that the various Councils were determining. Hence his startling conclusion for the age in which he wrote: 'The Nicene Dogma (Jesus is Divine) was maintained during the greater part of the fourth century:

1) not by the unswerving firmness of the Holy See, Councils or bishops, but
2) by the 'consensus fidelium' (consent of the Faithful).' (1)

By 'consulting the Faithful', Newman does not mean an intricate survey has to be taken before any definition necessarily, although it could be, but 'their belief, is sought for, as a testimony to that apostolical tradition, on which alone any doctrine can be defined'. (2)

During Newman's lifetime and in the century or so after his death, his sound scholarship and intuitions have been confirmed by extensive historical research particularly of the first and second centuries. Also Dollinger's criticism of Newman in chapter nine of projecting the Church of the 3rd & 4th centuries onto the first and second centuries has been shown to be true which lead us to a more nuanced view of episcopacy and laity. The tapping and probing hammers of the historians, archaeologists and scripture scholars have revealed graffiti that even Newman never knew. Nonetheless his basic conviction of the role of the laity in the Church has been validated many times over.

During the Second Vatican Council (1962–65) many remarked how the spirit of Newman hovered over that assembly. It was particularly in the sections on the laity that his contribution among others seemed to bear fruit. When the bishops assembled at Vatican II they had waded through seventy-two preparatory documents. They sent back seventy-one for inserting changes or total rewriting. One of those sent back was the one on Church which had delineated the Church as a pyramid with the pope at the head, then the bishops, the priests, religious and finally the laity. The document the bishops finally passed redesigned the document putting first the people

vii

of God, all the members of the Church of which all Catholics are members be they pope or peasant. We are all members, brothers and sisters by our baptism. This whole chapter was put before those on the pope, bishops and so on showing the early christian's idea of a community sharing authority with the Apostolic Authority.

The bishops deliberately reasserted the ancient order – the Church is the whole Body of Christ of which we are all members and those who have Apostolic Authority are the servants of all.

Other great documents of the Council such as the Church in the Modern World, the Laity and Revelation amplify much of the thought on the laity who are collaborators with the bishops and priests in spreading the Good News, who take the Gospel to their homes and workplaces and who are to be consulted. It is a step forward from Catholic Action, that valuable movement that sprang up in the Church before Vatican II spearheaded by people like Cardijn in which the laity were invited to co-operate with the hierarchy in the Church's apostolate. Now the Vatican II document veered more to saying it was their right to do these things. Yet it still fell short of stressing their right to help in governing of the Church, in choosing its leaders and giving advice on theological and moral matters in which celibate clergy particularly may lack expertise.

Since Vatican II the distinct emphasis of documents from Rome has been, 'we will run the Church and help to form you in your rightful mission to the world. You shouldn't be interfering in structures and telling us what the belief system or structures of the Church should be. With the growth of a more restricted idea of what Magisterium is in the last two centuries, it is our prerogative to judge, teach and alter structures.' No Catholic would ever dispute that it is the <u>ultimate</u> right of the pope and those in holy orders to pass final judgement on matters of belief. But there should be a free, open, informed and gradual process on the way to reaching those ultimate decisions and so make them as rich as they possibly can be and to prevent there being a narrow and often condemnatory document.

Curiously enough one of the best passages in emphasising the role and I would suggest the rights of the laity comes not in the aforementioned documents of Vatican II but in its document on Bishops when it admonishes: 'In exercising this pastoral care he (the bishop) should preserve for his faithful the share <u>proper to them in Church affairs</u>; he should also recognize their duty and <u>right</u> to collaborate actively in the building up of the Mystical Body of Christ." (3) Taken in the context of the documents after Vatican II however these words can seem to be a little hollow. The general thrust of Vatican II was for change and a return to the less structured systems of the early Church. Its documents however to avoid the open hostilities of Vatican I incorporated ideas of the more conservative minority bishops when they did not go against the majority decision. The ambivalence comes through in spelling out what the layman or laywomen's rights in building up the Church and being properly consulted could be or should be. Neither the official catechism nor recent documents spell out what rights belong to the laity within the Church. Consultation can be ineffective when it is done without real listening from the consulter or without the final result showing some important input from the consulted. Unfortunately in many cases as in other authoritarian regimes of history and the present, the consulters ask only those who will give predictable answers or make decisions as the result of a 'guided' process.

The protestant commentating on the document of the laity in Abbott's Documents of Vatican II was Mrs Theodore Wedel and back in 1965 she wrote:"A Protestant misses here a stronger emphasis on a share in the actual government of the Church. This may be an area where the Catholic Church will have to gradually make some changes. There is, however, a warm recognition of the fact that lay people have many skills which can be useful within the life of the Church." (4) Skills not rights or choices.

Twenty years later, there seemed to be very little substantial change when in the introduction of Concilium's The Teaching Authority of the Believers, J. B. Metz and E. Schillebeeckx drew attention to the 2nd Vatican Council documents in this area of lay rights and authority within the Church using in their introduction Karl Rahner's words 'a beginning of a beginning' as a 'stimulus to growth.' Things do not seem to have changed substantially since then. Metz and Schillebeeckx conclude their introduction by declaring: 'let us say that to discern and acknowledge the teaching authority of the faithful discussed here is an important step towards the Church's revitalisation as envisaged by the Council, and this in itself an indispensable and a decisive step forward in the growth to Christian Unity'. (5)

A lot of the present unrest in the Church seems to arise from withholding the rights of the laity and a yawning chasm growing between the Ultimate Authority and many believers, especially in the areas of contraception, homosexuality, ordination of women, divorce because they understand and feel they have no say in the destiny of the Church they love and find only shut doors when they ask to be heard.

It is the contention of this book that the laity were an important and necessary part of the shared authority in the Church, in the first few centuries. Even as that function and service were eroded in the next fifteen hundred years, when the hierarchical Church badly foundered as in 1046 and 1415 the laity rescued it. The unsteady nature of todays Church needs the same restoration and intervention.

My gratitude goes out to a number of people who have helped me in the production of this book especially to Chris Ruthe, Father Pat McCullough, Marie and Terry Stock, Laurel and Colin Chiles, Mary Thomas, Michelle McIntyre, Father Paul Chandler, and Rom Brady. Without their help and that of First Books, it would be a much poorer production.

I would like to say at the beginning of this book, I write it because I love the Church and want to see it return to its roots thereby increasing its efficiency and servanthood. I do not write the book to destroy the Church but remind it again of its origins and mission.

John Broadbent.

---

(1) Newman, J.H. <u>On Consulting the Faithful on Matters of Doctrine</u> (Ed. J. Coulson). p. 77
(2) Op Cit pp. 54-55
(3) Vatican II on <u>Bishops</u> 16(e) Abbott p. 409
(4) Abbott, W. S.J. (Ed) <u>The Documents of Vatican II</u>, London. Geoffrey Chapman. p. 524
(5) Concilium <u>The Teaching Authority of Believers.</u> p. xi

CHAPTER ONE

The apparent impasse in contemporary Catholicism

Ferment can often mean life in any given body. The creative juices flow. New life is engendered. In the Catholic Church at the moment, such life is going on. Even though in the Western parts of the world there is a marked falling off in numbers attending regular church services, there are movements, debates and discussions that show life and vigour. In South America much strengthening of the Church is occurring especially with base communities despite fundamentalist protestant missionaries' successes. In Africa and Asia there is marked expansion. But a lot of the ferment has reached an impasse that is causing frustration, and in some cases defecting or lapsing, as many feel their situations are not being considered fairly or listened to.

Why do I use the term impasse? Mainly because those in power in the Church do not seem to want to acknowledge this ferment or alternatively blame it on to the materialism and selfishness of the world outside the Church. They place locked doors in front of the solutions so many sincere catholics sense as the answers. Their argument is the doors are locked because behind them is the Tradition which is unalterable and "they" are powerless to change it. Many do not agree that the Tradition is as unalterable as the powerful Authority interprets it; but as they are the only authoritative interpreters of this Tradition from which there is no appeal the impasse grows greater.

What are some of these points of ferment that are creating this impasse?

The first is the polarization of the Church between what one would call the right and left wings. The right wing, like right wings everywhere holds a great reverence for the past and how things were done then. (Actually as we shall see it is to the more immediate past not the actual beginnings). It sees any alteration in the status quo as a betrayal of the glories of the previous generations and asserts it is heresy to suggest those in the past could have got it wrong. In the catholic case, it professes an unswerving loyalty to the pope and his departments in Rome, because they believe even some bishops have got it wrong and are not loyal enough to the pope. The left wing sees the Church must adapt to the times without departing from the Gospel

1

teachings of Jesus: in fact, as they reason, because the teachings of Jesus have been watered down by the past. They now need to be proclaimed without the baggage of centuries blinding the eyes of the searcher and being retained solely for the sake of the past generations that either assembled the baggage or remembered it. With the changing attitude in the past century or so towards women, sex and authoritarianism they call for a new look at older attitudes to these. Secular society has changed and often for the better by its change of attitude that indirectly has changed the Church as "signs of the times" mentioned in Vatican II.

Now is the time to go further; but officialdom is closing doors using Tradition and Authority as reasons.

The poles could be producing a healthy tension if such vituperation, lack of charity and mindless zealotry did not accompany them. Then the extreme right wing thinks Tradition exists in a vacuum needing few scholarly criticisms just as the extreme left can often claim modernity when it is no more than a new disguise for the old fashioned vices and habitual evils that have plagued humans from their beginning on earth. In between, the majority of catholics are caught in the middle and are confused.

The second point is the kind of bishops often appointed by Rome are not the leaders the catholic people wish or need at the present time. The catholic people, priests and religious do not have any real say in who are selected as bishops. The result is often a "safe" man who will obey the central authority not a creative leader. There are many exceptions and some, like Archbishop Romero, do change after selection. The autocratic system does need modification. Perhaps nothing has proved this more than the recent shocks in the catholic world of sexual abuse by some clergy and religious. More disturbing for many catholics have been episcopal cover-ups, lack of understanding of addictive paedophilia, apparent lack of compassion for victims whose lives could well have been ruined for the sake of institutional silence as well as the huge economic drain on the Church when challenged. It has brought home to catholics that the same cover-ups, which occur in any autocracy and bureaucracy, whether secular or ecclesiastical, lead to a refusal to admit to mistakes in order to prove the authoritative power is always right. In contrast, Jesus says let your answer be "yes" for "yes" and "no" for "no", the same Jesus who showed such profound compassion for children.

The whole situation makes catholics ask the question:- "Does Christ's body have to be manifested in this particular autocratic form or should I have some say in how it is run and how my resources which I gift are used?" The dissatisfaction with officials rumbles on underneath an often confused exterior.

2

The third point lies in the decreasing credibility of the Church among its members. I have used the adjective "unsteady" about the Church in this book's title. Many movements and the present general malaise have indicated this. One of the best summaries is given by Owen O'Sullivan, a capuchin missionary and historian, in his book entitled "The Silent Schism". He first of all surveys the general return to a centralized, conservative Church approach in the wake of a decade or so after Vatican II which affects the bishops who are squeezed between loyalty to the Pope and their local pastoral concerns, with priests and religious silent not out of acquiescence but a "feeling that there is no point in speaking because the Vatican "listens" with cotton wool in its ears". (1)

O'Sullivan then goes on to say:- "Among the lay men and women of the Church there is a widespread sense of directionless drift. It is not simply that they think they are not being listened to; they know it. Appeals to stay with the Church and change it from within ring hollow; at best, they are meaningless, because the power to make changes resides at the top, and there is little indication that those who hold power have any intention of sharing it: at worst, they mock people by inviting them to undertake the role of Sisyphus, the legendary figure of Greek mythology sentenced by the gods to push a rock up a hill, only for it to slip from his grasp as he reached the summit and roll all the way down to the valley below.

The young, in more than a few countries, have simply left the Church and gone elsewhere: drawn off by a popular culture without substance or content: or to the sects: or to simply abandoning formal links with any christian church, while, at the same time, often retaining a residual sense of loyalty to the christian faith itself in an undefined, inarticulate way, so that there is still a germ of hope." (2)

The fourth point is that if the credibility of the Church is suffering among its followers, its example continues to be eroded among christians and others outside the Church. O'Sullivan again summarizes it well when he says:- "At a wider level, the image of the Church vis-à-vis the world has changed. In the years after Vatican II it was seen as being open to the world, ready to engage in dialogue with it, prepared to see the world as a potential partner for the sake of humanity. Now it is seen as having reverted to its true reactionary type, back in the trenches slinging grenades over the top to its adversaries.

Within the Church, truth has been replaced by fear and dialogue by dictation. The path of the pilgrim church over the past twenty-five years or more is littered with the debris of shattered hopes and lost or even squandered opportunities. We have lost a sense of priorities to such an extent that catholic identity, instead of being focused on love of Jesus, centres instead on secondary issues like contraception.

The Church at the end of the second millennium is more polarized, alienated and divided than it has been for a very long time, perhaps since the Reformation." (3)

Much of the apprehension among other christians could be dissipated by the obvious picture of a Church that has a sense of priorities, as O'Sullivan has put it, and one that consults its own members widely as well taking into account well proven contemporary study. Many non-catholic churches have been weakened by a laissez-faire liberalism that seems to cut out all definite teaching and long for a Church that has a definite model respecting its Tradition but open to the "signs of the times".

The fifth point means a different kind of control in an acceptance in reality of Vatican II's teaching on conscience. It of course flatly contradicted much of what had been taught before, especially Gregory XVI's condemnation of freedom of conscience "Mirari Vos" of 1832. Since Vatican II many catholics have watered conscience down to: "What I feel or what I am convinced of" forgetting the Council was talking about an informed conscience – one that has read up about the Church's teaching, got advice from competent people and prayed very much about it. If that has been done then thunderous denunciations of moral acts that some have conscientiously come to accept do little good except alienate. By the Church unravelling her constant Tradition but also by placing priorities on its various teachings it can give guidance to those forming their consciences as to what is the nature and gravity of sin.

The sixth point is a general dissatisfaction with the Church's sexual ethics which seem to be unable to take on board both some of modern psychology's findings and a sharper exegesis of the Bible. Writing at the end of the seventies (a decade or so after Vatican II) Jack Dominian, the noted catholic english psychologist, commented:- "A decade of openness has made the subject of human sexuality much less of a taboo even within the Church......On the one hand, there exists the most revolutionary and promising statement of marriage and the family in the documents of Vatican II, on the other hand there have been two most traditional pronouncements regarding human sexuality, namely Humanae Vitae and the Declaration on Sexual Ethics, which have left most Roman Catholics, particularly the young, puzzled and frustrated. A great number of them are firmly convinced that in many specific areas the Church has simply lost control over this topic...... no one would disagree there is a real crisis" (4)

The seventh point of ferment are gender issues. Rome's recent statements on women are far more positive than in the preceding centuries; but the issues of women's ordination to priesthood and power sharing at top levels are still forbidden to be expressed publicly. The well-known franciscan spiritual writer Richard Rohr, has expressed the male patriarchy that seems to be taken as unchangeable in the Church's hierarchical structure; " 'woman stuff' is the hidden energy behind almost all of the justice issues. The movement towards non-violence and disarmament, the movement against homelessness and refugee problems, the raping of the earth and its resources, sexual and physical abuse, the idolatry of profit and corporation, the rejection of the poor, none of these will move beyond the present impasse until the underlying issues of power, prestige and possessions are exposed for the lie that they are.

Humanity's capacity to disguise its own darkness seems endless. Patriarchal logic is only logic in favour of the system and the status quo – which is proudly, called the 'real world' ". (5)

Many women have left the Church. Many more have stayed in, loyal but dissenting.

These are some of the important points causing ferment in the Church with many people banging their fists against a brick wall. One can go through many practical answers to these points. Most, I fear, are short term. This book has been written to suggest two long-term solutions for beginning to improve the various situations that confront today's Church. One is the restoration of the laity's rights as practiced in the early Church of being properly "consulted" on matters of doctrine and governance as mentioned by Newman in the forward. The second is to implement a teaching of Vatican II, the Hierarchy of Truths, to protect the Tradition from becoming merely a victim of democratic process, lobbying or agitation. Both are needed as I hope will be shown.

In the next few chapters we will see the evidence of the laity's shared authority and rights in the first few centuries and then trace their erosion in the next fifteen hundred years.

(1) O'Sullivan, O. The Silent Schism. Dublin, Gill and MacMillan. 1997. p. 31

(2) Ibid, pp. 31 and 32

(3) Ibid, p. 32

(4) Dominian, J. Proposals for a new sexual ethic. London, Darton, Longman and Todd. 1977. p. 20

(5) Rohr, R. Ed. J. B. Feister. Radical Grace. Cincinnati, St. Anthony Messenger Press. pp. 278-279

CHAPTER TWO

The Tradition and how it began to be passed down

For many catholics and orthodox what has been received as Tradition means a fairly orderly passing down of eternal truths in an institution very much the same in its hierarchical structure as it is today. Monika Hellwig, the distinguished american theologian, puts it well when she says:- "Because most Catholics have assumed a static and unified Church organization, it was also easy to assume that the pattern was more or less set by Christ and should never be changed. But when men study history and suddenly realize that it was all changing all the time, and that it looked very different indeed at some times, they have to ask further questions about what is the divine and necessary pattern of the Church, and what is simply a human attempt to organize life in a Christian community as best meets the need. Whatever falls in the latter category could, of course, be changed again and in the same way, when the needs of the times changed." (1)

That is why I would see an evaluation of the impact recent first and second centuries' studies have made on Church doctrine and polity as important. It is not just a return to the past for the sake of the past - interesting enough as this may be. The evaluation would not exclude the process of development and a deepening discernment of what the original deposit or content from the Gospels and oral tradition contained. That has gone on in the Church's life for centuries. It would not claim necessarily that the first and second centuries were a golden age. They contained their mixture of sinners and saints as all ages have. A close reading of Corinthians and other Pauline letters as those of James and John should soon dispel this myth. But it would claim that those christians who actually heard Jesus or the apostles and implemented these teachings in their lives and writings were closer to the sources of our Tradition, knew Christ and those who knew Christ. I would argue that if you look back at the shared ideas of christian communities underlying the structures, you would find out the minds and intentions of those who knew what Jesus and the apostles taught and thought. This should be interpreted as modern historical and scriptural studies seem to indicate that Jesus and the apostles passed on no fixed office as the varieties of these structures indicate. However, to say that the apostles and early christian communities intended their communities to be structureless would be going too far according to experts. Where this seemed to be tried in the "John" communities of the three epistles, chaos seemed to reign heightened by a fierce individualism as each person thought his or her message was the only authentic one.

If elements of that tradition were lost for centuries or as we now know were gradually discarded in practice for the sake of greater emphases or from threats from outside, elements for instance such as the priesthood of all believers or diversity and pluralism, these same elements may well be worth looking at to see if they have a message for the Church and ecumenism today. If history finds more appropriate structures to suit the political and cultural circumstances of a later age then let us not be bound by them either. If these have been created forgetful of a more ancient past or, even more, based on false information, then a return to the origins helps us rediscover the possibilities for the present.

I still believe that the Church's claim to be "the pillar and ground of truth" does not mean the Church teaches equally well all truths at all times, nor need it mean the Church gives more emphasis to those truths that are more important than others consistently. History, I think, demands that if something important were forgotten, the obligations of truth need to be satisfied, however upsetting, and these important factors be re-evaluated.

The first century A.D. is too complex an area to attempt a full investigation of the findings and slowly built conclusions that scholarly work has pieced together about the beginning and formation of the Tradition. All one can do is to summarize some of the more important of these with their implications. In this task I am trying to use the findings of the more moderate scholars, catholic and protestant.

The first thing to note by the amateur is that except for mainly the fundamentalist christians there is almost universal agreement that the kind of history written in the New Testament, and for that matter the Old, is how the Jews and most ancient people wrote history in their times. How they meant it to be interpreted then becomes of immediate concern. It is not the same as the last few centuries' evolution in the West of scientific history which attempts to report as objectively and factually as possible. Pope Pius XII (1939-1958) instructed well when he said ("Divino Afflante Spiritu" 1943) that history can only be unrolled by finding out first the literary genres (contemporary ways of writing and thinking) of the people. The Gospels particularly seem written to proclaim Jesus as he really is and lead people to learn from and love him. To this, history in the factual and historical Western sense takes second place. Therefore to look for literal interpretation only without taking into consideration the main way first century A.D. jews wrote is often to miss the wood for the trees.

On the other hand to claim this was all made up by the early christians is most untrue. One has to consider how truth is conveyed by myth, an important adjunct to scripture studies.

Even though scientific history as the Western world knows it today is of recent centuries evolution, both catholic and protestant experience prior to the modern world was often to take every story in the Gospel as literally true to the finest detail or to interpret the passage allegorically using the person or events as symbols.

Scripture scholars, divided as it may be on the precise meaning of "Kingdom", show that the Kingdom Jesus came to proclaim is far wider than the Church although, of course, it includes it. The Church should be a living sign of that Kingdom. The further question can be asked, "Did Jesus really found the Church?" Most scripture scholars would say he anticipated the Kingdom coming in a fairly immediate future. Some from that have drawn the conclusion he had no idea of founding a lasting Church. Yet he did call his disciples to follow him and seemingly did so to a degree in his lifetime, although most scholars would say the definite "sending forth" was after the Resurrection.

Did Jesus in his lifetime before the Resurrection envision a separate movement from judaism? Many would say "no". However, the experience of the Resurrection fortified in the apostles' and their followers' minds the necessity of some definite community to continue on his message and its more universal dimension after Pentecost. As one scholar has recently remarked:- "In the eyes of their jewish contemporaries, the earliest believers must have been regarded as jews who lived devout and modest lives but who held some eccentric beliefs." (2)

The expectation of Jesus' imminent return made the early christian community in Jerusalem put off the long-term discussions about accepting non-jews without circumcision, food and other prescriptions. Sooner or later, as time passed and no second coming of Jesus seemed imminent, definite conclusions would be forced on a reluctant christian community.

What comes through to me even before definite structures begin to form or are accepted more universally in the second century A.D. are the three undergirding principles arising from the way the apostles or their immediate disciples acted in the first century – Community (Koinonia [Greek] in Paul) with shared authority, unity but diversity and the Scriptures as a reference point. All three are very important and seem to be the three constants if we are looking for principles that underlay structures. I am not here talking of doctrine which theologians have sorted out and will continue to sort out for many years to come. I am meaning indicators, seminal ideas, undergirding truths which will evolve and were evolving into the structures we begin to find in place by the end of the second century A.D.

1. Community (Koinonia [Greek] in Paul) with shared authority (Apostolic Authority) or as Van Jersel will soon describe it as, "synodal" authority – an authority in which all share but where already a group or one man has a final say but has been put in place not only for his or their leadership qualities but because he or they believe and give witness to the Jesus the Apostles taught. John Mahoney describes such a "Koinonia" well:-

"That work of revealing God's sons and daughters is summed up in the equally Pauline idea of *Koinoni*a, or 'the fellowship of the Holy Spirit' (2 Cor. 13:14), which has come into such prominence in recent years as almost a rediscovery made by the ecumenical movement about the nature of christian community. Entirely absent from the Old Testament as a description of men's relationship with God, or with each other in God's purpose, the concept contains layers of significance for the christian community in its regular appearances in Acts and the Pauline and other Epistles. The term *Koinonia* and its variants denote a passive and active sharing in God's gifts by individuals and among individuals, characteristic of the earliest disciples (Acts 2: 42) and of their material help collected for the Jerusalem church (Rom. 15: 26), as well as of spiritual blessings in which the gentiles 'have come to share' (Rom. 15: 27). It is expressive, further, of a corporate solidarity (Gal. 2: 9), and a solidarity in something received, whether the fellowship of Christ (1 Cor. 1: 9) or of his sufferings (Phil. 3: 10), or of his body and blood in the Eucharist (1 Cor. 10: 16). And not only is it also a fellowship imparted by the Spirit (2 Cor. 13: 14; Phil. 2: 1) to all Christ's followers, but it is a gift of God which finds its climax in fellowship 'with the Father and the Son' (1 John 1: 30) to 'become partakers *(koinonoi* of the divine nature' itself (2 Pet. 1: 4)…The Church lives in *Koinonia* and is a community in which all members, lay or ordained, contribute their gifts to the life of the whole." (3)

There were great differences in how the communities exercised authority, who in the community exercised it and whether they were appointed from outside or, as seems in most cases, chosen within the community. In biblical documents that scripture scholars would date as written before the Fall of Jerusalem (70 A.D.) there seem to be presbyters or elders probably originating from the customary Jewish system in some places. Yet in Pauline communities before that date very seldom (Philippians is an exception) are officiants given names other than "co-workers" or "those who are placed above you". In the Johannine communities still, twenty years after 70 A.D., there was as absolute a democracy as one could find in local christian communities on the basis of each baptized person possessing the Holy Spirit. In the later Pauline communities after the same date the names of official titles such as episkopos (superintendent later bishop) and presbyter (elder) seem interchangeable.

Underlying all these structures expressing how the authority possessed originally by the apostles was exercised in their lifetime stood the belief as the first letter of Peter Chapter 2 Verse 9 (probably 70-80 A.D.) expressed it of "the priesthood of all the Faithful". This was reinforced by another book of Scripture, the Epistle to the Hebrews. In this, Jesus was the only High Priest. All christians participated in that priesthood. The various attempts at interpreting the authority question, given the basic teaching of "all participating in the priesthood of Jesus Christ", undergirded Petrine and later Pauline communities of having elders/bishops just as having no offices seemed an extreme interpretation of the same principle in the Johannine communities.

The late Raymond Brown, the american scripture scholar, did a superb analysis of these Johannine communities in his Community of the Beloved Disciple in which he says the Holy Spirit, the Paraclete "relativized the teaching office of any church 'official'." (4) This Johannine community disappears somewhere in the 2nd century. Brown concludes:- "The lesson that the Pauline churches learned (as we see in the Pastorals) [Titus and Timothy] may also have been learned by some of the author's adherents in other Johannine churches, namely that authoritative presbyter – bishops serving as teachers were a bulwark against those who presented a doctrine which "did not agree with the sound words of our Lord Jesus Christ and the teaching which accords with goodness (1 Tim. 6: 3)." (5)

For those communities (the majority apparently) who had authority structures this authority seemed to be exercised with the understanding of 1 Peter and Hebrews that there was still in place shared authority where each person's part in the priesthood of Jesus Christ was understood and respected. The word "priest" was never used of anyone in the local church except Jesus Christ and then only of bishops in the 3rd century A.D. and presbyters in the 4th.

Who then had the say in the New Testament churches? Who had the binding authority? A noted catholic New Testament scholar, Bas Van Iersel, after examining the exercise of authority particularly in Matthew, Acts of the Apostles, Paul and Titus and Timothy concludes: "With the exception of the pastoral letters, the image presented in the New Testament is unexpectedly and strikingly homogeneous. In matters of doctrine and morals, the assembled community and of individual officials in the community is ultimately responsible for making decisions. There is even possibly a trace in the texts that we have considered of a procedure in which decisions are taken by majority vote in the absence of unanimity. The legitimisation of this authority is based in various ways on a reference back to the origin of Christianity." (6)

In his opinion, Van Iersel observed "that a synodal (i.e. all participating model of the Church is more in accordance with the New Testament and that the pastoral letters (Paul to Timothy and Titus) provide an exception to the rule)." (7)

The earlier Pauline communities get as close as any to a normative community that spells out in great detail what 1 Peter is asserting about each baptized person sharing in the priesthood of Jesus Christ. Paul in 1 Corinthians, and several other places, points out how each baptized person in the community has been given a special gift or charism for the building up of that community. Some are teachers, some prophets, some are administrators and so on. The interaction of these people and gifts constitute the part of the body of Christ in that particular place.

A pioneer catholic american scripture scholar added his summary of authority in the New Testament when he said it "is conceived in a way which must be called democratic rather than absolute. Authority in the Church belongs to the whole Church and not to particular offices. The New Testament is strangely silent both on commissions to command and on exhortations to obedience and submissiveness to Church authority. If exhortations to submissiveness are addressed to anyone in particular, they are addressed to the officers of the Church. Both the idea and the use of authority in the New Testament show no signs of rigorous control of the members by authority. Since the mission of the Church is the responsibility of all the members of the Church, all members have a concern in the exercise of authority." (8)

Over and above all variously named officials there remains this constant factor - the participation of all the priestly people in the running and decision making of the community.

Luis Bermejo, the well known theologian teaching in India, citing a long list of scholars in agreement with him, states:- "Given the flexibility of ministerial functions in the New Testament and the practical equivalence of both the titles, presbyter and episkopos (bishop), the unavoidable conclusion is that the classical threefold and distinct ministry of bishop, presbyter and deacon is an ecclesiastical creation of the later Church rather than a biblical dictum. No monarchical bishop in the modern sense of the expression can be found in the New Testament." (9)

Nevertheless as we shall see there was always in each of these communities, except perhaps the Johannines, a person or persons holding Apostolic Authority or the ultimate authority after wide consultation of a Church of shared authority who can make ultimate decisions.

2. Unity in Diversity. The second undergirding principle of the early christian communities was Unity in Diversity. It arises from the actions and convictions of the first century christians. It occurred first with the dispute between the "hellenists" and the "hebrews" in Acts (Acts chapters 6-15). Scholars are more or less agreed that the "hellenists" were Jews with experience or roots from abroad culturally and linguistically greek / roman. They also assert that their disagreements were not just over bigger or larger portions for their widows (Acts 6). With their exposure to other ways of thought at home, these jews were not so dependent on Temple worship and many of the stricter prescriptions. It would seem that Stephen's martyrdom was as much a part of his interpretation of the teaching of Christ as in dying for Christ himself (Acts 7). Only the "hellenist" not the "hebrew" christians were scattered from Jerusalem after Stephen's death evangelising particularly in Samaria (Acts 8) and even to Phoenicia and Antioch in Syria (Acts 11). The Jerusalem community (the "hebrews") then retained its quite Jewish character and had no reason to scatter. The apostles stayed in Jerusalem (Acts 8, 1)

This brings us to a further aspect of the first century Church carried on into the second century - its pluralism or tolerance within the wider christian community of differing theological viewpoints. There seems to have been no real break between the "hellenist" and "hebrew" christians - tension perhaps - but a tolerance with each other's differing thrusts.

The ultimate explosion of opinion was between the jewish christians and the christians favouring little or no accommodation to mosaic law prescriptions led by Paul and of course pioneered by Stephen. Acts 15 has the meeting of the predominant parties and the practical resolution of the polarized factions in the sense of toleration of diversity with small concessions made to both parties.

If Galatians, as many scripture scholars hold, was written by Paul after the presumed date of this agreement or council in Jerusalem which the apostles attended, there was still much tension in the aftermath. It meant, which the Western Church would probably find hard to live with today, two christian families in one street, one following the jewish prescriptions not against Christ's teaching, the other following none of the prescriptions; but both families worshipping together at the sabbath Eucharist.

These rulings of the agreement or council of Jerusalem became less an issue with the decreasing influence of jewish christians numerically and, after the fall of Jerusalem (70 A.D.) by the jewish religion's gradually alienating the christian sect within it. However, the pluriformity of opinion continued in directions other than the mosaic law and this was reflected in the Jerusalem and Pauline communities.

This diversity too was reflected in the Scriptures of the first century as recent scholarship on the first century has come up with after intensive work done on the Four Gospels. There is serious doubt whether they were written by Matthew, Mark, Luke and John which names were ascribed to them later than when they were first circulated. Many scholars prefer to speak of the Matthean, Marcan, Lucan and Johannine communities from which they arose.

We now know many sayings of Jesus, both oral and written, were circulating from the time of his death and resurrection. It was the genius of the four writers of the inspired Gospels to use or not use many of these "sayings" and weld them together as lives of Jesus. Exhaustive studies have shown them to give four different faces of Christ. Underlying these, one can probe and uncover different theologies and different emphases. If one were to add the probable completion of Luke's Gospel - the Acts of the Apostles - we have some glimpse of the evolving church communities towards the end of the first century A.D. Most scripture scholars and theologians would agree with J. Dunn's research: "Our study has also forced us to recognize a marked degree of diversity within first century Christianity. We can no longer doubt that there are many different expressions of Christianity within the New Testament." (10)

A far greater diversity than one would have imagined even half a century ago emerges. Yet despite that diversity there is an underlying unity. "By accepting the twenty-seven books of the New Testament as her canon (rule) of scripture, the church has chosen to live with diversity and with the tensions which sometimes come in the wake of diversity" comments Cwiekowski, an outstanding american church historian. He adds: "No single understanding of Christ and no one expression of Church fully exhaust the mystery of Christ or the richness and variety of life that come when the spirit dwells among Christ's followers." (11) Conversely, by investigating those books (many of which have been found in this century) which the Church consciously rejected, we can form a judgement of where the parameters of diversity within unity can be drawn and where "History" begins.

Yet always there was a striving for that underlying unity best exemplified by Peter's moderating influence (Acts 15) with James and the "jewish" christians tugging one way and Paul's communities the other. James tries as best he can to accommodate to the non-jews and Paul. Paul tries desperately to prove that unity by bringing the collection from the gentile world to James and the other apostles in Jerusalem. The tension of diversity creates a dynamism of its own in the Church, and when this tension between unity and diversity is removed in the name of order, or even worse uniformity in the name of unity, or disintegrates into division rather than diversity, then the Church has lost an essential part of its inner life which was there from the beginning. As Cwiekowski adds: "When these two poles of unity and diversity are ignored, something very basic to the reality of the Church is neglected and the Church as a whole suffers from such neglect." (12)

Which is where the statement made in this Book's title is pertinent – why have we come in this day and age in the Church to the threshold of saying lay people have rights in the Church but withhold from them the rights actively to participate in the decision making and election of the ministers who exercise the ultimate authority? The Church by not taking into account the good of the informed consultation with its lay members will arrive at a uniform way of thought and acting alright but will suffer an impoverishment of a well informed judgement creating an imbalance and even more importantly a stifling of the Holy Spirit.

3. Scripture, its use in the early Church. Right from the earliest days of christianity when Scripture meant the Old Testament and before the New Testament was written and in various stages of writing, Scripture had its honoured status, as it had among the jews, as the Word of the Lord. It was the backdrop to all belief. Communally and individually, the believer met his or her God and his or her Saviour in the written word. As Tradition developed and the New Testament Canon became generally accepted, many dozens of other writings, some claiming apostolicity, were generally discarded. The veneration for the Word and its importance in determining true belief and Tradition persisted.

Already in a shadowy yet discernible form these three underpinning ideas are indicated in the christian communities founded and taught by the apostles. Even when they are concretized fairly accurately by Irenaeus' building blocks at the end of the second century A.D., the seminal ideas are often wider than the building blocks proposed in the second century. That is why it has always been hard to pin Tradition down to a set of laws or facts. However these three undergirding ideas – Community with shared authority, Unity in diversity, and Scripture – are solidly based at the beginnings of the Church. They need always to be kept in balance. Taken separately each can lead to a danger. The community/synodal principle can by itself lead to division or chaos in any one community (such as when we will see the roman church wrote to the corinthian church) and therefore has to be balanced by the Unity in diversity principle (where diversity can go too far as gnosticism and montanism were to prove) and by the Scriptures which by themselves can be read literally and taken out of context as many aberrations in history show. All three underpinnings are necessary but need to be kept in balance to preserve the integrity of the Tradition passed down.

For christians the weekly Eucharist brought together the Scriptures with a homily explaining them, the mass and the sharing with one's fellow brothers and sisters. They became steeped in the Scriptures and everything became measured against them. Yves Congar O.P. one of the great exponents on the theology of the Church in the twentieth century, commented on the unity of the leader and the whole community expressed in the worship of these early christians: "The celebrant, that is, the president of the assembly and the head of the community, speaks in the name of all, for he is one with all its members. Several letters dating from the subapostolic period are written by the community and by its head, and the two are inseparably linked." (13)

Always for all the Church's teachings and structures, Scriptures would always be the litmus paper and ultimate testing ground of all teaching. Vatican II echoed this teaching in its document Dei Verbum when it said the Church's teaching office "is not above God's word, but serves it." (14)

So the first and early second century A.D. saw the Tradition passed down in various ways and through various channels. Remember again, we are looking at how it was passed down rather than what was passed down. Even though the ways and channels varied there seemed to be, emerging from New Testament scholars and the historians of the early Church, several truths or factors all these early christian communities held in common to express their convictions about institutional form. These I have called the three undergirding principles of the institutional Church. A return to these would help to set the Church on its journey into the twenty first century.

Karl Rahner, one of the great catholic theologians of the last century, says Vatican II (1962-65) began the third stage of the Church's evolution. The first was what was taking place in the first century, a transition from jewish christianity to a gentile Church. The second stage from the second century to our own day has been the successful "europeanization" of the Church beginning with its adaptation to the greco-roman world. The third stage imaged in Vatican II by a world-wide episcopate, vernacular in the liturgy and the Church's opening out positively to the world initiates, says Rahner, an entry into a truly Catholic Church from the europeanization of the second stage. By 2000 A.D. a considerable majority of catholics will come from Latin America, Africa and Asia. (15) Already the diversity in unity they increasingly portray has firm foundations in the first century A.D.

Like the first evolution, the second to the third evolution will be accompanied by its trials and sufferings, its good people battling each other in what each considers the "true" cause. We can never seem to learn from our history and thus go on repeating the same mistakes because we fail to know and understand our true past.

❧ ❧

If the Church existed for the first hundred years with great diversity even among its authority structures, cannot our present ones be thought through again and be patterned on less absolute models?

A recurring mistake particularly within catholic theology is to think that a later development is necessarily an improvement on an earlier one. While this can be the case often it is necessary to examine the reasons why this development took place which can be cultural or historical and may not now suit this present age. The fact that the Church was at its earlier stages more democratic and less uniform can surely be returned to if a future age so wishes. Not that the present writer thinks bishops should be done away with but that different ways of looking at the office can be looked back to and a flexibility may be in order that is not only true to our origins but more importantly more just to those who suffered being left out of an evolution in which by rights they had a part.

1. Hellwig, Monika. What Are The Theologians Saying? Cincinnati, Pflaum/Standard. 1970. p. 27
2. Cwiekowski, F J. The Beginning Of The Church. Mahwah, Paulist Press, 1987. p. 74
3. Mahoney, J. The Making of Moral Theology. Oxford, Clarendon Press. 1989 pp. 343-344
4. Brown, R. The Community of the Beloved Disciple. London, Geoffrey Chapman. 1979. p. 141
5. Ibid, p. 159
6. Van Iersel, B. "Who According To The New Testament Has The Say In The Church?" Concilium, Vol. 148. 1981. p. 15
7. Ibid, p. 1
8. McKenzie, J. Authority in the Church. London, Geoffrey Chapman. 1966 p. 85
9. Bermejo, L. Towards Christian Reunion. Anand, India, Gujarat Sahitja Prakash. 1984. pp. 198-199
10. Dunn, J. Unity And Diversity In The New Testament. London, S.C.M. Press, 1977. p. 372
11. Cwiekowski, F J. The Beginning Of The Church. p. 197
12. Ibid, p. 198
13. Congar, Y. Power and Poverty in the Church. London, Geoffrey Chapman. 1964. p. 42
14. Abbott, W, S.J. (Ed.). The Documents of Vatican II. London, Geoffrey Chapman. 1966. p. 118
15. Rahner, Karl. "Concern for the Church" in Vol. 20, Theological Investigations (transl. Edward Quinn). London, Darton, Longman and Todd. 1981. pp. 78 and 83

CHAPTER THREE

The transition from the First Century to Second Century Church and forces that helped to shape it.

At the turn of the 2nd Century, the same features of unity and diversity, pluriformity of theologies and structures and evolution of authority were present. Recent study of that interesting period has reinforced conviction on that score. My question is still to ask after examining the main evidence from the second century A.D. how can we be so certain about some of the theoretical and structural assumptions we presently have about continuity from the early church?

Karl Rahner, for instance, with the humility that often marks a great mind, saw towards the end of his life that while there must always be an Apostolic Ministry in the Church "the triad which is current among us of bishop, priest and deacon, therefore is regarded as jus divinum (divine law) to the extent that one office in the church which she must have of her very nature has such a hierarchical structure, but it is not assumed that the dividing up of this one office is the only possible way it could be divided" (1). Rahner continues that "...There is no reason to conclude that the Church could not confer sacramentally other kinds or levels of participation in the one pastoral ministry of the Church. In light of the teaching during the Middle Ages about the sacramentality of minor orders, a negative opinion is not even probable. From all this, it follows that it is not a priori certain that Protestant Churches wishing to be united with Rome would have to adopt that division of pastoral ministry which now exists in the Roman Church." (2)

Rahner, aware of the historical studies going on in his time, saw that the church's undisputed doctrines on apostolic succession and the bishops' role to be the sole teachers, rulers and high priests each of his own diocese and collectively of all the churches could be subjected to a degree of modification.

Vatican II, aware of the intricacies of the same problem, took on board recent research. We can see this comparing the Council of Trent's (1545-63) statement on Holy Orders with Vatican II's (1962-1965).

19

Council of Trent

"If anyone says that in the Catholic Church there is not hierarchy by divine ordinance, which consists of bishops, priests and ministers, let that person be anathema."

Vatican II

Ch. 3 Dogm. Const. Church "Thus the divinely instituted ministry as expressed in different degrees by those who even from ancient times have been called bishops, priests and deacons."

Every Roman document chooses its words with extreme care. One can notice the outlined phrases in Vatican II, acknowledging modern scholarship but keeping a link with what Trent had said four centuries before. "Hierarchy" was changed into "ecclesiastical ministry" and it was this ministry which was of divine origin, not the Hierarchy spelt out as bishops, priests and ministers (deacons) and it was the named three-tiered ministry that came from ancient times not necessarily from the very beginning.

Very little christian documentation had come down to us from the second century A.D. unlike the first century during which most or all of the New Testament was written. This was partly because many christian books were destroyed purposely in the roman persecutions, partly because of the fragility of the parchment on which the literature was written, partly because many manuscripts were destroyed in the barbarian invasions in Western Europe, but also partly because the "orthodox" or "catholic" party became the victors and destroyed much of the "heretical" literature. (3) This nowadays induces much caution, because the victors wrote what they understood the "heretics" were saying. Anyone experienced in history knows that need not be the same thing as what the "heretics" were in fact saying. History is often determined by the winners who can suppress the losers' case.

As a high school student or seminarian I studied the literature that existed at the turn of the first and second centuries A.D. As we saw it, the Council of Trent was right, namely, that everything was operating the same then as now. The hierarchy was well in place as we know it and this all seemed confirmed by the existing documents. Recent research has shown this not to be so.

The Literature was divided roughly into four segments. The first was a small number of writings at the beginning of the 2nd century A.D. - Ignatius of Antioch, Clement of Rome, Didache, possibly Barnabas, the Epistles to

20

Titus and Timothy (some scholars put these well into the 2nd century) plus Polycarp.

The second segment are the writings usually dated in the period slightly after the first segment and up to the middle of the 2nd century. Some of these are now non-existent such as Hegessipus and Papias which were known to 4th century writers such as Eusebius, the historian. Hegessipus bolsters up the claim to Apostolic succession of bishops and Papias gathers together a lot of interesting but often muddled facts. The Shepherd of Hermas and the martyrdom of Polycarp are works we still possess.

Hermas particularly has been described "as one of the most obscure and puzzling documents to come down to us from early Christianity".(4) It consists of visions and what Hermas calls mandates and similitudes. Its value lies in the inference that in the roman church (where it was written) the "prophet" could still take his (or her) place with the presbyters (5) and that Rome (as a revised Clement or an Ignatius of Antioch suggested) has still a college of presbyters as its ultimate authority not a bishop. It reflects too the growing rigorism in the early Church and a stricter attitude to reconciliation perhaps because of many defections. (6) It still kept a roman middle way avoiding extremes. There were those who said none of the serious sins (usually classified as murder, apostasy and adultery) could be forgiven after baptism. The other extreme would seem to be those who said sin can be forgiven after baptism time after time if accompanied by sincere sorrow. Hermas allows one forgiveness only of these serious sins after baptism which became the later official Roman position.

The third segment are the apologists or those christians who wrote in defence of christianity to the pagan world the greatest of whom was St Justin. They wrote mainly in the second half of the second century, although some may be dated a little earlier. St Justin, for instance, gave a remarkable description of the Eucharist which parallels closely with today's celebration. They are valuable teachers of doctrine, exemplars of apostolic zeal and had a deep realization of the contemporary pagan world. They often presented christianity as a 'wisdom'.

Their arguments do not affect the general thrust of this book for or against to any great degree. But their enthusiastic and deep seated faith, when they must have been aware of the serious rifts and divisions within christianity, would suggest a common core of teaching, ethical living and worship they knew the converts could join in any part of the Roman Empire. As Robert Wilken adds: "There was not, in the language of the 1980 U.S. Presidential campaign, a single issue test of Christian identity, yet it is apparent that Christians (and others) had a sense of belonging to an identifiable group with distinct bounds." (7)

The fourth segment are many apocryphal writings traceable to the 2nd century. They were books often claiming to be inspired Scripture and using apostles' names but never accepted by all the christian communities (though for a time by some) as inspired. The possible reason for constant rejections was that many were obviously gnostic in tone. The one who processed much of this literature and can be thought of as being the first christian theologian is Irenaeus who lived on into the early third century A.D. He was an Easterner (meaning from the Middle East or Asia) who became bishop of Lyons in France. It was his attempt at synthesising christian teaching and defining the boundaries more exactly against the gnostics and his defence of bishops as going back to the time of the apostles in succession that make his works the "catholic" culmination of 2nd century teaching.

The first segment of writers were obviously then the most important for apologetic purposes. They were certainly used by roman catholics and orthodox to prove the similarities between present church structures and those of the immediate generations after the apostles.

Perhaps the most important of these first segment writings are the seven letters of St Ignatius of Antioch (+ c.109 A.D.) an aged, heroic and saintly bishop taken to Rome to be eaten by the wild beasts on account of his faith. The letters show the existence of one bishop as well as presbyters and deacons as the norm in each local church in his particular area of Asia Minor.

Then there was a letter of Clement I, the fourth pope, bishop of Rome, addressed to the corinthians showing the papacy exercising the papal solicitude for all the churches writing to Corinth to tell the christians there they should accept back the leaders they had apparently driven out even though these had done nothing seriously wrong. Clement apparently ended with a gentle threat of excommunication if the corinthians did not accept back their leaders. Unlike most other documents, he implied that the officials were appointed.

In our apologetics study there was one little disparity that did not quite fit in - the "Didache" or teaching of the twelve apostles. It was known to the early Church, disappeared and was found in a greek orthodox monastery towards the end of the nineteenth century gradually disseminating into the Western (roman catholic and protestant) christianity. This writing gave an account of a fairly simple living Christian community at the convergence of the first and second centuries with its own rules, regulations and aphorisms. The lists of officials did not exactly correspond with the three-tiered system Ignatius of Antioch was writing about; but bishops (several) and deacons were mentioned, although not at the top of the list. The chief officials would seem to have been "Apostles" and "Prophets" who could preside at the Eucharist - not what one would expect with the contemporary Ignatius and

Clement showing one bishop over each community. But then there is always an exception.

* * * * * *

One of the turning points in second century christian scholarship came with the realization that the bishop/presbyter/deacon system was not universally in place by the end of the first century. As we have seen things were far more diverse structurally. Then how could it be that in 90-110 A.D. things were so certain in Clement and Ignatius? Or were they?

As Raymond Brown has remarked: "I Clement has been a storm centre of recent scholarship. The battle over the unimpassioned pages of I Clement" Brown adds "is often a surrogate for a battle between the impassioned descendants of the Reformers and of Trent..." (8) As the storm subsides and a reasonably objective picture begins to form, it was found that Clement's name was only appended to the letter seventy years after it was written. The constant use of the "we" (far too early for the papal royal "we") in the letter brought most scholars to the conclusion that it was a letter from the college of presbyters in Rome writing to the corinthians. No bishop or Clement of Rome by name is mentioned in the text; although curiously enough the corinthians are asked to take back their "leaders". A scholar as moderate as Cwiekowski commenting on the shift of opinion that regards the letter of Clement as a proof of papal primacy says: "Today Catholic scholars regard Rome's solicitude at this time differently: it was a continuation of the apostolic care and guidance once associated with Peter and Paul but exercised in the last decades of the first century through the community most closely identified with the two principal leaders of the early church." (9) The letter also showed with its military and hierarchical comparisons the roman sense of order which was to influence the Church down to our own day.

Another scriptural contribution to the debate was the work accomplished by scholars on the Pauline Epistles to Titus and Timothy. The direct Pauline authorship was generally discounted although they could have been written by Paul's followers, unlike the authentic ones. There was a general consensus that the type of bishops mentioned in these epistles were not the Ignatius of Antioch type bishop, head of the local community, a model for the churches of all the centuries that followed, but a legatine type of bishop appointed by presumably one of the twelve apostles who made and unmade the bishops/leaders in his area. It almost foreshadowed the papal legate of the Middle Ages. Scripture scholars also pointed out the terms "bishop" and "presbyter" were used interchangeably thus proving an evolving situation rather than a fixed one.

When these findings were combined with the strange little "Didache" where bishops were on a lower scale than "Apostles" and "Prophets", although they may well have been the mainstay of the local community, one was forced to the conclusion that ministry (in the sense of official) was still in a fluid state even around 100 A.D., although it was obviously firming up. The Johannine community with its more democratic form of acknowledging everyone's sharing in the authority of the community baptized in the Spirit was also contemporary in the documents I have already mentioned, thus reinforcing this claim of fluidity.

Raymond Brown summarizes much of the argument: "An older generation of Roman Catholic scholars assumed that the single-bishop practice was already in place in Rome in the 90's or earlier; and they opined that, as fourth pope (third from Peter), Clement was exercising the primacy of the bishop of Rome in giving directions to the church of Corinth. The failure of Clement to use his own name or speak personally should have called that theory into question from the start, were there not other decisive evidence against it." (10)

That then makes the seven letters of Ignatius of Antioch the oddity rather than the norm as it was considered half a century ago. Scholars remarked too that six of the letters were addressed to the bishops of each church except the letter to the church of Rome where Ignatius was heading for martyrdom. In this letter to the Romans, unlike the other six, no bishop is mentioned which seemed to confirm the scholarly research on the letter of the church of Rome to the Corinthians (Clement) that Rome was ministered to by a college of presbyters. The situation was still the same at whatever date (some place it as late as 140-150 A.D.) the Shepherd of Hermas written in Rome is placed.

An eminent Catholic patrologist, Robert Joly, has revisited the whole controversy surrounding the authenticity of the letters of Ignatius, especially the dating around 109 A.D. (11). It needs revisiting now because with more and more research Ignatius' churches seem ahead of where other churches were at about 100-110 A.D. When it was thought that Lightfoot, the noted anglican scholar, had proved for all time the authenticity of seven of the supposed Ignatian letters and that they really could have been and were written at the time claimed, it was also assumed Ignatius, Clement, Titus and Timothy were all showing monarchical bishops as we have now. Lightfoot's arguments seemed conclusive to most of the scholarly world. Joly was not so sure.

Joly's arguments have still not been generally accepted by patrologists and theologians; but they have raised enough suspicion to make scholars much more careful about asserting that Ignatius is a witness to the three-tiered system of bishop / presbyter and deacon in a certain area of the

Church at the junction of the two centuries – the only written witness for decades as far as one can tell.

Later generations would say Titus and Timothy's use of "bishop" was meant to be the same as Ignatius' with one bishop for each diocese as we have it now. The name St Clement was attached to the letter from the church of Rome to the church of Corinth showing it was a letter from a bishop (successor of St Peter) whereas it was basically from a college of presbyters. What are we to say to all future "Tradition" based on the assumption that these monarch bishops who alone were successors of the apostles could alone determine the Faith of the Church, especially when they ceased being chosen by the other members of the church and after an historical process had become above their churches rather than "with" their churches? Surely "Tradition", the conservatives would say, supports the bishops' sole right to determine what future teaching would say. But is it so clear?

Given what we have seen, does all "episkope" (Greek = supervision, authority) disappear into the office of episkopos (bishop, superintendent, supervisor) when this office becomes accepted as monarchical by the supposed majority party about 200 A.D.?

Given too, the scriptural testimony and evidence from early christian writings that the democratic elements of all the priestly people having a say in the Church was still there in 200 A.D., and even for several centuries later, to balance out the slow assumption of monarchic rule. At the very least they could control the election of the monarch bishop. But it was not a political matter only, it was a deeply theological one, as already pointed out, that became lost with the over-emphasis on bishops.

The later assumption of "Tradition" that all Apostolic Authority resided in this one man does not do justice to the historical evidence of the time and is based on selected works often taken out of their historical context as we have already seen and are to see again. By the placing of all authority into the hands of a one man ruler it is my contention that checks and balances of the first, second and even later centuries were slowly lost to the detriment of a diversity (not a disunity) needed for fuller Church functioning. When bishops assembled in synod they were there to represent the local church, i.e. its particular teachings and customs in the light of Christ. There has been a slow erosion of that vital concept - often in the name of "Tradition".

The origin of the word the sacred writers of the New Testament used for church ("ekklesia" in greek, the language of the New Testament), although used only twice in Matthew for all the four Gospels but used constantly by Paul in his mission to the non-jews, is important. They would, of course, be influenced greatly by the jewish septuagint writers two centuries earlier who translated the hebrew "kahal" into the greek "ekklesia". "Kahal" had meant the religious assembly of all the Israelites called together and the appropriate translation was considered to be the word the Greeks used in a more democratic age of the city states for the whole assembly of citizens who met together in the city square enjoying full rights. Thus the word implied both the dignity of the members and the legality of the assembly. (12) Too much weight can be placed on the original choice of a word; but the usage and meaning has its own significance when other choices are available.

Yves Congar constantly stresses in his writings that Apostolic Authority was grounded and rooted in all its members. The vital question of who, in matters of dispute, gave the ultimate judgement in this shared Apostolic Authority of the first two centuries was complex as we have seen and solved probably much later than imagined in one particular way. Even when solved it still left several interrelated checks and balances in place. History, while often giving them lip service, was effectively to banish them for over a millennium and then in the Roman Catholic church's case restore them more in theory than in practice.

Robert Joly's thesis of Ignatius being authored fifty years or so after its purported date of 100-110 was notable for the intervention of a highly respected and eminent catholic patrologist in a field which up to then had been fairly polemical often on a catholic basis. Even if Joly's thesis is not sustained, it shows only one section of the churches had monarchic episcopacy in the form we know it today.

Carolyn Osiek sums it up well when she states: "One of the key questions in the church of the late first century was what to rely on as authentic teaching once all the first generation were gone? Of course different communities gave different answers to that question: some shifted their confidence more heavily toward internal sensitivity to the Spirit as exemplified by the Johannine and gnostic communities and radical Paulinism. Some moved toward the radical religions' interpretation of history, emphasizing a coming direct intervention of God (Revelation and apocalyptic Christianity). Still others began to rely on a succession of teachers as a guarantee of legitimacy (Lukan and Matthean groups, the conservative Paulinism of the Pastoral Epistles). It is no accident of history that those communities which developed stable systems of self perpetuation survived and became the dominant form of Christianity." (13)

Raymond Brown, when looking at the complexity of those who exercised ultimate or binding authority in the Church in the first century and a half until all "catholic" churches had one bishop at the turn of the third century, makes an invaluable distinction between "episkope" (valid Apostolic Authority) and "episkopos" (bishop, superintendent, overseer). There was always "episkope" or Apostolic Authority in every christian community, often exercised by differently named officials or even the whole community itself as the Johannine and perhaps even the Matthean communities seem to have been. Episcopal christian churches (catholic, orthodox, anglican mainly) who constitute the majority of all christian churches maintain that the evolution from a variety of officials exercising "episkope" to one "episkopos" presiding over the community was a natural and inevitable one. (14) How inevitable was it, given the fragmented evolution we now know that took place? We wonder even more when shortly we look at some of the lesser known literature of the second century much of which has only come to light in recent decades.

One thing, however, is certain. All these known expressions of searching for an ultimate sanction for authority across the spectrum from the most democratic to the most authoritarian contained the underlying premise that the infusion of the Holy Spirit had to be controlled by some who knew the apostles or had been appointed by them or knew those who had been taught the Jesus the apostles knew and who also by their own holiness, leadership qualities and balance could establish authentically the Jesus the apostles taught. It was what basically theology calls Apostolic Authority. This, of course, was always subject in some fashion to the community's reaction and endorsement. In a world where shared power by a whole community was rare and where power was seen as exclusive to one body of class or opinion or one ruler, it was quite extraordinary to find the democratic elements in many christian communities lasted so long. Apostolic Authority was a multi-faceted expression, but was traceable in all the christian communities.

Conclusion: What therefore emerged by 200 A.D. in the 'catholic' christian communities was not one man rule therefore quashing the community/synodal idea of 'episkope'; but one man rule for reasons we will possibly see tempered still by the community/synodal cluster of ideas. The bishop was still elected by his presbyters and people, taken from their midst, and was supported by them in his decisions while he in his turn consulted them. There are many indications of this (cf Cyprian pp. 58 & 59).

It is when the cluster of ideas begin to disappear around the bishop who is the appraiser of the Tradition for his community and in consultation with his neighbouring bishops for the communities of the region that a big difference sets in. When the ideas of consultation and election begin to fade, when the appraiser (bishop) is appointed by a power outside the community and fails to know the faith of the local church and is often appointed as a reward for loyalty or even venality or royal blood or whatever then you have a distortion of the appraiser and thus a weakening of the appraised doctrine on which he has to decide, because the Holy Spirit's working through an underpinning idea is partially blocked. The thing appraised must of its nature suffer.

Soon the episkopos will absorb all the authority of the episkope as well as many charisms in it that are better separate for the balance of the community. But does he have that full authority without the sharing of charisms so envisioned?

Not only should the selection for episkopos be by the local community because of his leadership qualities but because of his teaching the Jesus the apostles taught (Apostolicity). Apostolicity seemed to have a further arm in that those communities founded by the apostles were to be consulted about the tradition they had received from a most authentic source, an apostle himself. This was especially true of Rome where the apostles Peter and Paul had shed their blood and helped build up the church which was the Capital of the Empire. We see Irenaeus hurrying to get there from Lyons to forestall two of its bishops who on different occasions were going to excommunicate churches that had different customs from them. Was the bishop of Rome important because Rome was the capital of all the Empire or because it contained the Tradition of the Apostles Peter and Paul? Perhaps both. In any case, and experts can be found on either side, Rome became the court of last appeal when decisions were being made about heresy. Earlier the roman church had shown its solicitude for Corinth (p. 22). Now it seemed to exercise more and more its solicitude for all churches.

When episkope developed into episkopos by the end of second century all the Gospel ideas surrounding episkope were channelled into the one office. When all the factors were in balance there was no need to doubt the diminishment and efficacy of the appraiser/leaders powers. When one by one these factors were removed, the diminishment of power is one reason for seeing a defect in the appraiser/leader.

So while "episkope" (one of the undergirding ideas) was always there and "episkopos" is a very valid expression of "episkope" it was so in relation to all the cluster of ideas surrounding "episkope". "Episkopos" or bishop became accepted as the sole expression of "episkope" to the point that when the surrounding cluster of ideas were eroded century by century, the office remained as the sole appraiser/leader. One can validly ask "Is this the only way Tradition could develop". This prompts the further question:- "Does the Holy Spirit work fully when the principle of appraisal/leadership is compromised?"

♣ ♣

What forced the sharing christian communities, many of whom were governed by colleges of presbyters, into one man leadership? Probably by 150 A.D. and certainly by 200 A.D. the monarch bishop was present in every one of the churches.

There are no doubt several reasons; but some of the most convincing seem to be the need to combat heresy, certainly gnosticism, but even to a certain extent montanism.

Recent finds of gnostic literature particularly at Nag-Hammadi in Egypt in 1945-46 have indicated that perhaps gnostic christian communities lived near "catholic" christian ones before "catholic" christian communities began their persecution of gnostics, especially once the Roman Empire began to tolerate christianity from the beginning of the fourth century A.D. (15)

Fascinating glimpses of Jesus emerged - making love to Mary Magdalen, giving secret instructions to his disciples now revealed only in these special "Gospels". Some of the writings speak of the feminine element in the divine, celebrating God as Father and Mother.

As Joseph Tyson remarks: "The practice of writing Gospels was popular well into the third century." (16) We will see why "catholic" christianity came to reject them. The Gospel of James, for instance, has a heavy emphasis on proving to the reader that a celibate life was most pleasing to God. The Gospel of Thomas contains some 114 sayings of Jesus and has distinct gnostic leanings. As do the various Infancy gospels about the miraculous child Jesus. The Gospel of the Ebionites gives great support for the retention of jewish customs within a christian setting.

Allied to the Gospels were many letters, Acts and Apocalypses which were often read in various christian communities. In general many of the letters that were "catholic" in character survived. Those that had gnostic tendencies were the ones later zealously destroyed. Many of these, of which only fragments were extant up until now, were found in whole or in part in the Nag- Hammadi scrolls.

It forced the christian churches before the end of the second century to draw a line especially with such extreme gnostic groups such as "marcionites" and "valentinians" understandably to root out the enemy from within. The need for a strong one man rule to facilitate this became obvious.

Pagels, the english gnostic scholar, summarizes well, I think, the dangers the "catholic/orthodox" christian saw in these many and diverse gnostic thrusts.

"Orthodox Jews and Christians insist that a chasm separates humanity from its creator: God is wholly other. But some of the Gnostics who wrote these gospels contradict this: self-knowledge is knowledge of God; the self and the divine are identical." (17)

Pagels shows the remarkable individualism and existentialism of much of gnostic teaching. "Second" she continues "the 'living Jesus' of these texts speaks of illusion and enlightenment, not of sin and repentance, like the Jesus of the New Testament. Instead of coming to save us from sin, he comes as a guide who opens access to spiritual understanding. But when the

29

disciple attains enlightenment, Jesus no longer serves as his spiritual master: the two have become equal - even identical." (18)

Origen, the brilliant christian thinker of the 3rd century, was to express the catholic/orthodox criticism when he declared that God would not have offered a way of salvation accessible only to an intellectual or spiritual elite.

"Third" concludes Pagels "orthodox Christians believe that Jesus is Lord and Son of God in a unique way: he remains forever distinct from the rest of humanity whom he came to save. Yet the gnostic Gospel of Thomas relates that as soon as Thomas recognizes him, Jesus says to Thomas that they have both received their being from the same source: 'Jesus said, 'I am not your master. Because you have drunk, you have become drunk from the bubbling stream which I have measured out…He who will drink from my mouth will become as I am: I myself shall become he, and the things that are hidden will be revealed to him." (19)

Pagels goes on to discuss the possible connection between eastern religions and gnosticism which could have existed in the second century.

Orthodox/catholic christianity would have seen in the Jesus the gnostics presented as a Jesus it did not believe was the real Christ presented and taught by the apostles. In fact the word "apostolic" was used by early christianity to say precisely that - "are you teaching the same Jesus the apostles taught?" It was the essential component they would have looked for in their leaders/leader that they/he should have taught the same Jesus the apostles taught. Together with this attribute they would look in their presbyters or bishop for the charism of leadership that he or they could oversee all the other charisms and draw them together in a unity. He/they would also know when the Jesus presented was not the Jesus the apostles taught and would know where to draw the line.

Commenting on the situation, Rudolf Schnakenburg adds: "In the struggle against false teaching, however, those who held office and were committed to the sound teaching of the apostolic tradition were bound to gain in significance. This led to a development in which, from the second century onwards, the communities tended more and more to become separated into "shepherds and flocks", with an increasing stress on the "monarchical" episcopate. None the less, the co-operation and co-responsibility of the whole community, so prominent in the New Testament times, were indispensable elements in the life of the Church, which must be taken even more seriously into account today." (20)

Just as in times of war one person leadership, even in democracies, has usually to be strengthened, so in the Church when under siege. In the same way christian communities were threatened with persecution by the romans without and the gnostics and as we shall see montanists within. Committees are notorious for uninspiring leadership. Monarchies and charismatic one man or one woman leadership show the human need people have of focusing their aspirations and placing their commitment in the hands of one leader.

Gnosticism then would have been a major factor in the gradual change to one man rule. The importance of the Nag-Hammadi find lies in the fact that we now know much more precisely the extent and depth of christian/gnostic teachings (as distinct from what often amounted to others' assessment of them) and how they could have wrecked catholic/orthodox christianity. We can also see how as one strong, negative factor they served to fashion and build the catholic/orthodox centre into the Church as we know it today.

Negatively too we can look at the literature and the movements catholic/orthodox christianity consciously rejected what it did not want to say. Undoubtedly the Church until recently did not have access to most of these writings due to the "zeal" of the "catholic" christians who destroyed them before they corrupted other christians. In defence of, but not justification for this action, it must be realized that most christians would probably have been illiterate (which is not the same thing as saying they would be unintelligent) and may well have been confused by exposure to these "unorthodox" writings.

* * * * * *

A second important movement in that same fashioning process was montanism. The prophetic charism and the charisms of speaking in tongues and their interpretation would seem to have diminished, but not necessarily to have disappeared in the mid-second century Church.

Carolyn Osiek's commentary on Hermas (a work which can be variously placed by scholars 120-150 A.D.) and his visions encapsulates the presbyteral authority in tension with prophecy well when she concludes: "...there is no conflict to be seen (in Hermas) between prophetic and presbyteral authority, though they are probably distinct. Hermas intends to promulgate a vision backed up by the presbyters, but there is no indication that there is one. To say that he needs their approval for either inner or outer validation may be going too far." (21)

It would be fairly obvious that as order became firmer in most christian communities, the prophetic and allied charisms would come more under control. The experience of modern pentecostal churches would serve to confirm the point. This would seem to be the setting for the rise and popularity of montanism beginning in the second half of the second century. Whatever diminution had occurred in the office/charism of prophecy, montanism restored with its emphasis on prophecy and private revelations.

31

The churches' reactions to this movement were varied, because some seemed to see in it a reinvigoration of the gift of prophecy which was losing ground and was a valid charism in the early churches. Others saw it as a challenge to the growing bishops' authority by the prophet setting himself against/above episcopal authority. Ultimately the latter group won out and montanism began to be perceived as "heresy".

Our documentation is one-sided. We do not possess the writings of Montanus to confirm or deny this aspect, only his alleged quotes from the pens of his enemies.

In Phrygia, Montanus (c.160-170 A.D.) began proclaiming himself the New Prophet, the mouthpiece of the Holy Spirit. Together with two women, Priscilla and Maximilla, they prophesied the time and place of the second coming of Christ and when this did not happen their movement's enthusiastic followers kept it going as a movement in which the prophet was directly inspired by the Holy Spirit. It would seem the bishop in Rome early in montanism's spread became opposed to what he saw were its potential dangers. Many other bishops viewed the movement with the same unease as many of today's bishops have regarded the charismatic movement in their own churches. Others would say, "If it helps people pray, leave them alone." Such a bishop was the bishop in Lyons in Gaul who may well have dispatched Irenaeus to Rome in 177 A.D. to plead with its bishop to be more tolerant to the montanists. While Irenaeus was away, an incipient persecution had intensified and he returned to find his bishop martyred and he himself elected bishop. He was by origin from Asia Minor and was to become the formidable opponent of gnosticism.

Unlike many of the gnostics the montanists sought out martyrdom and fasting to prepare for the second coming of Christ. They may well have died out in decades; but probably the conversion of Tertullian, one of the greatest christian thinkers of the early third century, to montanism helped to perpetuate its growth for several centuries. It is interesting that during this period from catholicism to montanism, Tertullian, an original staunch defender of mono-episcopacy became a fierce critic of episcopacy.

There has been a lot of modern research on montanism. Von Campenhausen has pointed out that in the early churches the "dialectic tension" between charismatic freedom and orderly structure had a valid part to play in the ministry and building up of the Church. "Prophecy was a gift of the Spirit manifested in charismatic freedom, yet it was not operated in isolation but as part of the ongoing life of the larger community of believers, but it was not to be understood as official and charismatic"…the co-existence of these various kinds of authority is not felt to be a problem." (22)

Montanus, many modern scholars have argued, was not so much against order as preaching against the downgrading and absorption of the prophetic function into the official ministry structure in so many of the christian communities. One of Montanus' contemporary critics seems to be castigating him for his emphasis on the laity and each person's charism in the Church. One wonders how much of the balance of the early Church was being lost with a slow de-emphasis on the laity's position vis-a-vis the growing bishops' movement.

Two centuries later Eusebius the historian's contention that Montanus had a new kind of prophecy and ecstasy has been critically re-examined and not been seen as correct. In fact, what Montanus could have been doing was restoring prophecy and speaking in tongues that was being fast forgotten in christian communities. (23)

Whatever the strength of the re-thinking on gnosticism and montanism by highlighting lacks in many of the christian communities, their potentiality for disruption and divisiveness could only help to reinforce the need for what was probably the average 'catholic' christian to find a stronger, ultimate Apostolic Authority in his community and what better than as Chadwick, the pre-eminent historian of the early Church, expresses it "the manifest necessity of a single man as the focus of unity." (24)

* * * * * *

While many historians point out how the stress of gnosticism and montanism paralleled the rise of bishops in the Church and, as has been implied, helped it, no-one to my knowledge has looked at the political mind-caste of the christians regarding their own structures. A great deal of controversy has gone on about the likely social strata of early christians and this, if agreement could be reached, would give us perhaps an indication of the educational background of the communities. Whatever their degree of sophistication, most christians by the second century A.D. would have little or no experience in the political world that surrounded them of what we now today call democracy or some participation in the powers that govern them.

Some of the greek city states, now cities within the Roman Empire, had retained some degree of all male, non-slave, citizen participation (25) which may well have been why the Pauline communities of Ephesus, Iconium, Thessalonica and Corinth in the first century manifested more obviously this more democratic element than the other christian communities. But as the second century wore on the democratic elements in most of the Mediterranean cultures were gradually subsumed, like Rome itself, into the military and mob features of the later Roman Empire. The influences of a more dictatorial and authoritarian political culture around them could well have been a factor in the security the average christians of the late second century felt was best expressed in one man rule.

The Empire's political structure was what the vast majority of christian people experienced and it had become by the second century A.D. monarchical, dictatorial and increasingly militarily controlled.

There had been democratic elements in the Roman republic before 14 B.C. when Augustus assumed the role of Emperor. The Senate was the supreme authority of the Empire, except in the times of great unrest when a dictator ruled for emergencies' sake. The Senate which represented the privileged and often hereditary classes was balanced and counterchecked by tribunes, knights, the law, questors and a growing number of people with full citizenship. Even at the beginning of the Empire, many of these more democratic checks and balances had some control over the Emperor. But as the Emperors grew stronger and divinization of their office (which caused so much trouble to the early christians) grew, they became virtually dictators, often made or unmade by the army.

A recent history commenting on the period says: "...in the imperial government the senate became merely an audience to which decisions might be announced for acclamation. All laws and appointments were made by the Emperor...the government thus reverted to the oriental pattern - a despotism resting on control of the army and acting through a royal council composed of executives arbitrarily appointed by the king. The Greek experiment was abandoned. Even in law, trial by jury died out. All that survived was a literary tradition from which subsequent ages would draw inspiration." (26)

The roman citizens of the second and third century A.D. experienced only autocracy in their secular life and they carried this mental framework with them into their religious sphere. With no experience of any other form of political structures and a conviction that anarchy would prevail if this autocracy collapsed, the christian carried this realization through to the forum of his or her own community where if too much diversity were tolerated, gnosticism, montanism, the fear of Imperial persecution could erode the spirit of the group and its commitment to the Jesus of the Gospels.

Those christians who more and more adopted the presbyteral system of government probably drew on a democratic strain within judaism that first occurred during the exile in Babylon and became popular among the dispersed jews of the known world - the synagogue run by elders. The system was adopted because of distance from the only Temple and its priesthood in Jerusalem. Despite all the positive elements involved in this system of elders, its weaknesses would become apparent when the presbyters had to decide about the Jesus the Apostles taught. When they were divided about the interpretation, did the majority vote hold? How do we weigh the value of this teacher, this prophet, as against what the tradition of the apostles seemed to point to? When gnosticism began to infiltrate christian communities, and even some of the presbyters were gnostic, where did you draw the line? How binding were the rules of neighbouring christian communities on your own community? These and a thousand other questions must have come to upset the tranquillity of a committed but still human group of christians. Moreover, if a number of baptized people had very little formal education of any sort, how skilled were they in understanding the intellectual arguments and nuances of interpretation demanded for solving certain crises? More importantly with people unskilled in exercising democratic processes in ordinary life, would they not opt especially in times of crisis for the only political security they knew, one man rule?

Given too the roman paterfamilias, the father of the family's gentle but firm sway and the patriarchal system of many of the mediterranean peoples, the system the majority of peoples within the Roman Empire felt gave them the most security was a paternalistic one where "one person knew best". Paternalism would flourish especially if christians included a number of not very well educated people. Thus the drift and then the swift universal adoption of one man rule, particularly under stress, is explicable also in cultural terms.

As said above, the general sharing of Christ's priesthood was kept in place particularly by the community's right to choose its own local leader (fairly democratic for the age they lived in). By the beginning of the third century, if not earlier, orthodoxy was ensured by two or more neighbouring bishops coming in to confirm that the elected man was catholic/orthodox and showing their approval of this aspect by laying hands on him by ordination.

Gnosticism and montanism not only helped to shape a one man episcopate for each church for defence purposes but also forced the churches to finally find the point where diversity could no longer be tolerated without interfering with the unity and integrity of belief. Gnosticism was probably the more insidious, because it in its various forms took away the uniqueness of Jesus Christ. Montanism may well have resembled our present charismatic movements and perhaps even revived the increasingly dormant charism of prophecy; but when it began to say the prophet with his direct line to the Holy Spirit was superior to the elected leader, the diversity part in the unity could be stretched no further.

1. Rahner, K. Theological Investigations Vol. XIV, transl. David Bourke. London, Darton Longman and Todd. 1976. pp. 196-197
2. Rahner, K. "Open Questions in Dogma considered by the Institutional Church as Definitively Answered" in Catholic Mind. March 1979. p. 13.
3. "Orthodox" meaning true teaching and "catholic" meaning universal in both time and place are used of the mainstream Christians. In the second century as this "mainstream" is forming, the word "protocatholic" is sometimes used.
4. Osiek, C. "The early second century through the eyes of Hermas: continuity and change" p. 116 in Biblical Theology Bulletin, Vol. 20 No. 3. Fall 1990.
5. Ibid, p.119.
6. Ibid, p.117.
7. Wilken, R. "Diversity and Unity in Early Christianity", p.109 in The Second Century, Vol. I No. 2. Summer 1981.
8. Brown, R.E. and Meier, J.P. Rome and Antioch. New York, Ramsey, Paulist Press. 1983. pp. 176-177
9. Cwiekowski, F J. The Beginnings of the Church. Mahwah, Paulist Press. 1987, p. 182
10. Brown, R E and Meier, J P: Antioch and Rome. New York, Ramsey, Paulist Press. 1983, pp. 162-163
11. Joly, R. Le Dossier d'Ignace d'Antioch, (Bruxelles, Editions de l'universite de Bruxelles. 1979. The authenticity of Ignatius of Antioch's letters have been hotly contested; but the great anglican scholar, Lightfoot, proved to most scholars that seven of the letters were certainly written when they claimed to be. However an eminent jesuit patrologist, Robert Joly, still doubts that they were written by a bishop on his way to martyrdom in 110 A.D. He tries to show the theological arguments are anti-gnostic ones that fit more a later period. Why was Ignatius sent to Rome with an expensive cohort of soldiers (Paul was a roman citizen appealing directly to the Roman Emperor) when he could have been martyred in Antioch? There seems to have been no throwing the christians to the wild beasts before the reign of Marcus Aurelius (160-180 A.D.) Puzzling alterations in the letter of Polycarp, one of the bishops Ignatius saw on the way to Rome seem to have been made to fit in with the ignatian dating. Certainly Polycarp's church much later than the date of Ignatius' martyrdom seemed to be led by a college of presbyters. Irenaeus does not seem to have used Ignatius' letters and one

would think they would have been a trump card in his bid to reinforce the apostolic succession of monarch bishops. Another well-known patrologist, Rius-Camps, agrees with Joly for different reasons. Most of the rest of the world's patrologists remain unconvinced.

12. McKenzie, J. Dictionary of the Bible. London/Dublin. Geoffrey Chapman 1965. pp. 133-134

13. Osiek, C. "The early second century through the eyes of Hermas: continuity and change", p.118

14. Brown, R. "Episkope not episkopos: the New Testament Evidence" in Theological Studies, Vol. 41, No. 2. June 1980. pp. 322-338

15. Pagels, E. The Gnostic Gospels. Harmondsworth, Penguin. 1982. pp. 17-18

16. Tyson, W. A Study of Early Christianity. New York, Macmillan Co. 1973. p. 184

17. Pagels, E. The Gnostic Gospels. p. 19

18. Ibid, p.151

19. Ibid, p.19

20. Schnackenburg, R. "Community Co-operation in the New Testament", Concilium, Vol. 7 No. 8. Sept. 1972. p. 19

21. Osiek, C. Biblical Theological Bulletin, Vol. 20. Fall 1990 No. 3. p. 120

22. Campenhausen, Von. Ecclesiastic Authority and Spiritual Power in the Church of the First Three Centuries. London, A & C Black. 1969. p. 178

23. Eusebius. The History of the Church, Harmondsworth, Penguin Classics. pp. 218-219 also article David F. Wright "Why were the Montanists Condemned?" in "Themelios 2". 1976. pp. 15-22

24. Chadwick, H. The Early Church. Harmondsworth, Pelican History of the Church. 1967. Vol. I, p. 49

25. Sherwin-White, A. "The Roman Background of Early Christianity", Concilium Vol. 7 No. 3. p. 5

26. Bickerman, E J. and Morton Smith, "The Later Roman Empire" in The Columbia History of the World, Ed. J A Garraty and P Gay. New York, Harper & Row. 1972. pp. 227-228

CHAPTER FOUR

The rise of the middle "Catholic" Party in the second century reinforced by the Monarch Bishop.

How did this early catholic/orthodox centrist attitude rise in the Church and particularly through the episcopal system keep control? Many scripture scholars would see it as the middle position taken by Peter in Acts 15 between James' conformity to all that could be retained in the Old Testament that did not go against Christ and Paul's position of abolition of the Old Law. Peter's compromise of a modicum of jewish practice for the non-jews seemed to be accepted by James while many have doubts about Paul's acceptance of Peter's principle (cf Galatians seemingly written after the Apostles met in Jerusalem). Paul, however, in later life seems to have softened and was most insistent on bringing the collection from the gentile world to Jerusalem as a sign of the unity of all christians.

This middle ground between the Pauline and James churches many scholars have called the proto-catholic party that developed into the full blown "catholic" christian church of the third century onwards.

A skilled analysis is attempted when Brown and Meier proceed to a geographical analysis - the churches of Antioch and Rome originating in the first and continuing into the second century. These two biblical scholars on the basis of New Testament evidence built up pictures of what in Meier's case were the indications of the Antioch community and in Brown's case the Roman one. While their evidence was not totally conclusive, they felt there were enough indications of the contemporary churches in scriptural passages to admit of more than tentative conclusions. The Antioch and Roman communities had at least by tradition the presence of Peter and Paul at different times. More and more Scripture scholars placed the community of Matthew's Gospel in Antioch and located a community in Rome that favoured Peter's balancing of James' extreme jewish christian attitudes with Paul's no Old Testament Law for the gentiles teaching.

"We are convinced" they say in their preface, "that the somewhat-right-of-Paul strains that emerged at Antioch and Rome in association with Peter were a key factor in the emerging church catholic. Such an analysis does not detract from the enormous power and challenge of Paul's letters and thought; but it warns that a purely Pauline Christianity was not dominant in New Testament times and afterwards. To some, the failure of Paul to dominate represents the loss of Christian vitality. Others of us believe that the only Christianity that can do justice to a New Testament containing diversity is one that resists sectarian purism in favour of constructively holding together tensions. Blending Paul into a wider mix therefore is what made the Pauline Epistles biblical i.e. part of the Bible meant to guide, serve and challenge the church catholic." (1)

Meier, in a scholarly and convincing way, gives the proofs for Antioch as the base for the Matthean community. Matthew is the only New Testament Gospel that uses the word "church" even though several of the other New Testament writings do. (2) In Chapter 16 Matthew seems to be using it of Peter and the universal Church whereas Chapter 18 is much more how to deal with sin or breach of discipline in the local community - first on a one to one basis, then a warning from two or three others and finally judgement by the whole community. Rome at the time of Matthew's writing had apparently no one bishop successor of Peter (p. 23), so Meier goes through the contrasts between the binding and loosing power given to Peter by Jesus and the democratic initiatives of the local community where no officials are mentioned, concluding: "The ambivalence of Matthew's approach to church authority may be explained partly by the various traditions with which Matthew must work, partly by the fact that his church is a church in transition, a transition which has by no means ended, but perhaps most of all by Matthew's own indecisiveness about how much authoritative leadership is good for his church. He admires the rock of Ch. 16 vv 18-19 but seems unable or unwilling to have a local counterpart to this figure of universal ecclesiastical stability." (3)

Meier is, of course, rather hard put to it when he dates Matthew at about 85 A.D. to show how the three-tiered church of Ignatius of Antioch was unquestionably the accepted thing in that same Matthean church of Antioch community twenty years later if the usual date for Ignatius is accepted. Given what has been said about Ignatius by Joly, the disparity may not seem so inexplicable.

Brown in a similar manner gives a picture of the roman church. He gives ample proof that the dominant form of christianity in Rome in the '40s and early '50s was close to Jerusalem and judaism. He analyses the Letter of Paul to the Romans and its emphasis, written at the end of the 'fifties, to prove his point. The third generation, as he calls it, - the letter of Clement or the presbyters of Rome c.100 A.D. - showing a really moderate roman approach to a problem makes one ask what of the 'second generation' - the one between the Letter to the Romans and Clement? Brown draws on 1 Peter and the Epistle to the Hebrews, possibly written to christians in Rome sometime after 70 A.D. to partly answer that question. His conclusion? "...a Jewish/Gentile Christianity more conservative in its preservation of the Jewish Law and Cult than the Christianity of Paul in Galatians. Indeed, as with Antioch, so also with Rome, this Jewish/Gentile Christianity can plausibly be related to the image of Peter." (4)

When Brown examines the Letter of Clement specifically he points out "the close parallel made between submission to the presbyters and obedience to the civil leaders or military leaders. One gains from this parallelism reinforcement for the thesis that the roman church of necessity came quickly to terms with the awesome organization of the empire by duly appreciating the strength of the system." (5) Brown goes on to show how for Origen and Cyprian the Church was an organism comparable to the Roman state. In Clement especially not only is the admiration of imperial Rome underscored but the vital need for hierarchical order in the church a lesson probably needed by the corinthian church Clement was addressing which was more charismatic in its roots than the roman church as Paul's Epistles to that church show. "The revulsion shown in Roman Law for civil disobedience and schism" concludes Brown, "seems to have constituted an a fortiori argument for having no sympathy for schism in the church." (6)

Brown also discusses the thorny question of whether the apostles appointed their successors (whatever they were called) as seems apparent from 1 Clement 42:4 or even Titus 1:5 or, whether as seemed to happen in many Pauline or Didache communities, officials were appointed from and by the local church. He wisely decides: "The solution that seems most plausible is that I Clement has generalized an apostolic practice that was occasional but not consistent or universal." (7)

The Meier-Brown thesis is tantalizing - that Rome and Antioch preserved the Petrine middle position of keeping the best of the Jewish tradition and wedding it to the New Testament liberation by Christ's teaching. This they would contend is the middle way between James' circumcision mentality and Paul to the Galatian's freedom from the Law. In these two churches they would see the proto-catholic Church, holding undisputed sway through its bishops by the second half of the second century.

This development from diverse structures, particularly the presbyteral to one bishop for every local church, lacks explicit documentation. The vast majority of the documents remaining until recently implied as thoroughly as they could that there was a line of bishops stretching back to the time of the apostles. From existing documents and their comparison one with another, scholars have shown implicitly the development that actually took place. We have picked our way through these monumental theses to try and trace that development. But the lack of explicit documentation gives one good cause for wondering was there collusion between certain parts to create the impression of an "apostolic succession" of bishops? The negative factor is (particularly if the Joly thesis on Ignatius is correct) why create documents to prove something happened which in actual fact did not?

The colluding parties who are often called the proto-catholics would probably argue that it was difficult and confusing to tell uneducated people that there had always been Apostolic Authority in the churches although interpreted variously for quite a few decades, probably a century or more after Christ's death and resurrection. It was far better to claim a succession of bishops having Apostolic Authority teaching "catholic" doctrine from the earliest times and they would probably argue, even in those communities having a college of presbyters, that there was usually one who was chairman or secretary who represented the college corporately and in a certain sense the line was really there...such as perhaps Clement in the Roman presbyteral college of 100 A.D.

It could be argued that the silence about the fairly speedy transition to bishops was not worth mentioning, because everybody knew about it.

But the fact that no one recorded it and a deliberate attempt seemed to have been made to look as though the opposite had happened - that bishops were always there - makes one suspect not without some foundation a certain collusion was going on both in retaining some documents and destroying others thus creating a certain pre-determined impression.

With arguments such as these the catholic/orthodox party assembled three building blocks on which the future catholic/orthodox Church would be solidly grounded. The first was the bishops in every place as a living sign of unity within the community and a link with all the "catholic" communities outside. The second was the Scriptures of the Old and New Testament recognized by a general agreement. The New Testament books the communities judged as containing the same Jesus the apostles taught and the true 'Apostolic' teaching coming from his apostles became the criterion. These words were regarded in both Old and New Testaments as inspired by the Holy Spirit and enshrining for all times the real Jesus. The Muratorian fragment composed in about 200 A.D. and found by Muratori in 1740 gives a list of the biblical books the second century Church regarded as inspired. It corresponds nearly to the books of our own Bible. Another century or two passed before all the churches accepted our present Canon. It gave time for christians to live out those scriptures and discover that they really mediated Jesus to them. As said above, the books of the New Testament contained a diversity of theological approaches reflecting the early Church's concern for unity in diversity and an awareness that these scriptures would form the christians of the future. The third building block was the 'Rule of Faith'. A consensus point was emerging in the christian communities resulting from the public ritual preparation and questionnaires asked of converts to christianity before their baptism. These questionnaires and formulations became the basis of a doctrinal statement called the "Rule of Faith" and often corresponded roughly with what christians later were to call the Apostles Creed. Each community had various but similar essentials. These seemed to sharpen the unity in diversity principle by offering lines of demarcation to diversity where unity could be threatened.

These three building blocks were enunciated and well used by Irenaeus, bishop of Lyons, against the gnostics in his books at the end of the second century. Irenaeus may well have been one of the leading lights on this catholic/orthodox push; but one can only surmise. Certainly he is their best spokesperson.

But even with Irenaeus there is a realization of the Holy Spirit working in each baptized member of the Church and a realization of each baptized person's participation in the Church in which the presbyters and bishop after consulting all the priestly people have the ultimate authority. Iranaeus' bishop is one with his people not above them.

Was this mono-episcopal identification of the same canon of Scripture and Rule of Faith movement just another movement like the gnostic and montanist movements mentioned in the previous chapter? I think it was far more and tend to agree with Robert Wilken when he writes: "A 'center' was being shaped and formed during this period, and it is historically important to understand how and why this sense of communal identity emerged. I have suggested that this 'center' cannot be defined in doctrinal terms i.e. solely in terms of religious ideas, for it included among other things, behaviour and way of life, liturgical practice, even a sense of "belonging" of church if you will, and this sense of communal identity was present long before there were definable standards by which to measure it. Irenaeus' famous appeal at the beginning of book 3 of his Adversus Haereses to the fellowship of the bishops of leading cities and their continuity with earlier bishops is a striking illustration of the growing sense of communal identity. It is the task of the present generation of scholars, now that we have seen how diverse, how varied, how polychromatic early Christianity was, to take up again the task of comprehending what emerged as the dominant form of Christianity. For what came from this period did not result simply in another tradition, another strand of Christianity, one trajectory alongside of others, but the form that Christianity was to assume for two thousand years and which provides even today the foundation for the lives and beliefs of most Christians in East and West. Early Christianity is an exciting field of study because such investigation is not simply the examination of a past religion, but the study of the formative period of a religious movement which thrives in our own world and whose adherents continue to believe that what happened in those ancient times still reverberates in the present." (8)

Why, then, did Irenaeus write those words that have become the classic text for the continuity of the mono-episcopacy with the apostles? "It is within the power of all...who may wish to see the truth, to contemplate clearly the tradition of the apostles manifested throughout the whole world; and we are in a position to reckon up those who were by the apostles instituted bishops in the churches, and (to demonstrate) the successions of these men to our own times." (9) If they are not historically accurate as our studies seem to have indicated why did Irenaeus write them? In fact this quotation with the earlier understanding of Clement and Ignatius' and a sincere belief that St Paul himself was writing to Titus and Timothy was very much the proof of all subsequent ages that the bishops were successors of the apostles. Theologians would say that the Tradition is passed down despite those texts and they were only used as proofs to confirm the Tradition. Is it as simple as that? True Tradition is surely not just what is passed down but what is based squarely on fact and if the fact is subsequently proved to be untrue or far more complex than the words imply then all that follows has tainted development of the Tradition. Depending on its importance it can be called a distortion. If this is reinforced by texts used out of the proper historical context each generation is reinforced in a certain way of thinking which distorts truth and perhaps the truths built on it. Can this be called unchangeable Tradition? In other words, were the bishops (leaders and appraisers of the Tradition) apart from their apostolic communities the only true appraisers?

To those who wonder why I am labouring a point, let me just indicate that in the 1800 years since Irenaeus wrote these words, not just ultimate but the sole Apostolic Authority has been placed in the apostolic succession of bishops, particularly by the Roman Catholic Church. By the erosion of centuries, any checks and balances which Irenaeus would have understood have disappeared.

A virtual monopoly of authority and those who appoint it in the light of what we have seen about the early Church is unwarranted without the contextual checks and balances in place. Moreover it shows the danger of one line of development that de-emphasizes what early christianity regarded as important when that line of development results in an autocracy alien to what many scholars would regard as the true attitudes of the Jesus of the Gospels. Certainly further investigation of a development that edges out other factors is indicated when it owes more to historical, political and cultural elements taken together with the human hunger for power that have at least muddied the original springs of Revelation.

43

As has been seen there would seem to have always been Apostolic Authority in the churches whether exercised by the whole community, prophets, presbyters, bishops or whoever; but to posit that the development to bishops alone holding that authority was divine, and inevitable as the only outcome is I think to posit too much. At least the basis for the "Tradition" should be revisited if only for the sake of ecumenism or to give the presbyters and the laity their God given rights in a balanced community. More importantly, it needs revisiting for the sake of truth.

* * * * * *

Why then did a saint, and I am sure, an honest man like Irenaeus say those words quoted above when there were probably no bishops in the developed 2nd century sense around when the apostles died?

There are many learned authors who rush to explain Irenaeus' words in context.

(a) If Joly is incorrect and Ignatius flourished 100-110 A.D. then the time lapse might explain that if the shift to one bishop for each church was early in the second century, Irenaeus writing in 180-190 A.D. may have genuinely reflected that this is how things always were. It is very easy, some would say, to think even circumstances one grew up with and changed only in the generation before one was born were always there from the beginning. Even if this were correct, it still does not make the original facts untrue, but could explain Irenaeus' convictions. However, it does not explain why Irenaeus, who had apparently contact with many areas of the Church which were slower than his church to change to one man rule, did not know of the earlier tradition.

(b) Eric Jay, the learned anglican patrologist, was probably more correct and is not alone in showing that Irenaeus was talking more of a succession of teachers than a lineal succession of leaders. "...the practice of appointing one of the presbyters to occupy the Kathedra (teaching chair of office [Cathedral]) as the official guardian of the faith in the local Christian community had been adopted. The title of episkopos originally an alternative for presbyter, is now applied to him exclusively." (10)

Jay in another context mentions how the gnostic claim "to possess a corpus of truth derived secretly from the apostles through a succession of teachers" (11) helped to provoke the succession of teachers argument on the "catholic" side.

In the case of the Roman church, Irenaeus' list does not tally with the later official list of bishops drawn up by the "Liber Pontificalis" (List of

Popes) whose origin is probably two centuries after Irenaeus. Possibly Irenaeus was naming the secretary- chairperson-teacher not strictly in order. But it is worthy of note (Adv. Haer iii, 3) that in his Roman list he does not name St Peter as the first bishop. The church of Rome is founded on the Apostles Peter and Paul - an apostle is an office given by Jesus for all the church - and Linus etc. are the bishops.

McCue adds, I think, pertinently: "...and at least the Roman list identifies as bishops men (e.g. Clement) who it would seem were not bishops in the mono-episcopal sense. Thus the question of the point at which the individuals named begin to be bishops in the later sense, as contrasted simply with the eminent leaders, cannot be determined on the basis of the lists themselves." (12)

Even allowing for Jay's, McCue's and other scholars nuanced explanations such as the succession of teachers, successive generations placed a far different emphasis on the text of Irenaeus. It was constantly used as a proof of a lineal apostolic succession of bishops. Moreover, whatever Irenaeus intended in using such a passage (could it be an interpolation also?), the fact that it has been a principle cause of misrepresentation needs a readjustment or rather a re-contextualization for the sake of truth.

(c) Irenaeus is also strong on presbyteral succession as many students of the early christian writers would hold, a fact which would probably fit in well with the Rome of Clement and Hermas. Irenaeus speaks of tradition "which originates from the apostles, which is preserved by means 'of the successions of presbyters in the churches." (III, ii,2) and again: "It is incumbent to obey the presbyters who are in the church - those who, as I have shown, possess the succession of the episcopate have received the certain gift of truth." (iv, xxvi, 2) (13)

Jay hastens to add, quite apart from many presbyters failing to teach and live the truth, many bishops have been at fault, a fact Irenaeus does not seem to recognize. "Unhappily the history of the Church does not justify such confidence." He adds: "There have been heretical bishops, an awkward fact which was to provide the Church with difficult problems." (14)

My mention of presbyteral succession in Irenaeus as well as episcopal seems to highlight his wider grasp of the Apostles' teaching about Jesus' teaching being passed down by a wider body than just the bishops. It could not have died out altogether, for St Jerome (+420) was still teaching presbyteral succession much later. Coupled with his strong belief that each baptized person possessed the Holy Spirit and was part of the Church, it would be wrong to see Irenaeus as advocating the succession of bishops as the lone vehicle of the church's Tradition.

It should always be remembered that even with his teaching on Apostolic succession of bishops and presbyters, Irenaeus saw a wider apostolicity of apostolic succession with the whole Church. "Where the Church is, there is the Spirit of God;" says Irenaeus, "and where the Spirit of God is, there is the Church and all grace; and the Spirit is the truth. Those, therefore, who do not participate in the Spirit neither feed at their mother's breasts nor drink the bright fountain issuing from Christ's body." (15)

That wider context of the whole community being involved in apostolic succession was slowly thrust into the background and effectively became an unimportant factor in the Roman Catholic tradition and even to a lesser extent in the Anglican episcopal tradition. In the Eastern churches the concept of "sobornost" or as Johannes Remmers defines it "that only in the living community of the whole Church can the believer truly live and find the truth revealed to him - where all are tied together, organically by love" was always a much stronger tradition than in the West.

Remmers goes on to say: "Limiting the notion of apostolic succession in the Church to succession within the hierarchy must derive from this same mentality: the Church (i.e. hierarchy) is set up over against the People of God. But apostolic succession within the hierarchy which is meant to serve the People of God, can only be understood in relation to the apostolic succession of the whole people. It is only because apostolic succession resides in the whole Church that it can be applied to the servant hierarchy." (16)

Hans Kung agrees with this assessment pointing out that all baptized Christians are followers of the apostles and all constitute the temple of the Spirit, built on the foundation of the apostles." The whole Church "is the body of Christ, unified by the ministry of the Apostles." Kung goes on to say: "The whole Church is the new people of God, gathered by the apostles through the preaching of the Gospel of Jesus." That wider context will be lost in the Western Church as the centuries pass, will be revived at the Reformation but unfortunately became, among other things, a weapon of attacking the episcopal Churches by many Protestants with the result of only entrenching the Roman Catholic Church particularly in its narrower concept of Apostolic Succession. (17)

(d) An even wider context in which to read Irenaeus is to see how he viewed the other two building blocks. He saw the "Rule of Faith", the basis of the Apostles Creed, as a quite remarkable agreement of the baptismal formulas of all the churches scattered through the then known world. The Church he said "believes these points just as if she had but one soul, and one and the same heart, and she proclaims them, and teaches them, and hands them down, with perfect harmony, as if she possessed one mouth...although the languages of the world are different, yet the import of the tradition is one and the same...in Germany...in Spain...in Gaul...in the East...and in Libya." (Adv. Haer 1, x, 1) (18)

Irenaeus obviously saw this "universality" this "catholic" teaching or orthodoxy in striking contrast to the myriad gnostic theories and another sign of the Holy Spirit bringing all diversity into unity.

Irenaeus' reverence for Scripture as the inspired Word of God in which the Spirit continually leads the reader or hearer to a closer union with and understanding of Jesus is obviously tempered by the balancing act he has to perform vis-a-vis the gnostics. They were adept in twisting the Gospels and Epistles their own way. Marcion, for instance, constructed his "Jesus" by rejecting all the Old Testament and most of the New except St Paul's Epistles and parts of St Luke's Gospel. He made a Jesus completely abrogating what had gone before. Apostolic Tradition passed on a far more complex Jesus than this.

As the Nag-Hammadi scrolls underscore, the gnostics also produced their own gospels and writings to try and give an 'apostolic' stamp to their teaching and as the Canon or full list of the New Testament accepted by the 'catholic' churches had not yet been completely finalized, Irenaeus had to show the balancing effect of the "Rule of Faith" and the leadership of the bishops in manifesting the uniqueness of Jesus. He still, however, emphasizes the reading of the Scriptures and their regular and careful exposition.

In a way, the three undergirding factors now become institutionalised. Community Episkope (supervision) had eventuated in episkopos (one bishop for each local church). As long as the bishop was elected by his own presbyters and people, as he seemed to be, then the synodal principle of episkope was retained and the episkopos, one with his people, voiced the local church. When he went into synod with other bishops each representing his own communion of Koinonia the episkope principle of the early Church was still retained. It was only later developments which gradually isolated him from his roots in the charisms of his own community and weakened and diminished his role as the appraiser of Tradition.

The Unity in diversity principle can be seen in Irenaeus' second building block in the Rule of Faith which was the common questionnaire and answers constituting an affirmation of the catholic faith and the basic tenets of christianity which finally resulted in our Apostles Creed and later creeds. The Apostles Creed in its simpler statements of belief was saying thus far no further as far as diversity is concerned - these are the essentials; but within them diversity should still be retained. Unfortunately factors beyond anyone's control were happening that made for a certain uniformity

- the same system of ruling each community had emerged by the end of the second century, the jewish christian communities were becoming smaller in numbers and even perhaps heretical.

Irenaeus' confidence in bishops as Jay pointed out above was not born out by history. Sociologists and historians would point out there is an ingrained tendency for formulae to become ossified and lineal successors to end up defending institutional tradition rather than the "Tradition". The Holy Spirit of Jesus Christ would, of course, as Irenaeus knew, be with his Church until the end of time. If both formulae and episcopacy continually tested themselves against the good news of Jesus Christ then the building blocks set in place would work well. If they did not and often confused traditions with Tradition and displayed the general fear any institution has to change especially when powerful and wealthy, then the building blocks could be counter-productive. The final test could only be the measuring rod of Jesus Christ, his life and works. When the bishops' system failed christianity in the Middle Ages by constantly refusing to reform itself together with the by now autocratic papacy, then protestantism cut itself off from one building block, the episcopacy, and while retaining one of the others, the Creed, replaced the weight put on episcopacy by giving double the weight to Scripture. With anglicanism and certain other protestant churches, the title of bishop was kept but in a more reformed and controlled fashion.

The weight protestantism now put on Scripture was the deep christian conviction that only Jesus was the "foundation stone" of the church and that by abuse and misuse the untrammelled episcopal and papal building block could be and was dangerous to the unravelling of the christian message. Scripture was to prove a two-edged sword once some people took the principle of its private interpretation to the limits as did many of the anabaptists at the Reformation for instance. Nor could the reformers have envisioned the biblical criticism of the 18th to the 20th century which in turn caused an unforeseen uncertainty. However, the basic protestant contention was that the Bible was the ultimate criterion of Truth and Jesus Christ fulfilled that Truth in his person.

Basically the Roman Catholic position has its similarities. Luis Bermejo puts it well when he says: "Later stages of development, even if they are very ancient, are at times given preference over the very first stage which started the development. The church has been promised the guidance of the Spirit of Truth, but this is no reason to turn the various subsequent stages of this historical evolution into an absolute norm of orthodoxy. Only the New Testament remains and will always remain the exclusive Norma Normans (the supreme norm). The New Testament has to be received and interpreted within the totality of the Church's tradition, to be sure, but it should also be emphasized that it is the New Testament that has to judge subsequent history and tradition rather than be judged and interpreted by them." (19)

The Second Vatican Council puts it well when it says the Church's teaching office "is not above God's word, but serves it" (Dei Verbum, 10). (20) Scripture remains the tribunal above any other tribunal mediated in Roman Catholic Tradition through the Church.

The Bishops as successors of the apostles is a claim that is more complex than the claim sounds.

♣ ♣

There has been a tendency in Roman Catholic thinking on development of christian teaching, as Bermejo puts it "… to turn the various subsequent stages of this historical evolution into an absolute norm of orthodoxy." Thus, as he says "later stages of development, even if they are very ancient, are at times given preference over the very first stages which started the development." (21)

When one sees throughout the christian communities after and during apostolic times, despite the various names for officials and varying functions for the same name, a balance of charisms together with a pluriformity of communities as being of the essence of Church. When further one sees this exemplified in a most expressive way in the Pauline communities, one begins to see Church at its deepest level. After Charity, Faith and Hope binding these communities together and the Spirit of Christ constantly infusing them, the various charisms interacted to form the one Body of Christ.

There was the charism of Apostolic Authority which was one of leadership by faithfulness to the Jesus the apostles knew and taught combined with talents to lead such a community and "supervise" (episkope) all these charisms uniting them in one. Higher up in the list of charisms was prophecy which was the gift of him or her who possessed it to keep the community aware when even "apostolic" leadership drifted away from the Spirit of Christ. Teaching was also included. He or she who possessed it could draw on the riches of scripture and tradition and pass them on. Even the charism of administration is mentioned by St. Paul. The administrator could bring order to the community by regulating its ritual and supplies so that the practicalities could function. And so on for the speaking in tongues and many others.

The assumption seems to be in many roman catholic circles that these were gifts to the primitive churches until they evolved into a uniformity of officials particularly one bishop over one diocese and a later evolution when "teacher", "prophet" and other charisms became absorbed into one episcopal office. Long forgotten in practice was the charism of every baptized person to have a say and a function in his or her own community what Van Iersel in chapter two (p. 12) calls the synodal principle.

The same is assumed about unity in diversity or pluriformity which of its very nature must create tension. However, it is a healthy tension as Cwiekowski has noted above (p. 15) and when either the parameters of unity have not been spelt out or non- essential diversity has been crushed by uniformity in the name of unity "something very basic to the reality of the Church is neglected and the Church as a whole suffers from such neglect."

What Cwiekowski has said about pluriformity applies also to that balance of charisms so essential to the Church's life that while the Holy Spirit still works even when one charism (Apostolic Authority) has officially absorbed the others, their necessarily separate functioning needs to be brought together and listened to by Apostolic Authority as checks and balances. So often the Holy Spirit is hampered and sometimes stifled by the non-functioning of the other charisms. The Spirit will see to it that the main thrust of the Church will not deviate from the truth; but its proclamation can be so unbalanced without the seasoning and interaction of the other charisms that it can upset many parts of the Church greatly.

There is a tendency in any autocratic authority to act arrogantly, without proper consultation or being advised by only its own appointees, to pursue one ideology at the expense of a wider legitimate pluriformity, to assume it knows best what its subjects need (even the word "subject" should not be valid in a christian context) and to absolutize non-essentials. These have been the weak points of the powerful, whether ecclesiastical or lay, throughout history.

They therefore need the leavening of the prophets to point out whether Christ would have acted this way or whether the ever so reasoned conclusions are really so Gospel sound. The pleadings of a Catherine of Siena before an Urban V or Gregory XI are the calls Apostolic Authority constantly needs to lead it back to the Gospel. The teacher is also necessary to bring Apostolic Authority and christian community back to the real meaning of the Scriptures in the context in which they were written but also to the real Tradition which has often been distorted by traditions which now include forgeries as we will find out later. How valid is a tradition passed down which is based on a forgery sincerely believed at the time and which has had its subtle influences on the ongoing Tradition of the Church? Only some teachers can discern this and Apostolic Authority must concede its debt to these men and women, preparing to change if necessary.

How can Apostolic Authority or even prophets and teachers (especially if most of them are celibate) teach with integrity the full extensions of theology, morality and spirituality to lay-people unless they listen intently to what lay-people dedicated to the Gospel tell them of how these things operate in their own lives? The political ploy of listening to those lay people whom authority knows will agree with it does not deserve the name of consultation.

The interacting of all these charisms in the early Church was an essential ingredient of its identity and even when mono-episcopacy became the norm, the election of the bishop by his people and his obvious consultation of them in many instances did not abolish this identity.

Because some teachers became suspect (gnostics) in the second century did not abolish this charism. The outstanding school of Alexandria was largely run at its beginning by lay teachers. In fact, rather than bishops absorbing the office of teacher initially, many bishops of the third and fourth centuries were elected precisely because they were good teachers and again some prophets (montanists) who it was claimed put themselves above apostolic authority damaged that charism badly. So many prophets in the Church's history were recognized retrospectively and, if martyred, canonized a lot later. St Joan of Arc, John Hus and Savanarola fit well into this category. In a sense while the charism or office of "prophet" was not often recognized, the charism lived on in the independent critics of the bishops from the fourth century onwards.

Administrators were, of course, always recognized. It was not hard to see as the centuries wore on how these practical managers became bishops.

But the wisdom of spreading authority and giving it checks and balances although retaining Apostolic Authority as an ultimate decision maker was slowly eroded. When pluriformity as evidenced in decision making gradually swung from the ultimate decision making of authority to the initiating of decisions by a sole authority rather than a widely consulted one, the tolerance of diversity grew less until orthodoxy became equated with uniformity.

The words are bandied around today of "consulting" and "dialoguing"; but if Apostolic Authority is unprepared to consult widely and be prepared to be modified or altered by the results of its consultation, then the words become mere empty shells and frustration sets in with attendant reactions. If, as has happened, Authority puts stooges in important places and then "consults" them, an insult is offered to the Holy Spirit.

The Church was never meant to be a democracy in the sense of one person one vote. Raymond Brown's perceptions of the Johannine communities show that. But neither was it meant to be an autocracy where one party, however ideologically correct it may see itself to be, can seize power, crush all opposition and take control which has been possible through most of the Church's history especially by those who can manipulate the autocracy previous to a papal election. Somewhere between these two poles the Church of the centuries has been trying to find its most appropriate structures.

Even when as the next few chapters show, Apostolic Authority outstripped in its development all the other charisms to the extent that I would argue imbalance appeared and together with human weakness sent people scurrying in all directions for a solution that was already there, the Holy Spirit, as I will endeavour to show, tried to restore that balance. By now Apostolic Authority had built up such a wall of justification for its sole use of power that these attempts have throughout the centuries met with such frustration and opposition that they have often provoked well meaning people to extremes that were never originally intended. Apostolic Authority was unprepared to see things in any other way than it had determined which it had every right to do but and, here is the reason for this book, not as a sole arbiter but as a maker of decisions leavened and modified by many layers of dialogue and understanding of other viewpoints.

In the next few chapters I hope we will follow this development hand in hand with the growing imbalance especially in our Western and Roman Catholic Christianity so that we can see the answer is to restore the actual balance that has always been in our hands if we will only look for it and pray to find it.

♣ ♣

The history of 'dethroning" absolute systems should not have to be repeated in an ecclesiastical system. If absolutism refuses to change, it may provoke schism.

1. Brown, R.E. and Meier, J.P. <u>Antioch and Rome</u>, New York, Ramsey, Paulist Press. 1983. p. viii
2. Ibid, p. 66 sq
3. Ibid, pp. 71-72
4. Ibid, pp. 90-91
5. Ibid, p. 173
6. Ibid, p. 173
7. Ibid, p. 175
8. Wilken, R. "Diversity and Unity in Early Christianity" in <u>Second Century</u>, I. 1981. p. 110
9. Irenaeus. <u>Adversus Haereses</u> III, I probably written about 180-190 A.D.
10. Jay, E. <u>The Church</u>, Vol. I. London, SPCK. 1977. p. 47
11. Jay, E. "From Presbyter-Bishops to Bishops and Presbyters" <u>in Second Century</u>, Vol. I, No. 3. Fall 1981. p. 161
12. McCue, J. "The Roman Primacy in the Patristic Era", p.51 <u>in Papal Primacy and the Universal Church Lutherans and Catholics in Dialogue V</u> (Ed. Paul C Empie and T Austin Murphy). Minneapolis Minnesota, Augsburg Publishing. 1977
13. Jay, E. <u>The Church</u>. pp. 32, 33 and 47
14. Ibid, pp. 48 and 49
15. Ibid, p. 31
16. Remmers, J. "Apostolic Succession: an Attribute of the Whole Church', <u>Concilium</u> Vol. 4, No. 4. April 1968. pp. 20-21
17. Kung, H. <u>The Church</u>, London, Burns and Oates. 1968. p. 355
18. Jay, E. <u>The Church</u>, p. 44
19. Bermejo, L. <u>Towards Christian Reunion.</u> Anand, India, Gujarat Sahitja Prakash. 1984. p. 210
20. Abbott, W M. <u>The Documents of Vatican II.</u> London, Geoffrey Chapman. 1966. p. 118
21. Bermejo, L. <u>Towards Christian Reunion.</u> Anand, India, Gujarat Sahitya Prakash. 1984. p. 210)

CHAPTER FIVE

How the Monarch Bishop gradually became "above" the rest of the Community

The word "priest" in the christian churches of the first two centuries was reserved for Jesus Christ only. To emphasize the whole people's sharing in his priesthood, the "priestly people" of I Peter, no bishop or presbyter arrogated the title to himself.

By the third century A. D. the word "priest" in the sense of High Priest was being used of bishops. By the fourth century of presbyters. But the understanding was they were the leaders of a priestly people and it was safe to use the word of the community's leaders now that paganism with its priests was weakening and judaism had seen its priests disappear after the destruction of the Temple.

When the barbarians began coming into the Church often tribally and sometimes without too much preparation, their notions of their own priests and sacrifice coloured the christian use of the word for bishops and presbyters. Christian communities no longer elected their bishops (now chosen by the barbarian kings and nobility) so that the connotation of a priestly caste distinct from the people began to grow unchecked especially as there was an increasingly scarce access to the early christian writers.

As the Church increased in numbers in the third and fourth centuries A.D., developments took place which could claim to be a valid growth from the first two centuries as long as a balance was retained with the cluster of ideas that surrounded each development. Unfortunately this did not always happen and the development of certain ideas remained uneven.

By the middle of the fifth century A.D., the Western Roman Empire whose boundaries were roughly coterminous with what would be the central territories for the next millennium of the Western Church and the christian Middle Ages collapsed under the pressure of barbarian invasions. Many of the structures of the by now imperially supported and controlled Church collapsed too. However, numbers of the christian ex-roman citizens, serfs and slaves provided a substratum of "catholic" christians to marry with and modify the largely pagan and sometimes arian christian conquerors. The sixth to tenth centuries saw the gradual conversion of the majority of invaders to "catholic" christianity and the insertion into these cultures of Church power and authority based to a significant degree on how the Church had operated in Roman times. As feudalism began to grow in Western Europe at the same time, its hierarchical principle reinforced the gaps increasing between bishops, clergy and laity.

Because of the massive destruction of libraries by the barbarians, many early christian writings were totally destroyed or were handed down to posterity only in fragments. Much of the written christian heritage was forgotten because the remaining christians were so intent on survival that the lack of adequate or reliable documentation was barely noticed. Theology in Western Europe not only stood still but virtually few great works of christian origin were written in those "Dark Ages".

With the Eastern Roman or Byzantine Empire based on Constantinople, its links to the West geographically and culturally after the barbarian invasions were tenuous and became more so with their own muslim invasion from the seventh century A.D. For the last few centuries before the fall of Constantinople in 1453, the Eastern Empire's territory was diminished to a small geographical area surrounding that imperial city. The muslims were better respecters of Learning than most of the barbarians and translated their conquered libraries into arabic, retaining many early christian writings as well as the texts of the greek philosophers. These writings in their turn were to be brought back by the crusaders and travellers to Western Christianity and through the spanish muslim universities from the eleventh century onwards. These in their turn were to add fuel to the fire of mediaeval theology which had begun its exciting course. Eastern christianity was thereby kept more in tune with its roots, because much of its early literature was available.

Why then did I use the word "unfortunately" in the context of certain developments in the third and fourth century remaining uneven and not retaining their balance with the cluster of ideas surrounding them? Those centuries with their living Tradition could understand that even if a development gave a certain imbalance to an idea coming from the Gospels, other structures were still in place to check that idea from becoming too unbalanced. However, with an almost complete break (the barbarian invasions) in the Western churches from the past and the destruction of most of its written documents, the main ideas were, of course, passed down, but often without the nuances and complexities that the early Church had kept in place. While Tradition did not cease, there was a strong hiatus in the total Tradition.

It was only a matter of time before the bishops especially and priests became the sole arbiters of Church affairs from theology to discipline. The laity were left with nothing else than to obey. It was not so much that what was taught about priesthood was wrong; but it had become so badly distorted as to be out of proportion in its development and needing revision. Over a thousand years was to pass before this revision was attempted at Vatican II. In the meantime the structure wrought havoc among the faithful who came to see the Church as the hierarchy of bishops with the priests sharing their power and authority.

There was nothing wrong with the use of the word "priest" now applied to bishop and presbyter by third and fourth century christians as long as it retained the early christian notion of a priestly people gathered around the altar (as fourth century architecture denotes) with one designated by Apostolic Authority whom the whole people had elected from their number. He could be called a "priest" to reflect this idea. Without these historically and important nuances and complexities being understood, it came to signify a different role among the newly converted barbarians. While the development of the word "priest" was not against Apostolic Teaching, it needed the cluster of ideas surrounding it to retain the balance common to the early Church. The separate development of one idea and the almost obliteration of the cluster is what was to cause so much of the conflict within christianity.

Now the appraisers of teaching, the bishops (greek plural episkopoi) had in their persons all the authority originally placed in the community. Now it was exercised by one man - and as the Dark Ages wore on - often a man not chosen from the local community by its people: often a man given the office as a reward and an income by the ruler: a bishop who had little or no consultation with the local church and increasingly did not reside there. But the office of appraiser of this Tradition (now isolated from almost all of the relevant factors that gave him episkope or superintendency in the New Testament sense) had the sole say (or in a council with other similarly appointed bishops) over the appraised Tradition. Distortion was inevitable especially given the lack of theological training and often lack of christian commitment of many of the appointees.

The question of the development of the sacrament of orders is still a very controversial one as the writings of Schillebeeckx and Kung among others, show. It is not the intention of this book to enter into this intricate controversy. However, to show the complex roots of such an argument, Bermejo, the noted theologian teaching in India, says there were three ways he sees of calling men to ministry in the New Testament originally - (a) imposition of hands from those who have themselves been ordained (with the approval of the community), (b) designation by the church (i.e. by some of the members who have not themselves been ordained) with the approval of the community (c) designation by the church (i.e. by some of the members who have not themselves received any particular commission) with the approval of the church's ministers and (d) free, charismatic creation of ministers by the Spirit with the subsequent approval of the Church.(1)

* * * * * *

An inkling of the fast development of the bishop's priestly role and its gradual emergence is exemplified in the writings of St Cyprian, Bishop of Carthage in North Africa from 248 to 258.

Cyprian was an extraordinary man - a lawyer barely three or four years a christian when elected bishop. His legal training, his peculiar experiences, his deep faith and leadership qualities helped him shape a theology of Church which was to have an enormous effect on western catholic thinking even to this day. One wonders whether this illustrious martyr who may well have been excommunicated by the bishop of Rome if he had lived, who himself fell martyr before this happened, would have produced such a strictly delineated theology of Church if he had lived longer as a "catholic" christian. He spent so much of his short life as a bishop and a catholic with crises, there could not have been a great deal of time for reflection. Jay, the english patristics writer, says of him "...it is true to say that Cyprian's hierarchical and sacerdotal view of the Church was to dominate western christianity for centuries." (2)

He built on the writings of Tertullian (+c.220), his fellow North African, and Hippolytus (+236) before him when he referred to the bishop as "high priest". He went further by drawing a close parallel between the christian ministry and the hierarchical aaronic priesthood of judaism and its sacrificial functions. Before Cyprian, Hippolytus, especially, applied Old Testament imagery of priesthood to the New Testament ministers. Comment has already been made on the straining of ideas clustered around the whole people sharing the priestly worship or sacrifice of Jesus when one element of it - the "priest" leader - is emphasized.

Cyprian's notion of Church seemed to have been shaped very much by his North African experience. It is curious that while his hierarchical and sacerdotal views have dominated Western Christianity for centuries, as Jay says, the Western Church has adopted some of his views that suited and rejected others as bordering on heresy; but for Cyprian they held together as a unified system. Irenaeus and the "catholic" party had seen Bishops as one of the three building blocks in the "catholic" system. One always had to be cautious about Scripture, they reasoned, because even what had increasingly become the agreed Canon could be twisted by heretics to their own end. The Rule of Faith, fast becoming encapsulated in the Apostles' Creed with its definitive formulae often making it easier to clarify than Scripture, still needing a living interpreter who was, of course, the bishop. Even the Rule of Faith or Creed was capable of several interpretations as for instance "one baptism for the remission of sins" which Cyprian of Carthage and Stephen of Rome were to find out and about which they disagreed. For Cyprian with the apparent breakdown of the bishop principle in Carthage, uncertainty ensued even with the three building blocks in place. This is how it happened.

The custom mentioned when discussing Hermas (p. 21) of the Church's not forgiving sins, apostasy, adultery and murder, appears strange in the light of Matthew's Gospel of forgiving up to seventy times seven times, but understandable in the light of the Church's crisis experience during the time of persecution, flared up again in Carthage in the persecution of Decius in 249 A.D. Cyprian took the more benign policy shared with the bishop of Rome that the many apostates who had offered incense to the bust of the Divine Emperor in the height of persecution could be absolved after doing penance for one time only and then were able to return to the community. The clergy who had done so could not function until such a restoration. This angered the "rigorists" who maintained such sins committed after baptism could never be forgiven by the Church. One can sympathise with those who had family members martyred in the persecution feeling resentful against "these people getting away with it". In the light of what the Gospel says about reconciliation, however, their "christian" conduct leaves much to be questioned. These "rigorists" were now being called novatianists after Novatian who had led such a faction in Rome and had had himself consecrated bishop even though Cornelius, the legitimate bishop, had been duly elected and consecrated.

Another party, the "laxists" as they were called, perhaps nearer the Gospel than even Cyprian, believed that after appropriate penance, the grievous sinners could be reconciled more than once. Both sides elected bishops so that now there were three bishops in Carthage. The bishop building block was thus shown to be defective.

Cyprian's answer was quite definite. Only the bishop, he claimed, who has the "kathedra" or teaching chair in succession to his predecessor in office can claim to be the bishop. Many scholars would see this as denying the principle accepted in later centuries that a person is a bishop by having hands laid on him by a bishop in succession to other bishops. They would also see Cyprian's teaching as excluding the possibility of a bishop who has no properly constituted see.

Cyprian's solution led him to two further conclusions which were to have far-reaching effects on subsequent Church teaching. The first was that it was the episcopate that gave unity to the Church. Using the Matthew 16, 18 text of Peter being the rock on which the Church was founded (a text which was to be used lavishly in the centuries to come as the central text for papal claims but interestingly enough not used so in Cyprian's time) Cyprian connects it with the succession of bishops. He concludes "...thence, through the changes of times and successions, the ordering of bishops and the plan of the Church flow onwards; so that the Church is founded upon the bishops, and every act of the Church is controlled by these same rulers." (Ep XXXVI, I[XXXIII]) (3) Did he know when he wrote this how Apostolic Authority was ordered in the first century? His conclusion? "You ought to know that the bishop is in the Church, and the Church in the bishop; and if any one be not with the bishop, then he is not in the Church (the emphasis is mine)...the Church which is catholic and one is not cut or divided but is indeed connected and bound together by the cement of priests (sacerdotes in the third century = bishops) who cohere with one another." (4)

McCue, a noted american ecumenist, says it is in Cyprian "we have the apostles spoken of as bishops, all the bishops spoken of as successors of the apostles, and thus the distinction between apostolic and non-apostolic churches and between their bishops is eliminated." (5)

More importantly, it is in Cyprian that we find the germs of that concept of "college" of bishops so recently revived officially by the Church in Vatican II and never forgotten by the orthodox churches. The latin legal term Cyprian uses is a roman word for a joint ownership of property in which each owner is regarded not so much as possessing a share but is accountable for the whole. In other words while each bishop is responsible for his own diocese, he is also responsible in part for the whole Church. (6) This is not a real departure from the traditional idea of each local church of priestly people led by its bishop, because Cyprian kept in balance this idea with his famous saying: "I have made it a rule ever since the beginning of my episcopate, to make no decision merely on the strength of my own personal opinion without consulting you (the presbyters and deacons) and without the approbation of the people." (7)

Damage occurred when the Cyprian texts absolutizing the bishop's role and the hierarchical system were not taken in conjunction with his other texts where he also stresses his responsibility to his own people.

His second solution on the Church was much more selectively used and even bordered in some of its aspects on heresy. His first solution had equated the Church with the bishop who succeeded the other bishops on the "Kathedra" or teaching chair of his predecessors. Where the duly constituted bishop was, there was the Church. Against the novatianists who argued that a church which included, or was willing to include, former apostates in its communion and therefore lacked holiness and therefore ceased to be Church, Cyprian argued that there were worse crimes than apostasy and one of these was heresy. The novatianist by deceiving others into heresy was worse than the reformed apostate, for "while the lapsed has sinned but once, he sins daily." (8) Cyprian then drew the conclusion, because the novatianists had no real bishops to his way of thinking, that they were not Church and their sacraments were invalid, even baptism. Repentant novatianists would have to be rebaptized, because in Cyprian's opinion they had never really been baptized. (9)

Here Cyprian drew a sharp retort from Stephen, Bishop of Rome, who reminded him that his ancient church's custom and those of all the other churches was that when the Rule of Faith, the Apostles' Creed, said there was only one baptism for the remission of sins it meant precisely that. If even a heretic was baptized in the name of the Trinity, it was a valid baptism.

Before mutual excommunications were pronounced, the bishop of Rome and then Cyprian of Carthage were martyred. Cyprian's sacramentology still remained strong in North Africa and was revived by the donatists with whom St Augustine had to deal a century and a half later.

One important maxim that came out of this rigid doctrine of Cyprian's on the Church was "Outside the Church, there is no salvation." It is a maxim that has echoed down the ages at times to fire the zealots and the zealous to acts of murder, forced conversion and even tireless evangelism in the belief that in order to save souls from the inevitable Hell for all who died outside the Church, any act was justified. It is another example of the danger of a tradition developing along its own lines out of context with its own cluster of ideas.

One of the interesting texts in Cyprian's writings that has often been used apologetically by roman catholics is the so called "Papal Text" in which he asks if "he who deserts the throne of Peter, on which the Church is founded" can be sure he is in the Church?

Many scholars in the light of Cyprian's defiance of Stephen of Rome have called this a later interpolation in the documents. Others have argued because they are two different recensions, one a papal one, the other not containing the papal clause, Cyprian himself may well have changed the original after his quarrel with Stephen of Rome. (10)

* * * * * *

Bas Van Iersel's comments (p. 11) on the New Testament Church are apposite here. Except for the Pastorals, he notes the image presented is "unexpectedly and strikingly homogeneous." He summarizes the images by noting "that a synodal (i.e. all participating) model of the Church is more in accordance with the New Testament."

That synodal model remained in the background during the first few centuries in the Western Church and has always been the backbone of the Eastern churches. Cyprian surprisingly had this in his thoughts. He wrote to the Church in Spain: "And the bishop should be chosen in the presence of the people, who have most fully known the life of each one, and have looked into the doings of each one as respects his habitual conduct." He invoked the collegial principle so "that for the proper celebration of ordinations all the neighbouring bishops of the same province should assemble with the people for which a prelate is ordained." (11)

Cyprian's concept of the college of bishops is in a sense a synodal translation of all the local churches meeting together in the person of their bishops. The Holy Spirit was always seen as the Spirit inspiring each baptized person with his or her own diverse gifts for the ultimate purpose of creating unity but often through the pain and sharpening process of diversity. While Cyprian does not state it this way, each bishop then in turn brings the Spirit of Diversity to the college of bishops to arrive at, preferably by consensus, the Spirit of Unity.

In the years before Cyprian we see synods of bishops meeting in such a Spirit. Brian Daley, an american scholar, mentions that while "there is no documentary evidence for formal gatherings of bishops until the last forty years of the second century," the third century lists many more. Mansi, the famous historian of Councils, lists "over four hundred synods and meetings of bishops, Eastern and Western, known to have been held between the mid-second century and the pontificate of Gregory the Great." (12) Daley also mentions pertinently that the process of "reception" of the newer General Councils of the whole Church was going on in the provincial synods of bishops from after the General Council of Nicea (325). He instances the Emperor Leo I in 458 specifically asking the provincial synods throughout the Eastern Empire "to meet and consider whether or not they still wished to adhere to the Chalcedonian Christological formula." (13)

There was much confusion certainly in the East after the General Council of Ephesus in 431 about which of the two Councils that met there at the same time was the real one. "Through negotiations between the provincial synods of the Antiochine and Alexandrian churches, the unfinished Christological business of Ephesus was finally resolved in 433." (14) In the heyday of arianism "meetings were so frequent that the pagan historian Ammianus Marcellinus wryly observed that the public transportation system during the reign of Constantius II (337-361), was paralyzed by christian bishops travelling to and from their synods at the imperial expense." (15)

The burgeoning hierarchy followed on almost parallel lines to the roman administration (the vast majority of christians until the barbarian invasions were within the imperial borders) and the imperial nomenclature. The terms used today in the christian churches often correspond to Roman terms of geographical division and titles - diocese, archdiocese, metropolitan and so on. The local diocese and city were often coterminous with the roman territory. In time the bishops in the provincial capitals were called metropolitans and exercised a certain chairmanship, often possessing prerogatives which varied from province to province. Again slowly in the most important cities of the Empire (Rome, Alexandria and Antioch) the bishops of those dioceses began to be called patriarchs. In disciplinary matters and heresy these patriarchates acted as final courts of appeal from the diocesan and metropolitan sees in their territory. As this hierarchical system emerged, there seemed to be a general consensus that in matters of heresy, Rome was always a last court of appeal, especially if the patriarchal or metropolitan system appears heretical to the complainant. In the same way it became customary for inter-patriarchal communication to inform the other patriarchates of the heresies condemned in one patriarchate, because they affected the whole "catholic" world.

The Church of Rome's special importance, already seen, combined a "solicitude for all the churches" arising from its being the church in which the blood of Peter and Paul had been shed and their tradition left behind. How much of this was also because for the first three hundred years of christianity, Rome was the imperial capital and how often too its role of the patriarchate of the West was mixed with the other roles is a matter of dispute and a burning issue of ecumenism. (16)

In a sense this hierarchy arose from below. The synodal principle was the whole of this particular church with its own peculiar diversity (as well as the unity it shared with the others) electing a leader who had the charism of leadership and sometimes other charisms, such as teacher particularly, and who has also shown himself loyal to the Jesus the apostles taught. The community knew he possessed these gifts and elected him. The supposition then was because he represented the local church both in its unity and diversity, he, through the same process, could arrive at "catholic" unity for the whole Church with his fellow bishops elected in the same way. The status or office of bishop which at first glance might be considered an overemphasis by Cyprian was kept in balance by Cyprian's other teaching as personified by the way he acted in his local church. Later writers tended to use Cyprian's text as justification for the argument that the authority resided in the bishop.

* * * * * *

The shock of adjusting to being the favoured religion hit the Catholic Church after Constantine and Licinius' Edict of Milan in 313 A.D. The euphoria and gratitude bordering on sycophancy are found amply in the pages of that remarkable pioneering History of the Church ably written by Eusebius, bishop of Caeserea (+ 336). He may not have been highly regarded as a master of literature or even as an historian by modern day standards, but as a work of recording documentation and eye witness accounts combined with love of knowledge and a persevering ferreting out of information it is justly a classic. It also, as any history, especially a pioneering one, registers a bias. Among other things it contains the belief that the apostles travelled throughout the world preaching in various regions and it accepts unquestioningly that bishops whom he names followed the apostles at their deaths.

The early chapters of this book have shown us the situation was far more complex than that. If anything many scripture scholars today think most of the apostles remained in Jerusalem. All subsequent histories building on Eusebius, took the "facts" for granted. Again we have the situation where tradition has built on history partly through the prism of Eusebius' writings. This is another area where the facts are substantially true; but from their interpretation too much is claimed.

Eusebius and others recorded the radical transformation taking place in the early fourth century Church. Christians primarily because of persecution had not many buildings of worship, but because of large numbers now joining the Emperor's favoured religion, the thrusting of temples and other buildings including palaces (basilicas) as gifts on christian bishops, taxes set aside for them, the cultic needs of the newly "converted", the nature of the episcopacy and presbyterate subtly changed.

The theologies of Hippolytus and Cyprian among others had leant heavily on the Old Testament concept of priesthood, as applied to the New Testament ministers. The ground was laid for the increased cultic aspect of ministry opened up to it by the constantinian change. The designation "priest" slipped further down from bishop to presbyter. Clergy were given special privileges and exemptions. For possibly the first time in its history, the Church began to have and be able to afford a large scale full-time priesthood. The sabbath Eucharist gradually became celebrated more and more on certain weekdays until Eucharist was every day. The special places of worship became painted and adorned. Statues, not without opposition, began to appear in churches. Vestments began to be worn much to St Jerome's indignation and his sneers at the foppish younger priests. Elaborate and sometimes court-like ceremonial began to build on the already well drawn up rubrics of Hippolytus.

Even though most of the priests and perhaps some of the bishops continued to be married, the Old Testament levitical sexual purity before "sacrifice" started to become a factor together with the great reverence and respect from Gospel and Pauline times for freely chosen virginity. This induced many synods to favour celibacy for the clergy. Elements of rigorism and even manichaeism (the heresy speaking of the dualism and opposition between spirit and matter with matter being considered as evil) may have been other remote factors in these recommendations to clerical celibacy.

Bishops, because of their talents, began to be used by the Emperor for civic affairs. He invested their judicial decisions with civil authority. Their many immunities and imperial favours made them important people in the political world, culturally raising them little by little above their people instead of "with" them. The temptation to join the presbyterate for other than spiritual motives was now ever present.

While the Edict of Milan professed freedom of conscience for all to choose his or her religion, Constantine in the first ten years or so of his reign moved from an attitude of treating pagans equally towards increasing signs of favouritism towards christianity. Probably he saw christians as the answer to the moral decay of his empire even though (estimates vary) in his early reign christians may have numbered barely 10 to 15% of his subjects. He modified roman law to fit in with christian laws. Sunday, the day when christians assembled, was made a day of rest. Sexual offences, such as adultery and prostitution, were given heavier penalties. Slaves, orphans and widows were given greater consideration in the law.

But the price of all this, most bishops and presbyters did not reckon with until the infringements on the Church's freedom became more apparent as the century passed. The ground was already being laid for the clergy to emerge as a class, even a caste, to reinforce their cultic and absolute authority in the centuries to come. Many have seen in Constantine the birth of the Middle Ages. More severe critics have seen him as effecting the loss of christianity's innocence.

Constantine for his first decade or so was Emperor of only the western portion of the Empire, but given his aspirations for christianity as the moral force in his political renewal he was disturbed to find a schism, donatism, in his North African provinces. It was very similar to notavatianism reinforced now by Cyprian's exclusivist sacramentology. He lent his imperial troops to the bishops endeavouring to crush the schism. But as Tertullian, the great african writer, had enunciated a century earlier: "the blood of martyrs is the seed of Christians." By driving donatism underground, it spread more rapidly.

When he defeated Licinius in 324 A.D. and took over the eastern portion of the Empire, Constantine decided to build an eastern capital of his own at what would be called Constantinople and rule from there in the "new Rome". He lavished all his wealth on this magnificent city. Again he was disturbed to find in the East a more disintegrating factor for christianity than donatism was. This was arianism which in one form or another taught Jesus was not God equal with the Father. It had begun to split christianity right down the middle. Constantine's clear roman mind saw if his moral movement now lost its unity it would no longer serve his political purpose.

His solution, on advice, was a good one - the synodal one. In 325 A.D. he called a super-synod of all the bishops of the Church at Nicea, a town near where his new capital was being built, so that he could keep an eye on both the building and the bishops. Posterity was to call this the first General or Ecumenical Council of the Church. The emperors were to convoke these first seven General Councils which roman catholic, orthodox and many protestants (some adhere to the first four only) still respect as binding. The first four (Nicea 325, Constantinople I 381, Ephesus 431, Chalcedon 451) forged for all times the Church's doctrines on the Trinity and the co-equality of Jesus as God the Son together with the Holy Spirit with God the Father. They also spelt out in dogmatic terms how Jesus was both human and divine. The unifying principle of a General or Ecumenical (Universal) Council had been born.

If the New Testament synodal principle was kept in context, with all the people and presbyters together with their bishop coming to a consensus and his exercising his charism or office of ultimately interpreting apostolic teaching: if this was followed by their bishop representing the whole local church going into synod with all the other bishops provincially or in what would now be called a General Council, then the whole aspect of the early Church was kept in place. When as time passed, bishops were seen as solely the only authority to gather at General Councils with or without consulting their diocese or local church or when outside powers or non-representative controls exerted moral or physical pressure on the bishops or when there was barely an adequate representation of all the churches in the person of their bishops, then the Holy Spirit speaking through the supposed consensus of the Church may not be snuffed out but could be considerably stifled.

The theology of those early centuries worked out that in any of these eventualities a synodal basis was still demanded by what was coming to be called the consensus fidelium. The consent of all the Faithful was needed for the decisions of a General Council as lived in their faith and works after the Council's decrees had been published - a consent they recognized in their own beliefs and lives. We have seen this "reception" by provincial synods after General Councils mentioned by Daley (p. 61). In the Western or Roman Catholic Church this belief, although not entirely forgotten, became less and less effective until its revival by Vatican II, foreshadowed particularly by Cardinal Newman's works a century earlier. What often happened was that assent was demanded with an obedient touching of the forelock rather than a consent searched for as a right of those consenting. The principle of consensus fidelium was good but it became watered down by the processes of history. So in the end the priestly hierarchy ended up by claiming too much.

One needs to take into account how difficult it would have been for the Church in the West after the barbarian invasions to exercise a valid consent of the Faithful (consensus fidelium). Very much more than in the times of the Roman Empire where there were always pockets of sophisticated and educated people (experts differ on the percentages) within the christian communities, the barbarian masses were generally devoid of any formal education. Their "consent" would have been rudimentary which explains partially at least why the election of bishops fell into abeyance and consent of all the Faithful was rarely sought. In the Eastern churches this theological teaching of "consensus fidelium" was better kept both in theory and in practice. That, of course, explains the cultural reasons in the Church why this teaching of authority sharing by all fell into the background. Added to this would have been the response of the hierarchy (when it was educated) to mistrusting 'popular' religion and its excesses, especially in populations largely devoid of formal education.

When this lack was allied to the growing hierarchical systems in the Church together with the gradual formation of a priestly caste, then one can understand the slow setting aside of a very important tradition. Conversely, of course, stubborn religiosity or unwillingness to change could often be used if needed by the hierarchy as an argument for "consensus fidelium" in a people little educated in Theology or the Scriptures. Many christians in the first five centuries were not well-educated, but were soaked in the Scriptures from the Liturgy. The barbarians were probably less educated but a latin liturgy precluded often that same education and made 'consensus fidelium' more difficult.

As well as the consensus fidelium there was also the allied sensus fidelium, the living belief among the Faithful which can be tested at any time. The trouble was of course that at times the consensus fidelium could be used by the ignorant to oppose change because it preferred the status quo. The sensus fidelium could also be misused especially when and if forgeries and parasite ideas had shaped minds and made them think a particular teaching was unalterable and therefore opposed change. At their best however they were indicators pointing back to a time when lay people had a right to express their opinions and assist in decision making as the Holy Spirit worked through them also.

Nevertheless, the various findings point us to the predisposition in human beings to search with great intensity for the securities that religion offers. The wisdom of the roman catholic church as opposed to many of the protestant churches has been to utilize these human religious factors to great advantage throughout the centuries. What the roman catholic church has often forgotten, nor did it have until recently the scientific analysis at its disposal to act, was that all these factors, valuable and important as they were, have a hidden danger. As Exeler has pointed out "The tendency to pursue religious knowledge and ritualism for their own sake is not exactly a new phenomenon in Christianity. It is as old as the faith itself, and must therefore be constantly exposed and resisted. We find that prophets fought it when, for instance, they turned against a ritualistic penitential system which encouraged people to hope that they could be reconciled with God through religious practices instead of genuine conversion. We find it also in Jesus' conflict with some groups among his contemporaries that put external religious practice above an authentic inner life. The unmasking of this diminution of religious life will always remain one of the tasks of ecclesiastic renewal. These features are the most subtle obstacle to religious life because this busying oneself about religion can easily cover up the real failures in life, and because those who want to purge religious practice are often accused of being enemies…of the faith. We should not forget that Jesus was put to death by very pious people in the name of God and for the sake of religion." (17)

It is the bishops' role to discern and lead their peoples through the positive aspects as well as the dangers arising from religious criteria. The religious predispositions can be hi-jacked by a fundamentalist or "one issue" group. Such a group may think one ideology can save the world and all must be subordinated to it. It sees no good whatsoever in its enemies' arguments seeing opposing theories in totally black and white terms. As for pluralism or living in tension with other views and tolerating them but agreeing to their right to exist, it will have none of that. A bishop's role should be to preserve that balance of diversity in unity as lived in the early church.

The religious predispositions can make religion an end in itself. Instead of being a concomitant to christian growth and a strengthening of that growth to open out to more real challenges of christianity they can become a self-preserving cocoon, inward looking and abrasive to prophets.

This yearning for the sacred and cultic, quite valid in itself, emits danger signals when it predisposes to a cultic, sacral priesthood above the "lower class" christians in contrast with the Gospel values such as we have seen were put into place and lived by the early Church, not without certain tensions but kept largely in place. The predisposition to pedestalize the guru or leader and make a dependent discipleship may produce the apparent

67

benefit of strengthening community, fellowship and spiritual knowledge. It may well have been, together with the contemporary political and cultural elements, the predisposition to monoepiscopacy. It can, however, be inimical when the growth to spiritual and emotional maturity is blunted in order to create perpetual dependence.

When the power given to the coterie of leaders is used to cloak the clay feet of the "gods": when their financial benefits and comfortable living are reasons for clinging on to this power: when the headiness of the power itself makes the divine passing on of servant authority by Christ himself extend to divinize elements that are dependent on 'parasite' ideas from the contemporary culture or political structure: when christian authority, (often in the form of political power) becomes concentrated solely on one group within that community and that group fears the extension of authority might mean power sharing with another group hence forcing it to forsake its ideology: when there is a power play in fending off "non-priestly" opposition or keeping that opposition ignorant or allowing them to believe in a "golden age" that never existed: in a word forgetting Gospel priorities. When the question becomes one of retention of power and the special Gospel priority of servant authority is forgotten, then religious elements have taken over at the expense of christianity. It is the church's mission to hold these two things, religion and Christ's teaching, in balance and tension. There will always be a temptation to settle for the easier way, the religious one, which in time tends to predominate at the expense of Christ's teaching.

1. Bermejo, Luis. Towards Christian Reunion. Anand, India, Gujarat Sahitya Prakash. 1984. p. 186
2. Jay, Eric G. The Church. London, SPCK. 1977, Vol. I. p. 73
3. Ibid, p. 67
4. Ibid, pp. 67-68
5. McCue, James F., "The Roman Primacy in the Patristic Era" in Papal Primacy and the Universal Church. Minneapolis, Augsburg Publishing House. 1974. p. 58
6. Jay, Eric G. The Church. p. 70
7. McBrien, Richard P. Catholicism. San Francisco, Harper. 1994. p. 744
8. Jay, Eric G. The Church. London, SPCK. 1977 Vol. I. pp. 66-67
9. Cardman, Francine. "Cyprian and Rome: The Controversy over Baptism", Concilium. October 1982. p. 36 makes the point that neither Cyprian nor Stephen would demand rebaptism of a person who was baptized a "catholic", lapsed and then returned. However, for a person baptized in a schismatic or heretical church, Cyprian would demand rebaptism, Stephen would not.
10. Jay, Eric G. The Church. pp. 70-71
11. Ibid, p. 71
12. Daley, B. "Structures of Charity: Bishops' Gatherings and the See of Rome in the Early Church" in Episcopal Conferences, (Ed. Thomas J. Reese S.J.). Washington D.C., Georgetown University Press. 1989. p. 27
13. Ibid, p. 28
14. Ibid, p. 31
15. Ibid, p. 31. In many cities at the time there were three bishops: catholic, semi-arian and arian. Ibid, p. 28
16. In his The Bishop of Rome. London, SPCK. 1983. p. 52. J.M.R. Tillard attempting to unravel some of the bishop of Rome's history says: "We should, therefore, distinguish between the authority which properly belongs to the specific function (munus) of the bishop of Rome within the universal communion of churches and the claims produced by confusion between the several primacies enjoyed by the Roman see."
17. Albert Exeler quoted in J.B. Walker, Christianity an end to Magic. London, Darton, Longman and Todd. 1972. pp. 49-50

CHAPTER SIX

The Monarch Bishops begin to lose their roots in the episkope and tilt in a distorted fashion towards Centrism and Papacy

The third, fourth and fifth centuries witnessed the development of the bishop "building block" into provincial and General Councils on the synodal principle that we saw Von Iersel and other scripture scholars summarized as a root New Testament idea. The same centuries also gave evidence of the rapid development begun in the first two centuries - the roman church, or as we would say nowadays, the papal claims.

We have seen in previous chapters the acknowledged moral supremacy of the church of Rome. The letter of Clement (pp. 22-23) shows that early solicitude of the roman church where the apostles Peter and Paul had shed their blood. This was no doubt enhanced by its universal interest arising from the fact that it was the church at the centre of the Empire. For example, Irenaeus hurried to Rome from Lyons to put in a good word for the Montanists (p. 32).

When, in contrast to his predecessors, Victor, bishop of Rome (+ 199) was about to excommunicate the bishops of Asia Minor for not keeping Easter on Sunday, a tradition they claimed to have from St John the Apostle, Irenaeus and other bishops remonstrated with him pointed out differences of disciplinary custom had not, up to this point of time, been allowed to compromise Christian fellowship. They seemed to have won their point. (1) Their protest was based on the principle of diversity in unity.

Second century literature such as the letters of Ignatius of Antioch speak of the roman "presidency of love" (2) in all the churches. Irenaeus' writings of the need for agreement with the Church of Rome "on account of her more powerful origin"(3) from the apostles Peter and Paul.

The third century saw that solicitude again being exercised, although not always being appreciated by Stephen I, bishop of Rome (+ 257), in the churches of Spain, Gaul and North Africa (all by the way in what was developing as the Patriarchate of the West). We have seen earlier the conflict between Stephen and Cyprian of Carthage (p. 60), which earned Cyprian's retort: "For no one of us sets himself up as a bishop of bishops, or by tyrannical terror forces his colleagues to the necessity of obeying, in as much as every bishop in the free use of his liberty and power has the right of forming his own judgement and can no more be judged by another than he can himself judge another." (4)

Perhaps we have here another clue as to whether or not Cyprian's papal statement was changed by him after his fight with Stephen or was a later interpolation (p. 60)!

In this third century too we see the first bishop of Rome (Callistus + c.222) to use the Petrine text in Matthew 16: 18 (Christ calling Peter the "rock") to explain his authority, but to justify his right against the rigorists to full powers to absolve from all sins, but not his authority over all the churches as commentators have pointed out. Some, but not all agree. They have seen a reference to the Petrine text in Stephen of Rome and J M R Tillard, the famed canadian dominican, agrees with C Hoffstetter when he summarizes all the evidence stating: "From all this we conclude that the awareness of the roman church's competence, and that of its bishops, within the universal Church is older than the awareness that this position corresponds with the position of St Peter among the apostles." (5)

Rome in the first three centuries of christianity had assumed a role (and it had been largely accepted) as the last court of appeal regarding heresy or serious deviation from Tradition, because in itself it contained the traditions of the two great apostles martyred there. As patriarch of the West, Rome's bishop had, of course, more immediate power in Western Europe and North Africa. But except for the extreme cases mentioned above, other local churches functioned independently or had recourse to their own metropolitans or patriarchs.

* * * * * *

The fourth century saw a development from that early christian position. As Ullmann, the noted English historian says: "The convocation of this council (Nicea), its composition and the predominance of Eastern participants were portents. It is of some considerable significance in this context to note that in his opening address Constantine referred to Byzantium as "New Rome" - the opening bar of a major symphonic theme. If Constantinople was "New Rome", the implication was clear for Rome itself and consequently for the standing of its church. Constantinople had become the empire's governmental and political centre of gravity. This factor was to a very large extent to determine the path of the roman church." (6)

When Constantine's enormous benefactions and their consequent administration, and more particularly with his moving to Constantinople, with the need to arbitrate now in clerical courts, the roman bishops set up on the imperial model a chancery or curia with registers for incoming and outgoing mail and also to add to whatever archives that early church possessed. Even the style and composition of the letters followed the imperial model.

The church of Rome never lost her sense of being the centre of unity and the last court of appeal for all the churches. When arianism in the decades after Nicea attempted to wreck that unity and almost succeeded in doing so, the focus of unity and power became the Emperor. Because one of the bishops of Rome, Liberius, would not conform to the Arian Emperor, the Emperor exiled and possibly tortured him until he signed on the dotted line in 355 A.D., Rome could see a new need for unity arising in the Church. Chadwick remarks: "The conflict of the Arian controversy weakened the respect in which episcopal synods were held. They still enjoyed high reverence and authority, but not as much as they had before the controversy began since there had been too many instances of rival synods producing incompatible manifestos." (7) Rome perceived an extension of this charism of unity was needed over and above quarrelling synods.

Most historians trace the vital changes within the church of Rome to have occurred under Damasus (366-384) and his successor as bishop, Siricius (384-399). As Henry Chadwick comments: "It seemed to be a clear lesson of the Arian controversy that the whole church needed a much stricter discipline and more centralized control." (8) In many dioceses and local churches three bishops, an arian, semi-arian and catholic, had flourished for a long time. In the later years of Damasus, arianism was effectively vanquished as a powerful force when Theodosius I in 379 became Emperor in the East. He was a strictly orthodox catholic. Theodosius sent ahead a message before he reached Constantinople that the faith that must be subscribed to had to be that of Damasus, bishop of Rome and Peter, bishop of Alexandria (Constantinople had a heretical patriarch and Antioch an internal dispute over whom was patriarch). He called what we now know as the Second General Council at Constantinople in 381. Rome was at the time under a Western Emperor, Gratian, and it apparently sent no representative. Damasus regretted this although the Westerners in any case would probably not have had much say.

The second General Council was a two-edged sword. It condemned arianism and all the heresies the bishops of Rome had fought; but included a canon which stated: "The bishop of Constantinople shall have rank after the bishop of Rome because it is New Rome." Chadwick pertinently remarks: "This canon was resented both at Alexandria, long regarded as the second city of the empire, and at Rome because, although it conceded that Rome was the first see of Christendom, it implied that roman primacy depended on the city's secular standing." (9)

For good or for ill this was to be the controversial point between the Eastern and Western churches in the centuries to come - Rome reckoned on apostolic foundation particularly its own, Peter and Paul, as giving hierarchical precedence, the East in the main reckoned on civil importance although it did not disregard apostolic origins.

Damasus sprang into action. He called a synod in Rome in 382. While it accepted the credal formula of the General Council at Constantinople, it utterly rejected the canon on the Old and New Rome. Because of this, the Council's canons were only fully accepted by Rome two centuries later. The synod declared that the roman primacy over all other churches resulted not from a decree of any Council but from the Divine Will and the Lord's promise to St Peter.

Fortunately for Rome, but unfortunately for historians of Tradition, two documents emerged from the roman chancery at this time to further muddy the waters. The first was a misrepresentation copied probably in error by some curial clerk. He had mixed the decrees of the Council of Serdica (343) with the canons of the First General Council of Nicea (325). The Council of Serdica had been called near the borders of the Eastern and Western Empires to settle disputes about arianism. When the Eastern bishops saw it was not going to go their way, they left the Western bishops to meet by themselves. In the course of this meeting the Western bishops passed a canon saying that the bishop of Rome could appoint judges to hear appeals by bishops under censure in their own province.

As the bishops present were from the Western Patriarchate, their canon was natural enough and could have probably been duplicated in any other patriarchate. When it was switched to become a nicene canon, it was supposed to be a law of the universal Church. Chancery's use of it as such gave the impression it was a nicene canon until Pope Zosimus (417-419) used it against the north african bishops who had never heard of the Council of Serdica. They sent to the East for authentic texts and St Augustine informed an embarrassed Zosimus of the mix-up. Again one asks how important were these documents in forming a roman mind on papacy or reinforcing existing ideas?

Perhaps they were executed, as many forgeries were, to underscore the current conviction that "we cannot possibly be wrong" but just need a few more documents to prove it then their effect of exaggerating true Tradition is a distortion and results in claiming too much from a perfectly valid premise. If these documents were used, as well they might be, by most as authentic documents then the question is not "Is our Tradition wrong?", so much as how did these documents then accepted as Tradition shape and distort contemporary and therefore future Tradition? Equally, how far did the teachings that sprang from them influence in their turn dogmas regarded now as unalterable?

R W Southern, the English medieval historian, even though he is speaking of a slightly later period, pertinently puts "forgery" in perspective: "...it is important to understand the importance of forgeries as vehicles of ideas in this early period. They did not have the vulgar associations of modern forgeries. The primitive age had few records, but it had clear ideas of the past. These ideas were based on accumulated traditions, legends, pious fabrications, and above all on a reluctance to believe that the past is largely unknowable. Hence even learned and critical men easily believed that the past was like the present, only better; in a word that it was an idealized present. Documents were therefore drawn up in which the theories of the present were represented as the facts of the past. These documents were inspired by a strong fear of losing any possession that the saints, whose dominion embraced every church in christendom, could claim as their own. Everyone felt that it was safer to overstate a case and to give their church the benefit of every doubt, rather than lose something that could justly be claimed. The forgeries which are a conspicuous feature of the age, provided documentary proofs for claims which, in the minds of those who made them, scarcely needed to be justified. The pen corrected the corruptions of nature and restored the gross imperfections and injustices of the world to a primitive excellence. The falsehoods implicit in these documents did indeed raise moral problems of which contemporaries were not unaware but the authors believed that they enforced truths which could not be abandoned without grave danger to their souls. Forgeries, like art, brought order into the confusions and deficiencies of the present." (10)

If they were acted upon, as many forgeries were, to underscore the current conviction (we cannot possibly be wrong) and if it took just a few more documents to prove that position, they were added. This had the effect of exaggerating the true Tradition, so it became distorted resulting in it claiming too much although it proceeded from an originally valid premise. Those distorting documents shape and can further distort teachings many would consider unquestionable.

Constantly the historian has to be checking and double checking to ascertain the claimed contemporeity of the documents as well as the credulity of the users of the same writings in subsequent centuries. This dilemma certainly arises from the second document produced by chancery. We know now it was a blatant forgery, but was believed to be authentic at the time. There was found a purported letter of Clement, bishop of Rome, to St James, brother of Christ, written as most authentic early christian

74

documents were in Greek, but now translated by Rufinus of Aquilea into Latin. Quite apart from what we now know about Clement of Rome not being a bishop, most experts say the document was probably later than the second century. For those who may have thought Christ's words to Peter in Matthew 16: 18ff were to Peter only, they most certainly were not. At St Peter gathered the christians of Rome around him and spoke, translated by Rufinus into the legal latin of the roman last will and testament: "I impart to him (Clement)" said St Peter, "the authority of binding and loosing in order that whatever he (Clement) will decide upon earth, will be approved in Heaven, for he will bind what must be bound and he will loose what should be loosed." In roman custom last will dispositions were often announced in public so that there would be no doubt about the intention. It was added that while St Peter had been in Jerusalem and Antioch he did not institute a successor except in the Roman See. Even though every bishop succeeded to the totality of all the apostles, the bishop of Rome was the sole successor of the head of the apostles.

The importance of this forgery is difficult to estimate. Sufficient for the moment to say that from early in the fifth century onwards the Matthew text of Peter and the rock was uniformly interpreted by bishops of Rome and their curia (chancery) in this sense.

These ideas described above I have christened "parasite" ideas because they live off true ideas. They were used to help explain the true idea in language or philosophy that suit the contemporary scene admirably then in time take over the true idea to the point where the "parasite" idea becomes the main idea. The hebrew idea of "soul" which was much more inclusive than the greek word which was used in opposition to the body and more powerful than it took over in time as the main idea of soul.

A further extension of the "parasite" idea was in forgery. The forgery (parasite) idea, believed to be authentic, helped to shape the thinking on that subject and became incorporated in the tradition surrounding it. Just how much it shaped the tradition is often hard to assess. This exercise has to be done however, when re-assessing the Tradition from traditions.

The U.S. Anglican-Lutheran dialogue on Papal Primacy puts the situation well when it says: "Historical studies have opened new perspectives not only on the New Testament writing but also on other problems. It is now clear that the question of papal primacy cannot adequately be treated in terms of proof passages from scripture or as a matter of church law, but must be seen in the light of many factors - biblical, social, political, theological - which have contributed to the development of the theology structure and function of the modern papacy." (11)

Our knowledge already indicates the probable assumption there were few bishops in the sense of local churches in the first century. Irenaeus' list of the bishops of Rome compared to the much later written Book of the Popes (Liber Pontificalis) records a different order with the names Linus and Anacletus coming between Peter and Clement, showing that the letter of Clement to James was probably composed after the time of Irenaeus. The disparity of much earlier documentation, authentic, forged or possibly interpolated is something which has to be evaluated; but something that can never be altered is the repercussions such misinformation has had on the belief systems particularly of contemporary people with little or no education - a belief system which, of course, feeds into the stream of Tradition.

Armed with these chancery documents and, I feel sure, believing them, Damasus' successors acted on the principles far and wide. As Holmes and Bickers say: "Siricius (384-399) was the first to use the title "pope" in itself simply meaning "father" but highly significant when taken in conjunction with the practice of calling other bishops "sons". He began the system of decretals - decisions given by the Pope in a particular dispute, but which soon assumed a much wider validity and importance. (The term, incidentally, was a roman imperial chancery term). Innocent I (402-417) maintained that all major claims must be brought to Rome for judgement from which there could be no appeal." (12)

It was under Leo the Great (440-461) that the particular climax of these decades of endeavour bore fruit. He was the first pope to take the title of "Pontifix Maximus" (High Priest of the pagan state religion) which the increasingly weakened christian Western Emperors no longer used. He was the first pope to claim in a letter to one of his suffragans, the bishop of Thessalonica, who had exceeded his powers "that he was not called to plenitude of power but only to a share of (Leo's) responsibility." (13) This latin phrase "plenitudo postestatis" (fullness of power) became a canonical axiom to underpin so many papal claims up until our own times. Leo can certainly be called one of the important builders of the papal system.

While frightened imperial officials fled Rome before the onslaught of the barbarians, Leo organized food supplies and went out to meet Attila the Hun, negotiating a settlement. By skilful arguments he contended that as in roman legal opinion the person of the honoured ancestor took over the less worthy descendant who could say he acted in the name of the ancestor. From this it is deduced that authority belonged to the office. Despite unworthy bishops the office itself was not compromised. The bishops of Rome were therefore "Vicars of Peter" and his heirs. Just as the authority given to Peter by Christ was conveyed to the other apostles through Peter, reasoned Leo, so the authority of the bishops is derived, not immediately from Christ, but through the bishop of Rome. (14)

It was the fourth General Council of Chalcedon (451) that saw the climax of Leo's power. After the reading of his "tome" by his delegates (a tome that became to a large extent the accepted basis of the chalcedonian decree on Christ's person and nature) the bishops in eastern fashion and imagery exclaimed "Peter has spoken through the mouth of Leo", a wonderful defence mechanism for roman catholic apologists. However, they were far more hard headed than that one acclamation may infer.

While the papal delegates were away, they passed a motion reiterating the Second General Council of Constantinople's decree (381) on the privileges of Constantinople being the second patriarchate in honour on the grounds of its imperial status as the New Rome. Leo was so incensed at the passing of this motion by the Council that he withheld his ratification of the dogmatic definition for two years. It only served to allow the 'heresy' the Council had condemned to flourish and use the bishop of Rome's lack of approval for the Council as a proof for his non-acceptance of all its decrees.

The apparently ambiguous attitude of the Eastern bishops at Chalcedon reflected the very dilemma indicated above. They were prepared to accept the age old Petrine gift of unity for the sake of the Church together with Rome's time-honoured role as a last court of appeal against heresy. They were not prepared to accept, as they saw it, domination from the roman see that for them had no precedents in their Tradition. The eastern attitude is well described by Piepkorn, a prominent ecumenist: "The Easterners are willing to accord a kind of primacy, to the see of Rome on a political-historical basis. Thus, when the roman see enunciates its claim to universal primacy, the Eastern churches listen and politely refrain from explicitly rejecting these claims, in part at least out of a genuine respect for the see of Peter. The bishops of Rome in turn seem at least at times to have interpreted this Eastern silence as concurrence in the roman positions." (15)

This was basically the fundamental position between the Eastern and Western churches for the next six centuries. It helped precipitate the final break. This certainly makes one question where the "consensus fidelium" and the consensus of the other "catholic" churches lay in the roman church's developments in the fourth and fifth centuries. This is especially so when very few of the documents from and in the files of the curia seem ever to have arrived in the East. Presumably too with the collapse of most courier services as a result of the barbarian invasions in the West contact substantially decreased and little "consensus" would have been able to be given to most of the documentation from the West to which it would seem to have been mainly dispatched.

The confusion resulting from the mixing of the Serdican/Nicean decrees has been noted (p. 73). Unilateral declarations with the "catholic" churches had up until now always to be tested by the other churches in fact and in theory. This new "papal" way had never been the accepted way of teaching, nor did it seem to have been adequately "received" in any case.

What makes one query the "consensus fidelium" of the fourth and fifth centuries, I think, is the question of how well was this quite significant development in papal claims received in the Western churches? Holmes and Bickers comment quite accurately: "The absence of any significant rival to Rome in the West aided the popes who made full use of precedents to prove the antiquity of their claims." (16) Arles was one of the few metropolitans in the West to try and defy Rome; but Hilary, its bishop, engaged the wrong man when he challenged Leo the Great. Hilary, as Chadwick remarked, "was brought to submission by Pope Leo I but only with the help of a thunderous rescript from the Emperor Valentinian III, which decreed that all bishops in the Western provinces must submit to papal authority on the pain of secular penalties." (17) This rescript of one of the last of the Emperors of old Rome presiding in the last days over the disintegration of the Western Roman Empire was filed away with the growing arsenal of authentic and inauthentic documentation to be used, often completely out of context, a few centuries later by scribes and canon lawyers for whom the context was largely unknown or irrelevant.

But a stronger argument than Hilary of Arles' challenge to Leo I in 445 against the wholesale acceptance (consensus fidelium) by the West of these more subtle and dominant developments of the papacy was the question: "Which bishops or communities were in a normal atmosphere to "receive" or resist them?" At the very time that the papal chancery was building up a new slant on an old image, unacceptable to the Eastern Churches, Western metropolitans and most of their bishops were fortifying their towns against barbarian invasions, witnessing their rape and destruction and seeking out a survival in their ruins. In fact, survival was the predominant theme of the decades 400-450 A.D. for most Western Provinces - an atmosphere not conducive to measured theologising or parrying with the roman chancery's niceties.

The visigoths invaded Northern Italy at the beginning of the fifth century. The Rhine (denuded of troops for the defence of Italy) was crossed by many different barbarian troops in 406. Rome fell in 410. Spain had been overrun by a horde of vandals, sueves and alans in the previous year. A visigothic kingdom was set up in the south of France in 419, a vandal one in North Africa in 429. The invaders were scaling the walls of Hippo as St Augustine lay dying in 430. The burgundians and franks had set up their kingdoms before Leo became Pope in 440. During his episcopate the angles, saxons and jutes were consolidating their gains in Britain. A battleground of devastated cities, villages and estates was hardly a normal place for "reception" as the roman chancery's line took on a very distinctive pattern that was to colour the christian churches' advance until now.

"Reception" of this kind of development is, as we have seen, a moot point. If it were supposed to be an extension of the synodal principle of all participating in decision-making and consultation before Apostolic Authority ultimately decides and is then followed by a process of consultation before it is finally decided, then it lacks all these facets of the principle.

One wonders how far beyond the roman chancery and its neighbouring confines it was fully "received" remembering the petrine principle of unity was already accepted. Its development (or distortion?) is the subject under question. It was not very difficult for a later theology interlarded with platonic philosophical premises to highlight the universal absolutes of the papal "development" from papal letters and decrees and ignore the historical context of this "development". Particularly when much of this "theology" took place in the Dark Ages without informed sources to critique this "development" further enhanced by an atmosphere of religiosity and the "sacred". The laity became more of a class below the clergy and bishops, but in one respect they held a trump card, not in the sense of the "priestly people" taking responsibility but in the sense that kings and nobles gradually became the powerful who selected bishops and often used them for their own purposes.

Sometimes the external form of presbyters (now called canons of the cathedral chapter or some other clerical body) were used to elect the bishop. More often than not the chapter through power politics, bribes or outright simony was swayed by the local nobility to vote for a selected candidate. Many times the king or a local noble chose the new bishop outright, sometimes to reward a worthy man, sometimes to reward a courtier who needed revenue, sometimes to ensure an illegitimate son a living for life.

Powerful laity then gained ecclesiastical power in the five hundred years from 500-1000 A.D. that took away the whole idea of the bishop coming from the people and because of his election by them, being with his people. Now as a result of historical change the bishop was above his people and responsible to the king or local ruler. When it was a ruler as well disposed as Charlemagne, good bishops ensued. However, this seemed to be the exception rather than the rule so desirable an office and status with its power and material sinecures did the bishop have. The appraisers and leaders were now very different from those exercising episkope in the early Church.

The name of bishop, ensuring continuity by ordination, cloaked an entirely different concept from the early church and even that of the first five centuries— an official now unelected by most of the clergy and people of his diocese, often an outsider to this local church unaware of its theology and definitions and a determined autocrat.

Most civilizations have credited their kings or rulers with divine powers. When Rome ceased being a republic and became an Empire it did not take the Emperors long before they claimed divinity. It was this very point that christians in the early Church could not accept. They could not bring themselves to offer incense to the Emperor as a god that resulted in their intermittent but fierce persecution.

From the time of Tertullian, Hippolytus and Cyprian in the third century, Old Testament concepts were used as a basis for priesthood to apply to bishops and presbyters. From that time it became natural that the Old Testament concept of the rulers as anointed ones, like David, came to the fore. Constantine called himself "bishop" and "presbyter" as the anointed one of God with power to call the bishops together in council. (18) Soon the early barbarian kings were being anointed and consecrated to lead their kingdoms and God's church within their borders.

In other cultures and climes the divinity of the ruler was also of paramount importance. Few cultures were a theocracy governed by their priests in the name of God or gods. In either kind of culture, religion so permeated the civilization that the distinction between politics and religion were hard to unravel. "Christianity on the other hand, 'irrupted' into ancient civilization" explains Brian Tierney, the american historian, "that already had its own established hierarchy of government and its own sophisticated tradition of political thought based on non-christian concepts. In the early centuries, therefore, the Christian church had to develop its own structure of governing offices, sometimes parallel to, but always apart from, those of the secular hierarchy and from the first there was always the possibility of a conflict of loyalties." (19)

Tierney would see in this seed of the christian church implanted in Western European society one of the reasons, if not the main reason, for the peculiar path it has pursued in history differently from other civilizations. "The very existence of two power structures competing for men's allegiance instead of only one compelling obedience greatly enhanced the possibilities of human freedom. In practical life over and over again in the Middle Ages men found themselves having to make genuine choices according to conscience or self-interest between conflicting appeals to their loyalty." (20) Even Constantine's benevolent interference never quite unmoored the Church from its beginnings.

St Ambrose (+397) confronted the great Emperor Theodosius I after his massacres in Thessalonica refusing him entrance to Milan cathedral in 390. "Palaces belong to the Emperor, churches to the priesthood." So wrote Gelasius I (492-496), bishop of Rome, following in the footsteps of Leo I and the fifty years or so of curial theology before Leo. He had the added strength to be speaking in the vacuum created by the last Western Roman Emperor's deposition in 476 and before the ostrogoths finally tightened their grip on Italy which freed Gelasius from both the Eastern Emperor's tutelage and the later papal control by the ostrogothic kings. He now wrote to the Eastern Emperor (who in theory was still the Emperor of the Christian world): "Two there are, august emperor, by which this world is chiefly ruled, the sacred authority of the priesthood and the royal power. Of these the responsibility of the priests is more weighty in so far as they will answer for the kings of men themselves at the divine judgement." (21)

This highly controversial text of Gelasius was interpreted differently throughout the Middle Ages as to whether he was advocating a balanced dualism or insisting that priests had more responsibility than kings. At least one historian (Ullmann) maintains that the different latin words for authority (auctoritas) and power (Potestas) had different roman legal connotations - authority could mean an inherent right to rule - power only a delegated executive power to carry out instructions. Whatever Gelasius meant, the text came up constantly in the legal compendia for the next thousand years. The stage was being set for the mighty battle of the next millennium between the State and the Church. As Southern remarks in chapter seven (p. 109): "The sacred ruler, however, who seemed to contemporaries the strongest of all the products of the age, turned out to be of all things the most fragile."

In the meantime it is worthy of note that the Eastern Emperor in Constantinople assumed for the next thousand years the mantle of the Sacred Emperor. This has often been called 'Caesaropapism'. One of its greatest exponents was Justinian (527-565) who invaded the old Western Empire now under barbarian tutelage conquering a considerable portion of it. H Moss says of him that he "was not content to regulate the Church by detailed legislation: in doctrinal disputes he exerted to the full his Imperial prerogatives of convoking councils and assigning limits...though formally distinct, Church and State were actually one, and political considerations guided Justinian along the road into which his theological interests had already led him." (22)

This caesaropapism, with its many nuances, was the mark of the Eastern Empire until its downfall in 1453. How did the old Western Empire, now a number of barbarian kingdoms and principalities, avoid becoming the same?

* * * * * *

It is one of the great accidents of history (and some would say divine providence) that Constantine moved his capital from Rome to Constantinople. It left behind a certain power vacuum for when at times there was no Co-Emperor in the West resident in Rome, its bishop often assumed a leadership role in that city. Even when a co-emperor lived in Rome he was left effectively presiding over the steady demise of the Western Empire, particularly once the Goths crossed the Rhine. As civil officials fled and the bureaucracy broke down, the bishop of Rome assumed a more and more commanding hegemony over the city, especially when Ravenna became the effective Western imperial capital from about 400. This is the period of Damasus-Leo the Great seen above in whose curia a theology and ideology were developed. Whether it ever received the consensus fidelium or not is, as we have seen, highly debatable. There was no debate over the roman church's primacy among but not over the other churches. Nor was there debate over its acknowledged place in discerning true from false teaching - nor its rightful solicitude for all the churches. The Damasan-Leonine curial development is what seemed unilateral and claiming too much.

The power vacuum in Italy ceased with its conquest by the ostrogoths at the end of the fifth century. Although arian, they did not destroy the remaining Italo-Roman culture. The bishop of Rome, now increasingly called pope, had at least a moral superiority as the sole native representative of ancient unity. After 476 when the last of the nominal Western Roman Emperors abdicated, the bishop of Rome assumed a semi-independence under the ostrogoths and once again we find under Gelasius, as mentioned above, a roman challenge to the Eastern Emperor.

However, once Justinian and his brilliant general Belisarius conquered the ostrogoths in Italy the power base shifted to Constantinople through the Emperor's exarch in Ravenna. Belisarius had used the lombards to help in the invasion. The bishops of Rome remained fairly muted during this period and even during the lombard occupation of half of Italy after Justinian's death. They were still subject to the Eastern Emperor's exarch in Ravenna and at least two popes were dragged to Constantinople to be bullied in one case and martyred in the second (Virgilius and Martin I).

One of the few Popes able to rise above this was Gregory the Great (590-604). His moral leadership extended far beyond Rome and the Italian peninsula. Even though the missionary movement of converting Western Europe was not roman initiated, Gregory directed campaigns against paganism and heresy in Gaul, Italy and Sicily, taking a measure of control over its disparate elements. He sent Augustine to England where conversions of the various anglo-saxon kingdoms soon followed. The english monks in their turn had much to do with the reform of the gallic (french) church and conversion of the german peoples.

The lombards were gradually becoming catholic christians but still posed a threat to the papacy as did the Eastern Empire once the Emperor

Leo the Isaurian (717-740) supported the iconoclast heresy (no images including ikons in churches). Pope Gregory III (731-741) excommunicated him. The Emperor seized the papal estates in the south of Italy. The lombards seeing a weakened papacy, pressed their advantage. While Gregory's successor, Zachary (741-752) negotiated an uneasy peace, he realized something would have to be done as Rome was threatened by both an heretical Emperor and Lombards impatient for invasion. If either party struck at Rome, whatever independence the pope had could be lost.

The new pope, Stephen II (752-757), acted quickly. Events played into his hands. The papacy looked West to the strongest family of the time, the frankish mayor of the palace or effectively prime minister. One of them, Charles Martel, had driven the muslims back when they reached their highwater mark in Europe at Tours in France in 732. Rome had appealed to Charles for protection against the lombards in 739, an appeal he ignored because the lombards were his allies. Now his son, Pepin, wanted legitimation to be king of the franks. The kings had become more and more ineffectual and were mere palace rulers with the real power in the hands of the mayor. Pepin had sent a message to pope Zachary suggesting that the one who exercised sovereign rule should be king. Zachary agreed but died before he could act. Pepin and Stephen II needed each other. The pope agreed to the deposition of the token monarch and St Boniface, the english missionary, anointed Pepin as king. This was followed by a visit to Pepin by Stephen II as the lombard treaty had broken down. While at Pepin's court, the pope re-anointed Pepin as king. In return Pepin promised to fight the lombards for the pope and twice invaded Italy to reinforce his promise.

Why this intricate affair assumes such great importance was that once again a document, we now know was forged, surfaced in the curia - the Donation of Constantine. Eight hundred years passed before that forgery began to be critically evaluated and doubted. We can assume Pope Stephen II did not doubt its genuine origins. For him it was invaluable for his meeting with Pepin. It purported to be a letter of Constantine the Great to bishop Sylvester I of Rome saying that on leaving the city for the new Rome he not only left the Lateran Palace to the bishop of old Rome but "likewise all provinces, palaces and districts of the city of Rome and Italy, and of all the regions of the West; and, bequeathing them to the power and sway of him and the pontiffs, his successors, we do (by means of fixed imperial decision through this our divine, sacred and authoritative sanction) determine and decree that the same be placed at his disposal, and do lawfully grant it as a permanent possession to the holy Roman Church." (23)

It meant, in effect, a large portion of territory in central Italy now became the Papal States which lasted until 1870 and still continues in the hundred acres of Vatican City. It was based in the curial mind on the fact that territorial independence is a protection against manipulation of the papacy by any ruler. This is understandable in a period when popes had been imprisoned by ostrogothic power or dragged to Constantinople by imperial troops to answer for opposing the Emperor. The need for the papacy to have temporal power, still being ably defended when I was at the seminary in the 'fifties, could not have been expected to foresee that the United Nations or the World Council of Churches can still exercise moral prestige and leadership in the modern world without necessarily having temporal power. And could it have done so anyway in the eighth century?

Understandable as the historical circumstances were of the papal plight on the eighth century Italian peninsula, the papal temporal independence had at least an indirect effect on the growing papal theology. For a second time the curia had built up an arsenal of documentary evidence for papal prestige over all the other rulers by the inference and acceptance that the pope took over the Western Emperor's position. It is easy for us looking back in time to say: "But this is a secular advancement in power not a religious one!" We have inherited the western mind which delineates the different areas of Church and State. Most civilizations have not done so. Nor did the "roman" civilization that was gradually being accepted as the respectable authority by the young barbarian nations seeking some form of legitimation for a definite authority at the time. It meant the bishop of Rome had a prestige and status accorded no other bishop in the christian world. Beside him the patriarch of Constantinople looked more like a court chaplain even though his status was great in the christian East. Certainly the power of being a temporal ruler could not but enhance all the spiritual claims of the papacy. Brian Tierney summarizes this when he states: "Indeed, from the eighth century onward the essentially political claim of the popes to be rightful rulers of Rome came to be increasingly confused with an essentially theological claim that they were overlords of all christian kings by virtue of their supreme spiritual office." (24)

Mirgeler, the eminent german political scientist and historian, has remarked appositely: "...the Christianity which the Germanic peoples had to take over into their world was already a Christianity translated into Latin: a Christianity which had entered into a historical unity with the philosophy of later Antiquity and with the late Roman Empire. Augustine regarded what we call his theology as the logical fulfilment of platonic philosophy and Constantine saw in the christianization of the Roman Empire the logical conclusion of Diocletian's constitutional reforms. The result was that Antiquity appeared to the frankish rulers, not as an independent power, but rather as a philosophy interpreting dogmas and an Empire protecting and supporting the Church." (25)

This melding of newly converted barbarians with roman imperial greatness and protection must have been at the back of the minds of the papacy and curia when the desperate but understandable solution of the Papal States was mooted. It had, however, mixed results. The military aristocracy of the new Papal States began to assert itself more than it had been able to do under some sort of Eastern imperial control. The papacy now became a pawn in the hands of various factions. Pope Leo III (795-816) was set on by a gang who attempted to murder, or at least mutilate, him in 799. While the external independence of the papacy had been enhanced by the frankish protection, the internal control of "priestly" authority still needed some stronger backing from powerful laity. This would seem to be the background to Leo III's crowning of Charlemagne as first Holy Roman Emperor mentioned above in 800. (26)

A ruler as strong as Charlemagne could come down over the Alps when the roman and italian nobility were attempting to intimidate the popes; but once his Empire began to break up with his sons' ineptitude and the norsemen's invasions, weaker nonentities held the title of Emperor and were unable to help the popes. The papacy became exposed to the vagaries of the roman and italian mobs.

One commentator has mentioned that in the tenth century (896-999) there were thirty popes and anti-popes, one third of whom died of strangulation or poisoning. (27) For a long period of time two unscrupulous women effectively ruled Rome putting on the papal throne lovers and sons as young as John XI (931-936) a teenager. The infamous John XII (955-964), scion of the world of the nobility, was only twenty when elected. (28)

Typical of so many actions of those times was John X's (914-928) acceptance of the nomination of the count of Vermandois' five year old son as archbishop of Reims. (29) It highlighted not only simony, powerful lay control of episcopal elections, the venal use to which ecclesiastical offices were now put, but also the importance of the metropolitan or archiepiscopal sees as the "outposts" of the old Roman Empire. They had assumed a semi-patriarchal authority which was resented by their regional bishops who should have been their co-operators but were now assumed to be "under" them in the growing hierarchical and feudal systems. Once again a forgery to undermine these new powers of metropolitans was produced which was to be of great assistance to the papacy.

The False Decretals, which they are now rightly called, were more cunningly devised than many of their ilk because they mixed true documents with forged ones. Some sixty forged decretals were used from the early "popes" until the Emperor Constantine and some 10,000 changes in valid texts worked in like mosaics. The intent of these letters was, of course, to re-assert episcopal independence from metropolitans or archbishops but they did so by inserting into the balance of power greater papal control. They were, of course, believed to be authentic and formed the basis of many of the collections of canon law. They certainly helped shape the masterly work of Gratian (c.1200) to which all canonists look back as a source.

Again, when Gratian used these false decretals he used them sincerely believing they were genuine. Their forgeries were not discovered until two or three centuries later. (30) However, can we calculate how many of these misrepresentations helped to shape the attitude, ethos and certainties of the canon law of the middle ages especially as regards papal centrism and therefore enter and shape the tradition?

These False Decretals were used by the last of the three popes called "great", Nicholas I (858-867) and again entered the curial arsenal to be used as weapons in the great papal and church reform of the eleventh and twelfth centuries. (31)

The reform movements arose out of an abhorrence of the many evils of the Church - clerical concubinage, lay nobles claiming bishoprics, abbeys, parishes and shrines as personal possessions, payments for offices and even hereditary passing down of parishes and sinecures.

It was a broadly based movement headed by St Peter Damian (+1072) Humbert of the romans and the cluniac monks. After a time it gained the ears of a by now stronger imperial family, the Saxon Emperors. Its broad strategy was to reform the papacy at perhaps its worst stage of corruption in its long history. With a reformed papacy the next move was to take the election of bishops out of lay control and restrict it to clerical nomination. All the other reforms such as celibacy for clergy, prohibiting money for church office or sacraments would follow from papal and episcopal reform they reasoned.

Southern summarizes the mentality of what the reformers supposed the past to be: "They dedicated themselves to the task of restoring the papacy to the position which it had held in a remote past and ought to hold again. Above all, they wished to restore the papacy to the controlling and directing role in the church (as they thought) it had once had, and they wished to make the pope's temporal lordship an unambiguous force in European politics. As their minds travelled back into the past they saw traces of a former greatness which had been worn away by centuries of German tyranny, and among these ancient monuments of greatness the Donation of Constantine held a conspicuous place." (32)

Methods for reform divided the zealous. Peter Damian and others saw the practice of anointed kings as being part of the process of appointment which had now become traditional. Cardinal Humbert and his followers were intransigent and allowed no royal interference in episcopal appointments. The issue was confused, because in the growing feudal system in Europe episcopal estates, castles and knights were part of national or ducal resources so kings felt they had a stake in such appointments. (33)

For the time being whether Humbert liked it or not, the new Saxon Emperors were needed to clean up the mess in Rome. The Saxon Emperors re-established the custom of coming to Rome to be crowned by the pope. When the Emperor Henry III arrived there in 1046 there were three popes as a result of rival factions. He deposed the three. The german pope he left behind died after several months, probably because of poisoning. He sent another german pope to Rome. Within weeks he too was dead. He was more successful with his cousin, Leo IX (1049-54) who became the first real reforming pope of that period.

In 1059 papal elections were restricted to cardinals nominated by previous popes. It was hoped that this electoral change would provide for the independence of the papacy which would then spearhead reform. It produced, as hoped, reforming popes particularly when Cardinal Hildebrand was elected pope in 1073 as Gregory VII. Under several popes he had been the power behind the throne. He had also studied carefully the documentation in the curia and was convinced of the truth of all of it, authentic and forged. Some of his convictions appeared in his "Dictatus Papae" of 1075. The pope can be judged by no one, can depose emperors, bishops, alone can call General Councils. All princes shall kiss his feet - his legates have precedence over all bishops, a duly ordained pope is undoubtedly made a saint by the merits of St Peter. The roman church has never erred and never will err till the end of time. The roman church was founded by Christ alone. (34)

Gregory adopted the intransigent conclusions of Cardinal Humbert rather than the probably more practical conclusions of Peter Damian - neither kings nor nobility should have anything to do with episcopal nominations. Southern notes: "In the eighth century the popes had turned from the Byzantine emperor and committed their future to the new Carolingian family in the West. Now Gregory VII turned from the successor of the Carolingians and stood alone against the world." (35) Southern also adds that while Humbert and Gregory both made ample use of the Donation of Constantine, the document was an ambiguous one, because it had Constantine "*giving* the pope authority over the other churches and as himself *placing* on the pope's head the imperial crown." (36) On account of this it was used by subsequent canonists more as a title deed than an historical account.

The "Dictatus Papae" and Gregory's other claims rocked and divided Europe. The young Emperor Henry IV (1056-1106) led the reaction. He carried many bishops with him; but his excommunication and the rebellion of nobles wishing to usurp the imperial title brought Henry to his famous penance at Canossa where for three days in the snow he awaited Gregory's absolution. Once back in Germany, as Gregory had expected, Henry returned to his former stance.

Finally when imperial forces invaded the Papal States, Gregory called the norsemen in from south of his border only to find them his captors. He died in exile in 1085, to his followers a saint, to his enemies a madman claiming too much.

After endless quarrels and wars, the Concordat of Worms in 1122 compromised by making the Church responsible for the bishops' election and consecration, and the king for granting temporalities.

Gregory VII was a cluniac monk. The fact that Cluny had played a large part in the reform movement can be seen in the increasing centralization of the Church from the reform popes onwards. Cluny was virtually the first centralized religious order in the Church where all monasteries were dependent on the "mother" house unlike most other Benedictine monasteries which were autonomous. The idea was to prevent stagnation already apparent in many benedictine houses. Gregory and the reform popes did not immediately take over the appointment of all bishops in the Church, although by now it was apparent that whoever appointed bishops ruled the Church. The popes, respecting the rights of the local churches to elect their own bishops, kept in check, for a time, the right they assumed they possessed from the documentation in the curial archives (especially the interpretation many canonists were giving to Leo I's "plenitude of power") (p. 76) thus giving them full rights to appoint bishops who had only a share in this fullness. "The surprising thing is," Southern wryly comments, "not that the popes in the end asserted this right, but that they resisted so long, and only approached the final step by so many imperceptible movements." (37)

The papacy's first step was to ensure the legal recognition of the canons of the cathedral's right to elect their bishop. This was in place by the middle of the twelfth century. Secondly the popes assumed the right to be supervisors at these elections either in the person of a papal legate or in the case of a canonical defect such as a lack of a majority vote (fairly frequent in the Middle Ages) to have an appeal lodged at the papal court which in turn gave the papacy the right of selection.

Of course, many of the bishops protested at these extreme papal claims to supreme over-lordship. An anti-pope was set up against Gregory. Catholic Church historians have tended to blame this on to the obvious fact that the bishops were sycophantic royal appointees. No one would deny this must have had a bearing on the case; but with the fragmented documentation available to them and a strong arsenal of papal documents claiming to be "the" Tradition, they still sensed that the papal decrees were claiming too much. This was not just in the light of the recent past in which they had been appointed by the royalty and nobility but from what they knew from Scriptures and the Fathers (or early christian writers) about the early Church.

Many opponents of the extreme papal claims such as the "Anonymous" of York and the author of the "De Unitate Ecclesiae Conservanda" argued from the sacral nature of the king's anointing to his power to appoint bishops to exercise his right to make sure his priestly people (1 Peter 2:9 is quoted) had proper pastors. Pope Gelasius I was quoted often about there being two powers (p. 81) with a heavy interpretation that the priestly should not interfere with the royal sphere. (38)

A more moderate opponent, Hugh of Fleury, argued that the king "had the right to assent to an episcopal election on behalf of the lay folk, whose acceptance of a newly elected bishop was part of the established canonical procedure..." (39) In the light of what we have seen, Hugh of Fleury's argument regarding the people was more than just canonical. It was the basic traditional one never entirely lost sight of in the quagmire of conflicting and often misleading documents.

When we look back at the time of the death of Gregory VII in 1085 over the Church's first thousand years, we see that a quite extraordinary development of the synodal principle of sharing authority, accepted as basic in the early Church, was still relevant. We have come from a situation in early times of loosely affiliated local churches in which the priesthood of all the community was accepted while acknowledging a basic Apostolic Authority of some sort in their midst. These churches (by the end of the second century) had accepted one bishop elected by and responsible for each community. In this still retained balance of a priestly people, we have noted a concern and solicitude for all the churches shown in a special way by the church of Rome. This was based primarily but not solely in the Western Churches on the roman church's foundation by the martyrdom of Peter and Paul and in the Eastern churches it was Rome's importance as the imperial capital.

This uneasy balance was upset by the barbarian conquest of the Western Empire. Once again Western Europe became missionary territory in the second five hundred years while the Eastern churches shrank to a smaller area centred on Constantinople. Communications between the two parts of the Church become infrequent, haphazard and politically acerbic.

In the West as the barbarian nations came into the christian fold, the divinely anointed aspect of kingship was highlighted. Kings and nobles became the protectors of the Church and the appointers of bishops and other clergy as they built the Church into their feudal systems. The local churches had lost their autonomy as the whole priestly people of God to elect their leaders. More and more were appointed from outside and often with their office sold to the highest bidder. This system operated from an ignorance of the original synodal principle and its importance. It was one more example of the period losing contact with its roots.

Side by side with this development went the papal development, especially the decisive curial interventions of 381-461, 752-754 and the gregorian reform documents. Again in the light of what we have seen about the original church's operation, papal development is arguably a valid but disproportionate one if the balance of consulting local churches and their priestly people are not kept in place. A further imbalance is present if that development is tainted quite substantially by forgeries.

It is a quantum leap to the claim of Gregory VII from the practice of the centuries that preceded him - too big a leap to provide a smooth transition. From the eighth to the eleventh centuries Southern observes "Rome was seen as St Peter himself...they did not ignore the Pope but they quite simply looked through him to the first occupant of this throne." And the question must still be asked; where was the "consensus fidelium", if it were possible to ascertain, in all these rapid developments?

The papacy of those earlier centuries was a centre of unity, as Southern notes but "with the very slightest exercise of administrative authority. The affairs of the church received little direction from Rome. Monasteries and bishoprics were founded, and bishops and abbots were appointed by lay rulers without hindrance or objection; councils were summoned by kings; kings and bishops legislated for their local churches about tithes, ordeals, Sunday observance, penance; saints were raised to the altars - all without reference to Rome. Each bishop acted as an independent repository of faith and discipline." (40)

Gregory VII's "Dictatus Papae" is understandable in the context of a need for drastic change; but it is a very arguable development when one remembers both Gregory's reliance on curial documents many of which were inauthentic and his apparent lack of real knowledge of how the papacy of the first few centuries functioned. Gregory's reform may well have been the best possible solution for the Church of the time. Was it unchangeable Tradition for all times taken out of its historical and cultural context?

At this point it is worth asking whether this development should not be subject to certain criteria especially as Tradition is not just a passing down (with an admixture of error) but a checking from time to time that the received Tradition is accurate. The fact that it is "received" does not necessarily prove its Gospel quality when the "receivers" (through lack of education or believing everything that is passed down as true and absolute) react religiously and stubbornly to any opposition when the actual truth is more nuanced.

It then enters the stream of Tradition as have so many "parasite" ideas and is regarded as unchangeable. It would seem obvious that criteria should be established for assessing both Tradition and Reception. These will be discussed in chapter twelve.

* * * * * *

But what of the other patriarchs? Why did they tolerate this development of universal supremacy, control from Rome and the Western patriarchate? The fact is quite simply they did not. By the time of Gregory VII there were no Eastern churches linked with the Western church to protest. The patriarchates of Antioch, Alexandria and the later one of Jerusalem, had all been conquered by the islamic powers making them largely internationally ineffective. The Eastern patriarchate that had survived in a somewhat diminished form was Constantinople with whom Rome had been locked in controversy on many occasions. Some twenty years before Gregory VII's accession a number of these simmering differences once again surfaced because of the loss of southern Italy by the Eastern Empire to the norsemen, allies of the papacy. The clash of two patriarchal jurisdictions in the territory where there were still many greek clergy came to a head. All the old differences arose, especially when the papacy began to impose the latin rite in southern Italy. The patriarch of Constantinople retaliated by imposing the eastern rite on latin churches in his city. Pope Leo IX, now a prisoner of the norsemen, his former allies, sent the intransigent Cardinal Humbert to treat with the patriarch ostensibly to defuse the situation.

The many disagreements - differences of discipline on celibacy of clergy, leavened or unleavened bread in the Eucharist need not have occasioned great disputes, as such diversity had always been tolerated between patriarchates. The only serious doctrinal one the "Filioque" or the Holy Spirit proceeding from the Father and the Son had been adopted by Charlemagne.

Pope John Paul II has recently inferred that the "Filioque" may not now be seen as an insuperable barrier to union between the Eastern and Western churches.

The "Filioque" is an example of a "parasite" idea which many historians and theologians were already coming around to seeing as a result of historical research to be an honoured Western theological tradition and possibly the best explanation of the relationships within the Trinity. But many still regarded the "Filioque" as an absolute teaching of the Church and could point to its compulsory acceptance imposed on the greeks at the Second Council of Lyons (1274) and the Decree for reunion with the

Armenians in 1439. Certainly until recently its persistence as an absolute doctrine of the Church and necessary to confess caused untold misery to the peoples of the Eastern churches who believed just as adamantly that it was an addition never accepted in their patriarchates and to some of them it amounted to heresy.

The fact was that the "Filioque" is not found in the original texts of the Niceno-Constantinopolitan creeds. The Eastern tendency was to describe the relationships of the Three Persons in the Trinity as the Holy Spirit proceeding from the Father through the Son. In the West, particularly crystallized in the teaching of St Augustine, the Holy Spirit's procession from the Father and the Son (Filioque) met with general acceptance. There even seemed an implication from the Western formula that Jesus was as much God as the Father to counteract arian claims that Jesus was human only. Thus when Reccared, spanish visigothic king, became a catholic christian renouncing his arianism in 589 at the Third Council of Toledo, the spanish creeds included the "Filioque". Their influence spread throughout Europe and found a fervent advocate in Charlemagne who ordered the "Filioque" put into all creeds in his domains where they were not being used already and tried to persuade Pope Leo III to do the same for all the churches in the Western Patriarchate. The Pope, knowing the mind of the Eastern Churches, politely demurred and the roman creeds resisted its inclusion for two centuries. Pope Benedict VIII (1012-1024) crowned the Emperor St Henry II in 1014 who reacted strongly against the lack of "Filioque" in the roman creed. Benedict, who was heavily in debt to Henry for his military assistance, complied by its insertion.

Now the concept of the Father's love for the Son and the Son's for the Father resulting like love in marriage in a third Person, the Holy Spirit, is a beautiful one. When added to the Doctrine of the Trinity as an explanation it is also helpful. But it is still a "parasite" idea, however beautifully the development grew from the original absolute. If it is to become an absolute teaching of the Church it must be as we have seen from the Tradition "received" by the whole Church and not arise principally from the historical and political impositions just described.

Once again, the original idea of a legitimate diversity in a unity had been forgotten as something more basic than the uniform framing of creeds. Even worse, the stubborn persistence of thinking one school of theology was absolute, was apparent.

When, as we have seen above, Leo IX sent Cardinal Humbert to try and resolve the difficulties between East and West, he chose the wrong ambassador. Cardinal Humbert arrived in Constantinople and with the one-sided arrogance that marked many of the actions of his life, laid a bill of excommunication of the patriarch on the altar of Constantinople's cathedral during the patriarchal mass. He narrowly missed being lynched by the crowds. It was one of the great miscalculations of history and was probably done without the agreement of Leo IX.

Nonetheless, 1054 marked the more definitive break between the Eastern and Western churches that future history was to widen. By the time Gregory's more outlandish claims were made there was only his own patriarchate left to "receive" his teaching.

The claiming too much was done in a climate where historical accuracy was difficult or almost impossible to find. It was processed from a curial arsenal some of which had been forged. There was doubt whether the authentic documents had been "received" by the whole Church, either Eastern or Western. No one doubted the early rights and privileges accorded to the church of Rome nor its solicitude for all the other churches. What was open to challenge and discussion was the papacy's claiming too much.

Conclusion:

The Catholic Church or the Western patriarchate with which it was now left had taken an enormous jolt. Distortions abound in the Tradition it thought it relied on. How seriously can one receive such an affected Tradition, largely not 'received', as a valid Tradition? But it was in place to influence all later Tradition. There seemed to be a feeling about this that if it happened and was sanctioned by the highest authority then it was right. We have already seen that Tradition is far more complex than that. This later elevation of the papacy was not done in consultation with all the charisms of the Church. It destroyed any diversity that disagreed with it and it had questionable scriptural authority especially in the light of modern exegesis.

The Gregorian Reform was beneficial to the Church in that it reformed corruption. What was beneficial for the time was to stay much longer.

In such a papal tradition handed down (here I advisedly use a small 't') with not only distortions from forgeries, cultural and political elements affecting quite important understandings of essential doctrines but also feeling no real obligation to correct such distortions because it thought itself unalterable and unchanging Tradition, one gets to the heart of the problem this book has tried to highlight. The presumption always was that if anything really contrary to the original Revelation crept in, General Councils of bishops or the papacy would, in time, correct it.

In fact, they didn't in many instances. Negatively, roman catholics (and many other christians) believe that for the first four or five centuries the Church was prevented from teaching any wrong doctrine by the guidance of the Holy Spirit. If that was all the Church was teaching then all and good; but it was teaching so much more. Allied with the essential truths there was

93

so much interpretation and absolutization of the corollaries of essential truths, so much wrong or misleading teaching that was socially or culturally conditioned but taught as absolutely as the essential truths. Millions possibly were often misled and certainly could not or did not become the mature adult christians they should have become. Certainly there were always the sacraments and the basic helps the Church was founded to give, but again often presented in such a ritualistic and set form that the presence of the compassionate and loving Christ was often lost.

Was there an alternative to all this? Theoretically I think so. In practice it would probably have been impossible especially in the period of the Dark Ages (500-1000) to have had such an objective body to re-appraise the Tradition and dissociate it from the society in which it lived. When the Western Church returned to its roots, intellectually and spiritually, in the next five hundred years, this was more possible and as we shall see actually happened when the papacy began to collapse.

By then, however, the re-appraisal had to fight an entrenched papal system within the Church which while it might basically have had its roots in Revelation (as roman catholics believe) had extended its 'divine' aspects often through the distortion of the previous five hundred years or so to the point where it was hard to distinguish between what was essential to the papal office and what history had loaded it with.

When that papal entrenchment collapsed under its own momentum during the Babylonian captivity and the Great Schism something akin to restoring 'episkope' was attempted. The age was so unused to even small democratic participation that gradually because the papacy was restored not to its former glory as it hoped, but it provided a convenient backdrop to the growing nationalism of the kings - but kings who wanted an absolute support for their absolutism. Yes, there could have been an alternative and one was projected; but the refusal of the papacy to reform radically helped precipitate the second big break in the Church - the protestant reformation.

Is there a possibility of unwinding this tangled skein? Something more powerful than the ones inside and benefiting from the system is needed. How many of the ideas giving rise to a centralized papacy are based on forgeries, distortions, feudal monarchies as well as a valid development of the "Petrine" ministry given to the Church?

1. Attwater, Donald. <u>A Dictionary of the Popes.</u> London, the Catholic Book Club. 1939. pp. 11-12
2. Cayré, F. <u>Manual of Patrology.</u> Paris, Desclee. 1935 Vol. I. p. 68
3. Jay, Eric. <u>The Church.</u> London, SPCK. 1977, Vol. I. p. 45
4. Holmes, J D and Bickers, B W. <u>A Short History of the Catholic Church.</u> Tunbridge Wells, Burns and Oates. 1983. p. 38
5. Tillard, J.M.R. <u>The Bishop of Rome.</u> London. 1983. p. 87. Chadwick, H. in <u>The Early Church,</u> Harmondsworth, Pelican History of the Church, Vol. I, 1967, p. 238 summarizes scholarly opinion when he says: "But it was not until Damasus in 382 that this Petrine text seriously began to become important as providing a theological and scriptural foundation on which claims to primacy were based."
6. Ullmann, W. <u>A Short History of the Papacy in the Middle Ages,</u> London, Methven and Co. 1974, pp. 6 and 7
7. Chadwick, H. <u>The Early Church,</u> p. 238
8. Ibid, p. 238
9. Ibid, p. 151
10. Southern, R W. <u>Western Society and the Church in the Middle Ages.</u> Harmondsworth, Pelican History of the Church, Vol. II. Reprint 1976. pp. 92-93
11. Empie, Paul C. and Murphy, T. Austin (Ed). <u>Papal Primacy and the Universal Church - Lutherans and Catholics in Dialogue V.</u> Minneapolis, Augsburg Publishing House. p. 16
12. Holmes, J D. and Bickers, B W. <u>A Short History of the Catholic Church.</u> p. 39
13. Southern, R.W. <u>Western Society and the Church in the Middle Ages.</u> p. 157
14. Jay, Eric. <u>The Church,</u> Vol. I. p. 98
15. Piepkorn, Arthur Carl. "From Nicea to Leo the Great" in <u>Papal Primacy and the Universal Church - Lutherans and Catholics in Dialogue V.</u> p. 90
16. Holmes, J D and Bickers, B W. <u>A Short History of the Catholic Church.</u> p. 39
17. Chadwick, H. <u>The Early Church.</u> p. 242
18. Eusebius of Caeserea commenting on Constantine as Bishop quoted in J. Stevenson (Ed) <u>A New Eusebius.</u> London, SPCK. 1987. pp. 366-367
19. Tierney, Brian. <u>The Crisis of Church and State 1050-1300.</u> Englewood Cliffs, Prentice-Hall. 1964. p. 7

20. Ibid, p. 2
21. Ibid, p. 13 Letter of Gelasius I to the Emperor Anastasius 494.
22. Moss, H. St L. B. <u>The Birth of the Middle Ages 395-814.</u> Oxford University Press. 1963. pp. 112-113
23. Quoted in Tierney, Brian. <u>The Crisis of Church and State 1050-1300.</u> pp. 21-22
24. Ibid, p. 19
25. Mirgeler, Albert. <u>Mutations of Western Christianity.</u> London, Compass Books, Burns & Oates. 1964. p. 7
26. Attwater, Donald. <u>A Dictionary of the Popes.</u> p. 90
27. Ibid, p. 111
28. Ibid, pp. 121-124
29. Ibid, p. 119
30. Coriden, James. <u>An Introduction to Canon Law.</u> Mahwah, NJ, Paulist Press. 1991. p. 16
31. Fuhrmann, H. "False Decretals", (Catholic Encyclopedia, Vol. 5, p. 822). New York, McGraw-Hill Book Co. 1967. pp. 820-824
32. Southern, R W. <u>Western Society and the Church in the Middle Ages.</u> p. 101
33. Tierney, Brian. <u>The Crisis of Church and State 1050-1300.</u> pp. 34-35
34. Southern, R W. <u>Western Society and the Church in the Middle Ages.</u> p. 102
35. Ibid, p. 104
36. Ibid, p. 101
37. Ibid, p. 158
38. Tierney, Brian. <u>The Crisis of Church and State 1050-1300 in the Middle Ages.</u> pp. 76-82
39. Ibid, p. 76
40. Southern, R W. <u>Western Society and the Church in the Middle Ages.</u> p. 96

CHAPTER SEVEN

Distortion of Tradition developing the lay-clerical divide

If the Church perceived the barriers the gnostics placed in the way of discovering the true and unique Jesus of the Gospels and therefore became extremely cautious about using many outside religious philosophies and mystery religions, it also understood the value of using some philosophies, particularly the greek, that seemed to enhance, and better explain to contemporary men and women the uniqueness of Jesus. St Justin (+165), perhaps the greatest of the apologists, spoke of the "Logos spermatakos", the Word scattered among all cultures and peoples before and after Jesus that were fulfilled in his person. By this Justin meant that all that was good, true and beautiful in every culture, philosophy and religion had been placed there by God with the people of that culture apprehending, in a certain way, Jesus as its fulfilment.

Stoicism, for instance, taught that reason in each person was a spark of divinity. Virtue was acting according to reason. Passion could interpose on action an unwillingness or repugnance to follow reason. It was therefore necessary to control passion and let reason hold sway. There were many meeting points that became obvious to christians in interpreting what over previous centuries had become a well developed philosophy and accumulated wisdom. If one prescinded from certain pagan biases, the philosophy could add much to christians pursuing a deeper and more perfect life of virtue and communication with Christ.

Platonism too, or (as it was becoming) neo-platonism, with its insistence on the explanation of ideas, logic and virtues such as the cardinal ones of prudence, justice, fortitude and temperance, was seen as an ally in christian endeavour. Even the rather extreme dichotomy in platonism of soul and body (where souls are joined to bodies in consequence of some sin and matter was constantly fighting against the soul) created a certain dualism which found a ready echo within christianity as long as it was not taken too far. The idea of eternal laws and ideas and changelessness also appealed to the christian mind searching for a philosophy as a framework for its own eternal and unchanging ideas.

97

I label these ideas: the culture and thinking that surrounds them, "parasite" ideas - ideas that take life from a christian precept, often explaining it in a meaningful way to the age that adopts it. Sometimes they can absorb or dominate the christian idea to which they became married. Subsequently they came to be seen as indispensable to the christian idea itself. Suffice to say here that if in the second and third christian centuries the importance of using these philosophies was well recognized so was the necessity of separating the non-christian elements from the philosophy. The subsequent danger arose when gradually the two had become so well wedded, and the surrounding ideas changed and depths of the adopted philosophy were plumbed that had not been apparent at the time of the wedding then the Church frequently failed to make the distinction between what was the "parasite" idea from the initial christian idea and ended up defending both, even if by now the "parasite" idea may have become outmoded in another age or another culture.

These ancient philosophies pre-supposed a fixed universe with changeless laws. Change was present but it was superficial and an example of finiteness in a basically infinite world.

The most insidious and often unrecognized danger of "parasite" ideas is that they can mould the thinking of subsequent generations who think they are giving a "consensus fidelium" to Tradition when in fact they are assenting to embedded parasite ideas, as required of them by Authority. They can then underpin subsequent theologies, e.g. original sin (which is taken to be absolute causing future internal dissension among theologians and with Church Authorities). It is also very hard to pin down their snowballing effect at much later stages.

Whilst the Enlightenment produced challenges to the static mediaeval world shaped by the Church, the Church clung onto these ideas believing the "parasite" ideas indispensable to explain the Church's teaching.

If we are to consider the changes in the Church in the five hundred years (500 to 1000 A.D.) often referred to as the "Dark Ages", we see at work more than ever before in Western history the paramount influence of religion. The mass illiteracy of the barbarian peoples made them more prone to manipulation and superstition. Conversion to christianity was often not heartfelt because they followed their tribal chief externally but still carried on many superstitions within their newly adopted religion. The hiatus with the past caused by the destroying of most of the libraries of the West leaving behind very few documents and fragments (laboriously copied in the monasteries of the time) made Gospel values seem very dim in early medieval religion.

All this was accentuated by the growing isolation of East and West, especially after the muslim conquests of most of the Middle East and North

Africa in the seventh century followed soon after by Spain, Portugal and nearly all the islands of the Western Mediterranean, including ,Sicily. Southern notes: "The first thing that stands out in this period is the inferiority of western Europe to its Greek and Moslem neighbours - both the Greek and Islamic systems were immensely richer, more powerful, and intellectually more sophisticated than that of western Europe." (1)

The hiatus or break with the past in the West resulted in few theologians of real note - St Gregory the Great (+ 604), bishop of Rome being one of the few exceptions - flourishing during this period. The passing down (traditio) of the known past was then transmitted mainly by word of mouth without much reflection as to its context. This often had the resultant ossifying of much of the living theology into axioms and definitions. Written law began to have a disproportionate importance in christian Tradition. With little speculative theology, law began to be in some instances the interpreter and even formulator of the theology as we saw in the growing papal theology. This forced break with the past meant in effect there were few points of reference available to the Church from preceding centuries when she had to cope with the reconversion of most of Europe.

No visit to these Constantinian centuries leading up to the barbarian invasion and their new kingdoms would be complete without mentioning monasticism. From the very beginning of christianity, christians realized how much of a community religion theirs was. The often quoted passage from Acts IV: "There was one heart and soul in all the company of believers; none of them called any of his possessions his own, everything was shared in common" was perhaps difficult of realization in many communities. It certainly always remained an ideal.

Eusebius, the historian, quotes Philo (+ 40 A.D.) the jewish platonist philosopher, speaking of the therapeutrides, men and women, living joyfully in communities meditating on and praying from the Scriptures. Eusebius thinks Philo may well have been speaking of christian jews. (2) Whatever origin the therapeutrides may have had, by the end of the third century christians began to depart in large numbers to live in ascetic communities in the deserts of Egypt. Because they lived alone (greek monos) at first, their huts and later villages of huts were called monasteries. In time they became organized like soldiers under St Pachomius (+ 348) in large buildings. Just as the Western Empire was crumbling, St Benedict (+ 547) wrote his rule in Italy.

These monasteries were to become with the Friars in the Middle Ages, one of the most important powers in the next thousand years of Church History. Initially they may well have gone into the desert to search for ascetic and small intimate communities as many of the early christians of the first and second centuries could have been. With the huge numbers being admitted to a church replete with spacious buildings and material comforts, particularly after the persecutions ceased, these people yearned for a simpler and more ascetic way of life. Further on in the book we shall see how and why these monasteries and their monks came to play the dominant role in the Church that they did. Their asceticism (the root word means basically an "athlete" in greek) attracted admiration all over the christian world. Thousands of men and later women (who had their own monasteries) flocked to join them.

Dawson notes: "After the peace of the church when the supreme test of martyrdom was no longer demanded, the ascetics had come in the eyes of the Christian world to hold the positions the martyrs had formerly occupied as the living witnesses of the faith and the reality of the supernatural world. They were men who "had tasted the powers of the World to come" and, as we see in the Lausiac History and the other documents of primitive monasticism, they were regarded as the watchmen or guardians who "kept the walls" of the Christian City and repelled the attacks of its spiritual enemies." (3)

At times monasticism was seen as a rival to episcopal authority; but fortunately as so many of the bishops were drawn from the monasteries this diversity of community was tolerated within the unity of the diocese despite many tensions. In later centuries exemption from episcopal control became common. Many commentators have seen in the monk's role the continuation of the prophetic role from the early Church.

The ability to keep these monastic communities side by side with ordinary christian communities within the wider Church was again a sign of pluriformity in the early Church - diversity in unity.

One of the many ways monasticism influenced the Church was the ascetic spirituality it lived and propagated often by its very example, especially when it became later the missionary arm of the Church. The Church of Egypt as we see from its great thinkers such as Clement of Alexandria (+ c.215) and Origen (+254) was heavily influenced by neo-platonism and greek thinking just as Philo, the jewish platonist of Alexandria, was. This neo-platonist thirst for the absolute became so interwoven with christian perfection that it became difficult to disentangle one from the other.

Matthew Fox picks out the polarities of greek and hebrew spirituality well when he says for the greeks, especially platonists, the spiritual meant what is immaterial, for the hebrews what is life-giving: for the greeks the soul wars constantly with the body, for the hebrews soul and body make one person who is at war with evil in its many forms: for the greeks matter was sinful and at most tolerated, for the hebrews matter is God-made and holy. As regards pleasure the greeks said "Shun it in order to purify the soul"; the hebrews said "ecstasy can come from outside things as well as internal joy." For the greeks spirituality was private (God and me), for the hebrews it was political (God and us).

The greek christian theme centred so much around the Fall and humankind's need for redemption, whereas the hebrew theme centred around Creation - how good God's creation is and how we say thank you by enjoying and sharing the enjoyment of it. Pride and lust were for greeks capital sins to be put to death by mortification, the emphasis for the hebrews was on developing one's talents as the Creator desired - ascetic practices such as fasting and discipline are strictly means not ends. The greek tendency was to be negative towards the human person and human history, the hebrew saw God working in and through history and human beings sharing with Him His work on earth. Our work on earth for the greeks was to prepare for Heaven, for the hebrews it was to regard Heaven as the reward for a fully lived life on earth. (4)

As a school of christian spirituality, the platonist-monastic asceticism was and is a noble and venerable one. It has sanctified millions of souls and may still bring to perfection many more. But where the danger lay and became actualized was in regarding monastic spirituality not only as the most important school of christian spirituality but the only school. Its hardness and inaccessibility, often its negativity, led many to regard themselves as second-class spiritual citizens compared to the monks and clergy. All they felt they could do was to say prayers, attend worship and listen to the higher echelons. When this was combined with the growing hierarchical developments regarding clergy and laity in the spheres of worship, social status and privilege then a clearer line of demarcation between "professional" and lay christians began to emerge, a demarcation not found to the same extent, if at all, among the early christians.

The one who helped most to make this neo-platonist monastic spirituality seem the only authentic christian spirituality was a late fifth century or early sixth century syrian monk who wrote under the name of Dionysius the Areopagite purposely wanting people to think him the same Dionysius who became a christian as a result of St Paul's speech on the areopagus in Athens (Acts 17:34). Because his readers believed this for a thousand years until renaissance scholarship in the person of De Valla showed it was a work composed at least 450-500 years after the real Dionysius, it was followed faithfully as the original christian spirituality of the apostles and the early christians. It also saw in its platonist way the whole of the spiritual life from God downwards as a series of hierarchical echelons reinforcing already existing hierarchical attitudes. Monastic writers, too, like John Cassian (+435), quoted by St Benedict, exerted a tremendous influence on western monasticism and were strongly neo-platonist. Cassian's master, Evagrius of Pontus, taught, for instance, that human beings were really fallen angels given their bodies as punishment! (5)

Benedicta Ward, after speaking of the positive points of monasticism in general, summarizes the situation well when she writes: "The dangers of such a way of life have always been exclusivism and perfectionism, the creation of a little church for the perfect within the church, based on a dualistic view of the world and a contempt for the sacramental understanding of creation exercised by those outside its ranks." (6) Ward hastens to add this danger does not invariably exist, but can and has done so. When seminaries for the parish clergy came to be established after the Council of Trent (1545-1563), the only model the Church could think of was to train the future clergy in a monastic establishment in which monastic discipline and training apart from the world became a strange preparation for those who were to work all their lives among people. (7)

One can see here how a "parasite idea" can almost take over its christian companion. The main point, however, to note in this chapter is that a good spirituality (monastic) has claimed too much when it claimed to be the only christian spirituality and its repercussions reinforced by Augustine's neo-platonism are still with us. To claim too much is often to claim a unity which is not there in the christian message. Worse still it can stifle a diversity whose challenge is needed for a wider understanding of what christian unity is really about.

The magnificent intellect and faith of St Augustine of Hippo (354-430) towers over the millennium of Western Christianity after his death and on into the Reformation to our own day. His disproportionate influence on the West where his works were preserved with often a dearth of the main early christian writers as opposed to the East where because of the historical break after the barbarian invasions his works were scarcely known until the Middle Ages, came not only from his rare genius but also from the fact that his mind had no rival in the West until the intellects of Aquinas, Duns Scotus and Bonaventure some seven or eight hundred years later. By that time it was not always easy to disentangle Augustine's personal contribution to Western Theological Tradition from "the" Tradition. The "Filioque" controversy between the Eastern and Western Churches mentioned elsewhere probably had a lot to do with the West's intransigence towards the East and its conviction that its tradition on the Trinity, highly influenced by Augustine, if not initiated by him, was the real "tradition" even though not spelt out in the Nicene Creed. (8)

Libraries have been written on Augustine but what I want to note here is how his teaching on sexuality going hand in hand with the gradual development of monastic spirituality as "the" spirituality thereby implicitly putting most laity in the category of second class citizens endorsed this attitude in his theology viewing the body as a deterrent to that spiritual liberty to contemplate God to which his generous soul felt called. Peter de Rosa summarizes his attitude well when he says: "The truth is that he never shrugged off the flesh. He always harboured a deep distrust of it and a loathing he could never quite disguise. His experience of sex had been restricted to illicit loves from which he gained a sense of guilt and misery…'nothing' he wrote in his Soliloquies 'is so powerful in drawing the spirit of man downwards as the caresses of a woman and that physical intercourse which is part of marriage'. In fear, remembering his own falls, he never allowed women to set foot in his house or even speak with him except with witnesses present…the holy fountain of life, he said, was always dirtied by lust (libido) even in the tidy garden of marriage. His conviction that sexual appetite is of its nature evil became the great tradition of the church. Because of the Fall, man has been attacked at his own vulnerable point: sex. Even in marriage, it is vitiated by lust. This is the chief and inescapable penalty of Adam's fault. Lust can be justified only by the desire to procreate." (9) The result has been as de Rosa points out: "There is no pope, no theologian who did not follow Augustine's views on sex and marriage [in the West, of course – my own interpolation]. Through them, he influenced lay people for generation after generation." (10) One begins to see a heavy tradition developing that places too great an emphasis on virginity and compulsory celibacy and more importantly aided the growing inferiority of laity towards clergy and monks.

As mentioned earlier, the barbarian kingdoms were mostly pagan, some few arian. Their conversion aided by intermarriage between the barbarians and the remnants of the Roman Empire's christians was begun at first from the recently converted island of Hibernia (Ireland). Ireland had never been in the Roman Empire. St Patrick and other helpers, formed in the monasteries of southern France, converted Ireland in the last days of the imperial collapse. The Irish became fervent converts and took to monasticism in great numbers with penances that vied with those of the Desert Fathers. (11) Being tribal with few towns, the Irish gave their monasteries an importance far outweighing, in many cases, the power of the bishops. Abbots and even abbesses were known to have appointed bishops from their own monasteries.

These irish monks became the first thrust in a long but successful conversion of the many barbarian tribes. It was long not because the irish monks and their successors were in any way tardy, but because the initial wave of barbarians was followed by others, lombards, magyars, slavs and the dreaded norsemen. It was a half millennium of continuing instability except for the brief oases of Charlemagne's Empire and towards the end of the period, the Saxon Emperors.

Mirgeler points out the background of the tribal teutonic societies was matched in many ways by the same social background of their celtic evangelisers and a century or so later their anglo-saxon ones. It was a religion of tribal gods as protectors, of sacrifices and a cultic priesthood. When lack of depth in the theology of the irish and english monks was allied to instructing at times large numbers of not too willing converts, the culture and its religion left its mark on the catholicism of the 'Dark Ages'. (12) In its turn the monastic impress on the barbarian peoples who often in the early days were evangelized from monasteries made a significant contribution to their spirituality. (13)

The Sacrament of Reconciliation or Penance which in the first five hundred years was public in nature, (and this was breaking down anyway at the end of that period) was changed in its operation for the next fifteen hundred years. The irish monks introduced private confession between the confessor and penitent before absolution, based on lists of serious and less serious sins called Penitentiaries for weighing up how much penance was to be carried out after the sacrament, matching the tribal lists of offences with requisite punishments. These lists of sins had a great impact on catholic moral theology and the categorization of sins in the centuries that followed. Indirectly they also added to the growing legalism in the religion of this and subsequent periods.

More interestingly the "miracle world" of gods in the teutonic religions, as Mirgeler points out, resulted in the need of the barbarians to have their own saints for each tribe or monastery in their area. This became actualized in relics of the saints, particularly the martyrs. At first Rome with its veneration for tombs and corpses would send out only something that had come in close contact with the bodies of the martyrs as the letters of Gregory the Great reveal. However, the chain of events set in motion by the barbarian invasions during which the shrine churches of the martyrs outside the walls of the city of Rome presented a difficulty of access to the pilgrims in such dangerous times, and resulted in the bones of the martyrs being brought into the city parish churches. The most famous was the church of St Mary and all Martyrs, consecrated by Boniface IV of Rome in 609 in what had been the Pantheon, to which many of the bones had been brought. The custom of not sending out the actual bones was beginning to break down. With the removal of the skeletons from the actual tombs it became easier to dispatch bones to the missionaries in the field when requested. (14)

Relics soon became a roaring trade particularly, as Mirgeler points out, among the teutonic tribes. Even the parallel devotion in the Eastern Churches to ikons was better incorporated into the official liturgy than the widespread veneration of relics in the West. They were carried in processions, monasteries vying with each other to accentuate the virtues and heroic life of their own martyr saints. When lives of their patrons did not exist (which was in most cases, although the names were often attached to the bones), they were invented by the monks. Bollandist research on the origins of early martyr saints' lives has verified this. Horrific stories of virgins having eyes gouged out and breasts severed followed by their miraculous restoration before the inevitable martyrdom abound in popular lives of the saints.

This unbalanced spirituality with its neo-platonic, stoic and often manichaean influences, the undue adulation of the monastic virtues of obedience and humility (often confused with being trampled on by one's superiors) entered into the folklore of these simple faithful to confuse them often about the Gospel values of Jesus who in any case became more and more the warrior king, leader against evil, in the statuary and paintings of the time. In the era after the Council of Chalcedon's (451) teachings about Christ, in which many commentators would see a bias to his divinity rather than his humanity, despite the definition's attempt at balance. This necessitated the saints as intermediaries between an awesome God the Son and his votaries. Perhaps the saddest over-all effect was to give the impression to the laity that sanctity was something other-worldly and, if attempted, it could only be accomplished by full-time "professionals" like the monks and nuns or even the clergy. (15)

The monks had become the prophetical element in the Church as well as the first missionaries in the conversion of the barbarian peoples. Pseudo-Dionysius names the monks as the first of the three lower chains in his hierarchy. Together with other trends of cultic priesthood and clerical privilege, the "superior" spiritual state underscored a growing gap between the "professionals" and the "ordinary" members. Another factor that widened the gap between "professionals" and "lay" was the use of latin as the liturgical language. Both Eastern and Western Churches did not have a "sacred" language. However, because the greek, latin and syro-aramaic languages used in the liturgy had in both their secular and religious practice such a fine literary tradition and had been employed in theological debate with such precision developing a specialized vocabulary, it was understandable that a specialized language was considered to be needed in the liturgy. The early irish and english monks were fascinated with these languages so that when they came to evangelise the barbarians the liturgy was kept in latin. As Jungmann has pointed out it would have been difficult but not impossible to have composed a literary language for the missionary work and liturgy as Ulfilas, the arian, had done for the goths and as Cyril and Methodius were to do later for the slavs. (16) Most barbarians had a smattering of latin from the market place as well as from contacts with roman citizens. It was easier to keep the latin liturgy than invent a new literary alphabet from the barbarian spoken languages, especially when these new languages would preclude the necessary nuances and complexities of a developed theological language.

This retention of latin was apparently in its origins practical. But in time as it was not the language that the people used in their daily affairs, it gradually became a "sacred" language with all the mystique surrounding the cult, given the religious connotation regarding the sacred. More and more devotions to relics and saints as well as memorized prayers were seen to be the domain of the laity, whereas performing the cult and engaging in deep, silent prayer were the domain of the monks and clergy. This was reflected in the architecture. The altar, unlike that of the early christian church buildings, which was in the centre of the presbyters and bishop on one side and the lay people on the other, was now found at the end of the building in a special sacred place called the sanctuary (Old Testament and tribal connotations) separated from the laity by a communion rail at which they knelt (unlike the early christians who always stood at prayer) in reverence for the awesome bread which was the Body of Christ. They no longer received him in their hands but reverentially on their tongue. Increasingly communion became infrequent because of the sacred reverence due to the Body and Blood of Christ so that Church councils had to insist on communion's reception four times and then once a year. Because of numbers, the priest alone received the bread and wine, while the laity received the bread only, based on a positive argument that Jesus was fully present in either. It is not hard to see how the religious sacred character and ritualization of much of the early Church's more spontaneous gathering came about.

The priest isolated now at the altar, turned his back on the people in his sanctuary to mediate and intercede between them and God with outstretched arms instead of facing his people as he had done at an earlier period. Once again a growing chasm between laity and clergy emerged.

Another factor was what one might call the "quantification" of spiritual things. Not only were there huge lists of sins each with its own carefully measured penances, but certain prayers to be said at saints' shrines and devotions which were kept carefully on certain days and at certain hours. On feast days and during pilgrimages, processions would be held. Special blessings could be obtained when the relics were carried out of the church for veneration. As many of the lay people knelt at the end of the church building during a mass which went on in a sacred aura and sacred language up on the sanctuary, they believed Jesus came down into the bread and wine. However, they prayed by rote or even silently during this "ceremony" to their favourite saint or to Mary, Jesus' mother, who seemed much less remote than her Divine Son whose eyes flashed power and majesty. The Eucharist, or mass, became the priest's action at which lay people prayed their own prayers while he performed the official sacrifice for them instead of a sacrificial celebration which they all offered in their own language led by a celebrant deputed by the whole community.

But the quantification went further. The monks, especially, once Cluny was founded in 910, spent more and more hours praying for the Church and the world. A cluniac monk might be in choir for six hours or more a day. He had the time and expertise to pray for those who could only "say" prayers while they worked in the fields. One could offer gifts or money for the monks to pray for oneself. If one had money, one could leave it for masses and prayers to be said for one's soul after death. This vicarious intercession again underscored the growing gap within the Church.

As monks spent longer and longer in church, the benedictine ideal of one third of the day being spent in study, one third in prayer and one third in manual work became more difficult to fulfil. Until lay brothers were founded (at a later stage) to work in the fields, monks with so much time spent in church had to employ and pay lay labour. Their income was supplemented not only by gifts to the monastery but by money given for private masses. Monks who had been in the main unordained became priests to say a private mass at side altars erected along the walls of the abbey church. It encouraged a mentality already noted above that the more "sacred" masses one had said for him or her, the more prayers said for one, the more chance one had of gaining Heaven after death. This "quantification" of prayer and services became a mark of the medieval Church.

It all became so redolent of any other religion whether it be hinduism or buddhism (not that a knowledge of these was very common at the time) that while the symbols or names differed, the activities could be classified in the same categories. In itself this need not have been wrong, but it does show how the Church was ingenious enough to adapt herself to the cultures, aspirations and religious mentality of the people it converted. One of the greatest users of incredibly frightening stories of souls in purgatory coming back and clamouring for masses was Gregory the Great, because he knew how to pitch things at the level of the people. But so often the sacred, cultic, and cultural expressions became ends in themselves. The leaders, like Gregory the Great, were rare and often incapable of leading their people through and beyond a merely religious expression - because that was the level they were at themselves. The leaders knew little enough of the early beginnings of the Church except through the Scriptures and even here passages of Scripture were used selectively and literally to bolster the "status quo".

While bishops and clergy were encouraged to preach in the vernacular at masses, so often, however, through their own lack of education they were unable to preach to the people at any depth or ended up merely moralising. The glorious gothic churches and cathedrals began to be built and their stained glass taught Gospel stories and parables to fairly illiterate people. The dramas and the morality plays in church and on the steps outside, enabled people to understand the Gospel message and lives of the saints. The homily or sermon at mass was often left out with people on many occasions attending mumbled masses in latin of twelve to fifteen minutes length, two, three or four times a day, hopefully to draw close to God but seemingly to increase the amount of grace in their souls and obtain a higher place in Heaven. Quantification of spirituality and a cultic priesthood had come into their own.

In a growing feudal society where everyone knew his or her place and every action and cult had a price on it, the religious element of christianity seemed to have become an end rather than a means to further the Gospel. It highlights earlier remarks about the difficulty of how to find a consent of the faithful (consensus fidelium) with a now widening gap between clergy and laity. How much is there a consensus fidelium from a laity who seemed immersed in religion and its practices and who had little or no access to the limited literacy of the time, rather than a christian faith springing from the Gospels? One can begin to see more clearly how cultural and historical rather than theological factors have accounted for the practical lapse in the Western Church of "consensus fidelium" until Vatican II.

The collapse of at least a minority of reasonably articulate and literate laity had actually begun to occur before the barbarian invasions. Michael Grant summarizes the situation in the last days of the roman empire: "In the vain hope, then, of keeping their armies in the field, the imperial authorities ruined the poor and alienated the rich. They also alienated and then very largely destroyed the solid segment of the population that came in between - the middle class. This had once been the backbone of the Greek city-states, and later on it had fulfilled the same role in the Roman empire as well; since that too was a network of city-state communities. But the external invasions and internal rebellions of the third century A.D. had dealt this middle-class terrible physical blows, while the accompanying monetary inflation caused their endowments to vanish altogether. And then, from the next batch of emperors, those who came later on in the same century, and grimly pursued the enormous tasks of reconstruction, the old-fashioned ideals of this bourgeois section of the community received little sympathy. Their public work programmes cut to nothing or severely restricted, the cities of the empire began to assume a very dilapidated appearance; and then in the fourth and fifth centuries, despite contrary efforts by Julian and others, their position continued to worsen, and the old urban civilization, especially in the west, plunged into a sharp decline." (17)

It was understandable that the "laity" in the "Dark" and early "Middle" Ages became equated almost solely with the kings and nobles. As many of these were largely uneducated, grasping, venal and ambitious for themselves and their families, one can perhaps forgive our church history professor citing this period as a reason for not letting the "laity" have anything to do with the running of the Church.

Southern summarizes the period well when he says: "One result of this massive dependence on the supernatural was that the individual was of little account. The individual was swallowed up in his community or (if he were a great man) in his office. And both community and office drew their strength from the supernatural. The rules of life for monks and laymen alike emphasized the littleness of man, the impersonal majesty of the spiritual world, the dignity of an order which was only attainable in this life in symbolic ritual, and the peace of spirit which could be found only in a rigid discipline. Thus in a paradoxical way it came about that the feebleness of man, his insecurity, his weak grasp of the laws of nature, and his ineffectiveness in government, all combined to impose an extraordinary appearance of strength and stability on the products of this first period of the Middle Ages. In all that men did, whether in secular ceremonial or liturgy or building, they aimed at producing an image of an eternal world within a world of change. These creations were made to last for ever, and many of them survived the disappearance of the social and intellectual system which had brought them into being. Buildings, indeed, were easily pulled down when architectural tastes changed; but the elaborate liturgical routine of the Benedictine monasteries, the institution of the payment of tithes based on the legislation of the Old Testament, the organization of dioceses and parishes, the loyalty to Rome which developed in these centuries in the west, proved almost indestructible. These were the lasting contributions of this primitive age to the future. The sacred ruler, however, who seemed to contemporaries the strongest of all the products of the age, turned out to be of all things the most fragile." (18)

Conclusion:

We have seen how as the office of appraiser leaders became narrowed down and many material distortions such as forgeries, cultural and political factors entered the Tradition, it in its turn became more and more unbalanced. However in hindsight, at least most of these insertions were traceable even though their effects continued to shape the Tradition more than the teachers of Tradition realized. Less traceable and less obvious were the marriages of the philosophies and spiritualities from outside the Gospel which at a given time, enhanced Christ's teachings, but often later were retained within the Tradition.

The 'parasite' ideas became more and more entrenched in the passing down of the Tradition accompanied by a lack of history and scientific criticism to isolate them. These 'parasite' ideas formed the minds of many generations and were taken as inseparable from the true Tradition with which they existed and were there originally to explain.

How much of the present teaching of the Church on say artificial contraception comes from "parasite" ideas such as aristotelian teaching on Natural Law or the teaching forbidding women priests arises from the sociological status of women in roman and barbarian cultures?

1. Southern, R W. <u>Western Society and the Church in the Middle Ages</u>. Harmondsworth, Pelican History of the Church, Vol. II. reprint 1976. p. 27

2. Eusebius. <u>The History of the Church,</u> transl. G.A. Williamson. Harmondsworth, Pelican Classics. 1965. pp. 89-93

3. Dawson, Christopher. <u>Religion and the Rise of Western Culture.</u> Garden City, New York, Image Books, Doubleday and Co. 1958. p. 45

4. Fox, Matthew. <u>On Becoming a Musical Mystical Bear.</u> New York, Paramus Paulist Press/Deus Book. 1972. pp. XVIII-XX

5. Cuskelly, E J. <u>No Cowards in the Kingdom.</u> Melbourne, Spectrum. 1969. p. 104

6. Ward, Benedicta. "Monastic Spirituality, Monasticism" <u>in A Dictionary of Christian Spirituality.</u> p. 268

7. O'Donohoe, James A. "Tridentine Seminary Legislation – its Sources and its Formation". Louvain, Publications Universitaires de Louvain. 1957. (Biblio Ephemeridum Theologicarum Lovaniensium Vol IX)

8. Chadwick, Henry. <u>The Early Church</u> pp. 235-236

9. De Rosa, Peter. <u>Vicars of Christ, the Dark Side of the Papacy.</u> London, Corgi Books. 1989. p. 444

10. Ibid, p. 449

11. Dawson, Christopher. <u>Religion and World History.</u> Garden City, New York, Image Books, Doubleday and Co. 1975. pp. 185-186

12. Mirgeler, Albert. <u>Mutations of Western Christianity.</u> London, Compass Books, Burns and Oates. 1964. pp. 44-46

13. Ibid, pp. 66-81

14. Jungmann Josef A. S.J., <u>The Early Liturgy to the Time of Gregory the Great.</u> London, Darton, Longman & Todd. 1969. pp. 185-187

15. Muller, Alois. <u>Obedience in the Church.</u> London, Compass Books, Burns and Oates. 1966. pp. 40-41

16. Jungmann Josef A. S.J. <u>The Early Liturgy to the Time of Gregory the Great.</u> p. 207

17. Grant, Michael. <u>History of Rome.</u> London, Weidenfeld & Nicolson. 1981. p. 340

18. Southern, R.W. <u>Western Society and the Church in the Middle Ages</u>. Vol. II. reprint 1976. p. 33

CHAPTER EIGHT

Attempts to restore Balance to the Tradition in the

Middle Ages

An event of 12th February 1111 stands out in Church history. It could have happened only in the Middles Ages. As the cardinals, bishops, priests, roman and german nobility assembled in St Peter's in Rome for the crowning of the Emperor Henry V, Pope Paschal II made the following announcement, that from now on having received from the new Emperor that he had guaranteed he would give up investing bishops, the Church would renounce all her feudal rights within the Empire, yield up her lands and temporal jurisdiction and look for support only to tithes and personal offerings.

There was an outcry from those assembled not least from the german bishops who stood to lose huge feudal estates. The decision would have turned the social structure of Europe upside down; but the outcry spread throughout the Church and the pope had to back down. It was a noble and idealistic gesture. As Attwater commented: "Much could be said in favour of such a revolution - but the feudal prelates of the twelfth century were not the men to agree to it." (1)

The wealth of the Church both locally and in its centralized amalgamation in Rome was enormous. Much of it was, of course, necessary for vast administrative networks, and the generous support given to the poor, sick and needy. Nonetheless the extravagant life styles of many of the clergy, particularly the bishops, cardinals and popes, the relative comfort and security of many of the ascetics in the monasteries, lost the Church the respect and admiration of many lay people. It helped provoke some of the extreme reactions by the medieval christians to such institutional wealth.

For instance the poor men of Lyons and Waldensians (although small in numbers) reacted to the over-institutionalization and wealth of the Church by living in simpler and poorer communities. The albigensian movement, a part manichaean revival, reacted in the same way. While it, like the manichaeans, had the same disdain for material things it had also the "perfect"- the gurus who lived lives free of attachment to material goods and sex. What the many "comfortable" clergy and monks often forgot was that their lives, so often relatively materially better than the generality of their people, provoked an over-reaction in people who expected a more Gospel orientation.

The attempts at restoring balance to the Church in the Middle Ages provide interesting reflection. The Church was, and is, a balance of apostles, teachers, prophets, a priestly people united by an Apostolic Authority. When one section develops to such an extent, it outstrips one or all of other elements in what could be regarded as the Church's basic balance of its constitutional parts. The resulting imbalance causes the other elements to lurch unhealthily to one side.

Throughout the Church's life, the Spirit continues to work to restore the balance of the undergirding ideas mentioned previously. Sometimes it takes the form of schisms or even heresies of people who are provoked by the Church's lack of Gospel living. Those who are heretical are provoked too far and they try to fix on one great lack in the contemporary structure and in doing so they often create another imbalance by over-stressing a lack at the expense of the whole teaching. At other times the Spirit's intervention takes the form of movements within the Church led by prophetic figures who try to work from within such as Francis of Assisi, Catherine of Siena, Nicholas of Cusa and many others, who have had a deep sense of where the Church should be going and try in their own lives and movements they found to alter the direction.

In Church apologetics it is said the human element in the Church can, temporarily, but sometimes long term, give bad example to those inside and outside the Church. This truth can turn into an excuse when one of the factors may well be structural not just human weakness. If as a result of the imbalance shown above, developments of the other basic charisms and structures have become stunted and frustrated by this unilateral development then the justified reactions of those suffering from this impoverishment can cause division and, if frustrated more, can become an over-reaction. This over-reaction can be originally a reaction to the lack of Gospel values in Church leaders who when they resist correction, and use power to frustrate even legitimate objections, drive the objectors to an extreme polarization. Instead of the Church looking at Gospel values as the base of the protest, it became too intent on preserving the system that had evolved at times leavened with "parasite ideas" and admixed with conclusions from forgeries or ideas taken out of context.

What probably saved the Church from even greater reaction to its wealth was St Francis of Assisi (+1226) keeping his ascetic movement with its ideal of poverty within the Church. This enabled people with needs and desires seeking a purer and more ascetic life finding it within the Franciscan friars.

The older monasteries (with still many exceptions) had lost much of their ascetic bent. The friars particularly provided this outlet in the 13th and 14th centuries. The friar, as distinct from the monk, lived in a monastery dividing the time between his monastic life and his life outside, preaching, teaching or in many franciscan cases begging. The friars were among those who were prominent in the scholastic revival in theology as can be seen in the lives of Albert and Thomas Aquinas.

In the 14th century quarrelling over poverty ultimately occasioned a papal excommunication of the "spirituals" who took an extreme position on being without goods in reaction to the Church's possessing so many. Yet the prophetic "charism" in the Church was found so often in the ranks of friars and allied orders, men and women such as St Catherine of Siena, Eckhart, Tauler and Savanarola. At the same time the institutional Church used the friars notably the Dominicans to be judges in its Inquisition, an agent for Church and social control over deviants from the system whether heretics or witches. It reached its most frightening aspect in the Spanish Inquisition. The friars were also to the forefront as missionaries going to the New World with and after Columbus.

The prophetic charism was by no means confined to the friars. People like Joachim of Fiore (+1202) and St Bernard (+1153) provided the continuity of the prophet in the monastic community. St Bernard, for instance, upheld the power of the priestly over the secular. In his letter to one of his monks elected pope, Eugenius III, he lamented the riches and administration of the office admonishing "a Church weighed down by its victories." (2)

The teacher charism, also continued to be explored and in St Thomas Aquinas' case solved in a particular fashion. Many of the teachers in the 4th and 5th Centuries were elected bishops and continued their teaching as bishops in these centuries preceding. During the barbarian invasions bishops and teachers often became synonymous. (However, exceptions abounded. St Jerome and Pelagius, for instance, were regarded as teachers even though they were not bishops). During what one may term the following "non-creative" centuries the episcopal and teaching roles were often equated because now teaching was reduced to passing on fixed knowledge. Later cathedral schools with their teachers remained highly regarded in the period before scholasticism flourished.

With scholasticism, much of the teaching charism passed to the university professors many of whom were friars. While in the Western Church (and markedly in the roman catholic tradition) the charism of teacher remained clerical, in the Eastern churches a tradition was developed (sustained to this day) by the lay theologian or teacher.

St Thomas' solution, after theologising on the teacher's charism or role was twofold. The teaching or magisterium of the Church, he reasoned, was not entirely episcopal. It proceeded from two cathedras or chairs. It came from both the bishop's chair and from the professor's chair with, of course, the ultimate decision on either teaching resting with the bishop's chair. (Later we will see where the word magisterium in the narrower sense of only papal and episcopal teaching has become the normal usage in the last century or two). (3) It is important to note how St Thomas Aquinas used the word "cathedra" or chair giving more weight to some of the interpreters of St Irenaeus who see his idea of succession involving a succession of teachers instructing from the "cathedra" rather than that of just episcopal succession. (p. 44)

* * * * * *

Paschal II's teaching was a very slight aberration in the direction the papacy was taking from Gregory VII (+1085) to Boniface VIII (+1303). The century that followed Boniface was a sad one for papacy before its almost total collapse.

While historians argue about the extent of theocracy (government or state governed by God directly or through a priestly class) claimed by Boniface VIII's extreme decrees, there is no argument about the general theocratic trend. Eleven years after Pascal's renunciation of imperial lands and jurisdiction, the Concordat of Worms (1122) was signed. By this bishops were to be canonically elected but the ruler had the right to be present at the election and receive homage from the newly elected prelate for the feudal lands of the Church. The king retained a certain amount of power. As Tierney remarks "...royal theocracy had been defeated without papal theocracy becoming established." (4)

The Saxon Emperors were succeeded by the Hohenstaufen Emperors who provided much opposition to the Papacy. As Roman Emperors they claimed the right to Italy and Rome in particular. The Papacy saw that Rome in the control of any foreign ruler could take away its needed independence and the tug of war continued between the lawyer popes and the great Hohenstaufens, Frederick Barbarossa (+1190) and Frederick II (+1250). "The solution they [the Popes] adopted was to assert that any rights which the Emperor possessed in Rome were held from the pope as an overlord, that the emperor was a vassal or official of the papacy", but it was by no means clear "whether such words refer merely to papal rule over Rome itself or to some dream of universal sovereignty, and at times, no doubt, the ambiguity was wilful." (5) The Hohenstaufens resisted such pretensions with many a papal backing down but with the original provocative claims being filed away carefully in chancery.

Under the great Innocent III (1198-1216) this concept of universal sovereignty grew to a high point and was maintained by his successors. Tierney summarizes the mood of that era: "The doctrine that Christ had bestowed his own powers on St Peter and on St Peter's successors in the papacy was universally accepted; the further argument that such a divinely established authority was necessarily superior to any other power on earth seemed convincing to many; and even those who were unconvinced found it difficult to refute." (6)

In fairness to the fully developed papal theory under Innocent III, the basic ideas of the synodal principle were not entirely forgotten. When Innocent assembled the great 4th Lateran Council of 1215, perhaps "the greatest representative assembly of the medieval world. Some 400 bishops and over 800 Abbots attended from all parts of Christendom. Moreover, along with these prelates, Innocent also expressly summoned representatives of cathedral chapters and other collegiate churches, because, he wrote, matters concerning them were to be discussed at the Council. Christian lay-rulers were also invited to attend...some of the italian cities also sent envoys." (7)

Yet at the very moment of the papacy's greatest triumph, weapons were being forged to retaliate. The same Aristotle who had provided so many rational arguments for the scholastics provided the king's followers also with a philosophical theory of the state that required no appeal to theological premises. The same Roman Law that provided Gratian with one of his bases of Church Law could also be used to provide a very exalted theory of legislative sovereignty together with a wholly non-papal account of the origins of imperial authority. (8) Even Thomas Aquinas in his teaching on Natural Law provided a theory of an autonomous state, because humans had two ends or purposes, an eternal one and a natural one. He denied secular power was derived from the ecclesiastical and said each was supreme in its own proper sphere. (9)

The theory of the nation states was being forged by secular clerks ready to use it. When the balance within the feudal system began to tilt more to a centralized bureaucracy under a strong king rather than a dispersal of powers among nobles, such theories were put to use. In France particularly these theories converged especially under the powerful king, Philip the Fair (+1314).

Boniface VIII (1294-1303) the aged, aristocratic pope who opposed Philip reigned during this period of theocratic claims by the papacy. When Philip and his advisers, trained in Roman Law, taxed the french clergy for the war against England, Boniface retaliated by claiming lay rulers had no authority over ecclesiastical persons or goods within their own realms. His bull "Clericis Laicos" (1296) opens with the words: "That lay men have been very hostile to the clergy antiquity relates; and it is clearly proved by the experiences of the present time..." (10) Philip in his turn countered by stopping all french monies going to Rome. Boniface, financially embarrassed and worried at a revolt of some of his cardinals and "spiritual" franciscans at home, called a truce. Philip had won an easy victory. He began to taunt the pope by arresting one of the french bishops (against canon law) and brought him to trial. The pope responded by the famous bull "Unam Sanctam" (1302) which contained the now famous sentence: "We declare, state, define and pronounce that it is altogether necessary for salvation for every human creature to be subject to the Roman Pontiff." (11) In open and veiled ways Boniface claimed the subordination of the temporal jurisdiction to the spiritual.

Just as Boniface was drafting a bill of excommunication against Philip in his summer palace of Anagni in 1303, a gang of french knights and toughs attacked the old pope leaving him severely wounded. He died in Rome a few weeks later. After the short reign of Boniface's successor, a french pope Clement V (1305-1314) left Rome and started a long line of french popes at Avignon, very much beholden to the kings of France. Innocent III's dream of a universal society of ordered peace had come unstuck with the combination of a pope as obtuse as Boniface, and the new political thinking arising in Europe. Tierney concludes: "Certainly the combination of an exalted theory of papal overlordship with a persistent practice of using the spiritual authority of the popes to serve local political ends sapped the prestige of the Roman see to a degree that made possible the victory of Philip the Fair." (12) It is one more case of the papacy claiming too much thus provoking opposition rather than the wise use of legitimate authority which could have and did aid european unity on many occasions.

The vast centralized papal bureaucracy did not come to an end with Boniface. It merely moved to Avignon. But the papal prestige suffered a grievous blow from which it never fully recovered. The "Babylonian Captivity" at Avignon (1309-1377) was disastrous enough for the papacy. But when it was followed by the Great Schism (1378-1417) during which there were two and then three popes simultaneously all claiming the allegiance of christendom, the papacy had truly fallen on bad days.

Southern, has chartered the increasing flow of business at the curia. He lists ten letters a year at the time of Sylvester II (999-1003). By the time of John XXII (1316-1324), one of the Avignon popes, the volume had increased to 3,646 letters a year - monasteries seeking privileges and exemption from episcopal jurisdiction, litigation involving kings and bishops, nobles and clergy, papal appointments to ecclesiastical benefices, issues of indulgences and even international arbitration. The papacy became a bastion for feudal monarchs, bishops and monasteries looking for ultimate legitimation of their growing power against local interferences. As Southern remarks: "The real reason why governments sought jurisdiction was because it was the only practical way in which they could enforce their claim to lordship." (13)

Like all governments, ecclesiastical or lay, once the bureaucracy was there it grew. Despite the large fees of litigants and office seekers, money was soon absorbed in its turn by this vast machine. More and more bishops, funded by their local churches, absented themselves from their dioceses to head papal offices in the curia at the same time as others of their number were summoned by the king to fill similar roles at his court. Papal control over appointments of bishops grew from the indirect control at local cathedral chapter elections (p. 88) to greater direct control as a more centralized theocratic papacy saw itself as the source of power. Innocent III spent much time trying to get rival factions of electing canons of a cathedral to agree on their new bishop before finally nominating one himself. Gradually this kind of nomination grew until under John XXII (1316-1334) and Benedict XII (1334-1342), (Avignon popes) nomination of bishops became reserved to the pope alone in 1335 as did all "patriarchal, archiepiscopal and episcopal churches, all monasteries, priories, dignities, parsonages and offices, all canonries, prebends, churches and other ecclesiastical benefices…" (14)

That this took place without huge secular opposition as it would have done in the reigns of Gregory VII and Henry IV is well explained by Southern: "Rulers found it easier to deal with a single pope than with a complicated web of local interests represented by a cathedral chapter." (15) Originally local interests welcomed the papacy's intervention to protect them against the secular ruler's control. This now led to complete papal control. Nonetheless a working relationship between popes and kings emerged from the time of Gregory VII so that the two could divide the spoils. The papacy could refuse to nominate an "heretical" intruder but still use the "benefice" to reward curial officials and sympathisers. As the Middle Ages wore on, nephews, cousins and even illegitimate sons also benefited. In many ways the imperial and royal machines before Gregory VII which were replaced in the hope of reform by the much better organized papal machine had now both fallen victims to bureaucracy, nepotism and venality. The main difference to many was that the pope's opulence and power looked worse, as it was operated by "men of God" for the sake of the institution than rulers consumed by national or self interest.

The reformation of this international exchange in spiritual and temporal power sharing was difficult. Good people could envisage no other system replacing it and because the powerful benefiting from it, were the last to see its weaknesses. The "prophets" have been mentioned above. Their railings were not only against the riches and power of the system but also now against a french pope with a majority of french cardinals running the bureaucracy from France, often beholden to a french king. The whole independence or supposed objectivity of the papacy, especially during such a period of the 100 years' war between England and France (1338-1453), came into question. Saints like Catherine of Siena and Bridget of Sweden pleaded with and ultimately prevailed upon the ageing Gregory XI (1370-1378) to return to Rome, the centre of christendom, and his own bishopric. It seemed the Babylonian Captivity was at an end.

Some two months after his arrival in Rome, Gregory XI died. During the papal election there were instances of pressure and threats from the roman mob demanding a roman pope. The pope elected was a Neapolitan, Urban VI (1378-1389), who may well have commanded the respect of all if his irrational moods and tempers had not made many fear for his sanity. In any event it gave the french and a few italian cardinals an excuse (and many would agree a solid one) to flee Rome protesting an invalid election. They in turn elected another french pope, Clement VII. He was welcomed back to Avignon by the french king where the bureaucracy and most of the money still reposed. For the next forty years there were two popes. In the last few years of this period when cardinals of both popes met in defiance of their masters and elected what they hoped would be a legitimate pope, a third pope emerged. None of the three were willing to resign. The Church was split into two then three obediences.

* * * * * *

On the face of it the collapse of papal credibility was a disaster, yet in many ways it created an opportunity to think out once more the true nature of the Church. This was made more difficult because there was not at hand a large collection of authentic or scholarly corrected source materials. Any scholar had to wade through the huge imbalance created by a tradition which had mixed materials as well as mythology; all regarded with the same degree of certitude. This misleading mixture had shaped the Faith and Tradition of the previous centuries in the Western Church. There was, of course, enough known about the early Church and the first General Councils, despite the overlay placed upon them, to realize the needed agreement of all local churches and together with scriptural backing for the whole priestly people to be involved.

The immediate solution was to call for a General Council. Not just of bishops and cardinals who were divided into three obediences anyway, but also of the "teachers", the theologians, and the "prophets" abbots and friars, representative lay people who were, of course, mainly kings and nobility. The first attempt at Pavia (1409) was abortive. It elected the "real" pope who started a third line of papacy because the other two popes would not resign. The second attempt at Constance (1414-1417) was eminently successful and supported by the strong arm of the Holy Roman Emperor, Sigismund.

After sinking to the depths it is always a cause for a certain amount of astonishment that the papacy's restoration was accomplished on two major occasions by the imperial power. On both occasions no power or authority within the Church could seemingly have effected the needed solution. When the German Emperors deposed several unruly popes in Rome in the 1046-1059 period prior to the new edict on papal conclaves, they were the only ones who had the superior force to bring order to the roman mobs. Now when the Great Schism could not be resolved forty years after its inception, only a strong outside power could force the three popes to resign or be deposed.

In the November of 1414 the delegates began to assemble at Constance. The Council was to sit for almost four years and at its height some twenty-nine cardinals, one hundred and eighty-six bishops, more than one hundred abbots, three hundred and more doctors either of theology or law, eleven ruling princes, including the Emperor Sigismund, and ambassadors from twelve other princes were in attendance.

After the resignations of two of the three popes and the deposition of the third at the instigation of the Emperor, the vote was taken up by the "nations", five blocs of nationalities - french, german, italian, english and spanish - to prevent any one bloc being too powerful on all important points. When the time came in 1417 for the election of the true pope, Martin V, twenty-three cardinals and thirty delegates (six from each of the five nations) took part. It was agreed that this procedure would hold true only for this papal election.

Two decrees passed by Constance were significant. The first "Haec Sancta" declared the sacred synod of Constance formed itself into a General Council "legitimately assembled in the Holy Spirit" with power "immediately from Christ". This Council was to be obeyed by all of every rank and position, including even the pope himself "as to the extirpation of this schism and the reformation of the Church 'in head and in members'. Anyone who disobeyed the Council's decrees should 'be subjected to fitting penance and punished as appropriate' even a pope." (16) This decree continued to be a controversial one for centuries. Nevertheless, as Oakley remarks "there can be little doubt that the subsequent activity of the Council was grounded in the claims it advanced." (17) Conciliarism or what "Haec Sancta" decreed lived on in the Church, particularly France, and was finally for roman catholic theology knocked on the head at Vatican I Council in 1870.

"Frequens" decree had a short time effect. It called for frequent councils every five years. While this was complied with for a couple of decades, the cat and mouse game played by the papacy in bowing to the council when it was forced to for survival, ignoring it when it felt itself stronger, is an interesting study in complex politics. Eventually conciliarism ended up with a council losing its following among the catholic people and an anti-pope who came to heel in 1449. The council with political pressure dissolved itself. "Frequens" became a dead letter.

Many of the great minds of this period began to re-examine the basis of the Church's structures in order to reform the Church. Despite many inadequacies they probed deeper into the Church's constitution than had been done in the previous thousand years. This was especially true of the great contemporary thinkers Pierre d'Ailly and Jean Gerson of the University of Paris and Cardinal Nicholas of Cusa. The Holy Spirit was still working in the Church.

Particularly was this true of the thought of the mystic and humanist, Cardinal Nicholas of Cusa. In his "De Concordantia Catholica", Nicholas asserted the authority of general councils was superior to the pope's. His arguments prepared for the stormy Council of Basle (1431) were not accepted because of the continual in-fighting.

"The prelates, who represented local communities, were outnumbered many times over by private doctors of theology and law who often represented no one but themselves" comments Tierney. And he goes on to say, "the later leaders of the council turned away from Cusanus' (Cusanus latin for Nicholas of Cusa) complex arguments to assert again a simple identity between the power of the Church and that of council - regardless of its composition." (18) When Nicholas saw there was no immediate future in conciliarism after the Council of Basle self-destructed, to the delight of both royalty and papacy, he went over to the papacy as the only viable future for the Church and was made a cardinal. Yet he never revoked his ideas.

Nicholas' thought represented an attempt to apply the synodal principle at a critical moment of history. He asked the question "What is a General Council?" Bishops convoked by emperor or pope? Surely the authentic historical situation which the Council of Constance had shown was that a General Council was performing its true function when it represented the general body of the whole Church. After all, the bishops were supposedly there as elected by and representing their local churches. Nicholas of Cusa envisioned the Church as a pyramid rising to the apex, Christ, whose base was the faithful. The faithful elected their parish priest, by votes. The parish priests with the consent of the faithful and the metropolitan elected the bishops who met together in provincial councils which in turn elected the metropolitan. The provincial councils, bishops and metropolitan, in turn sent delegates to the pope who was required to make them cardinals. These cardinals should form a permanent general council.

Even though Nicholas said the council was not a general or ecumenical one unless the pope summoned it, should the council convene for the welfare of the whole Church and the pope ignore it then the council's authority became the greater.

Nicholas' reasons are interesting. He argued the pope had certain privileges from St Peter and the apostles, but others flowed from canons and secular rulers. It was a mixed authority; but by contrast general councils represented the universal Church with authority directly from God. Moreover, the judgement and wisdom of the combined cardinals and bishops would be less prone to error than that of a single man, i.e. the pope. Nicholas seemed to regard the pope as the chief executive officer of the ecclesiastical organization. (19)

Nicholas established the important principle to be discussed in the last chapter that the guidance of the Holy Spirit manifested itself through the consent of the community and that the elected bishop signified and represented his Church as a public person. This was significant because based on the knowledge available to him, Nicholas believed Christ had instituted bishops.

Many medieval thinkers contemporary with Nicholas of Cusa such as Ockham and Marsilio of Padua had thoughts on political theory relating to the state and church similar to Nicholas. Gerson defined a general council as "an assembly made by legitimate authority of every hierarchical state of the whole Catholic Church, no faithful person who seeks a hearing being excluded." (20) Tierney sums up the whole period well when he says: "In the end the ideas of the great medieval churchmen on representative government had more influence on the secular sphere than in the Church itself. The failure of Basle proved a council cut off from the people could not carry through the much needed reform of the Church; but the subsequent history of the Renaissance papacy showed that the popes could not reform the Church without a council that credibly represented the Christian world." (21)

No wonder royalty and papacy combined to oppose conciliarism - as it was perceived to undermine the autocracy of both systems!

The conciliarists, however, overplayed their hand in opposing a general council to the papacy. Perhaps it was their scholastic training that forced them to turn the situation into a black and white dynamic with papacy and council at opposite poles instead of seeing each one part of the synodal principle - the petrine charism serving to unite the Church balancing Christ's authority with the general council, bishops, priests and laity of the whole Church.

Support for the conciliar movement waned not just because people lost interest as many did after the papal crisis was over, nor because the conciliar party was outmanoeuvred by papal diplomacy and stonewalling, but mainly because the papacy had won as Oakley, the american historian, says "by accepting - helping sponsor, even - what amounted to a constitutional revolution of another type, and one that was determinative for the history of the papacy in particular and the Roman Catholic church in general right down to the nineteenth century." (22)

What was this constitutional revolution? During the Babylonian Captivity and the Great Schism many kings had struck deals with the papacy over certain matters. To give a simple example, by leaving a diocese vacant for a year or two, the revenues were divided and they were kept between the two of them pending the appointment of a bishop. The kings had also with a weakened papacy after Boniface VIII threatened to withdraw their taxes which the papacy needed for the lifeblood of its bureaucracy. In England especially during the one hundred years' war with France and a french pope, the english king could marshal national anti-papal feeling in refusing to pay papal taxes.

When there were two popes with two obediences, the kings learnt to play for privileges and exemptions from a weakened pope who often badly needed their support. This continued during the fifteenth century to the point where on the eve of the Reformation, many of the 'catholic' kings were in virtual control of their churches, nominated their own bishops and benefices with the pope keeping the prior right of refusing the nominated only if he were a "heretic". All the battles of the Middle Ages for papal supremacy and power in Europe were conceded to the kings who, as Oakley put it, "were willing to withdraw support from the conciliar idea that went with it. Possession of the actual substance of power mattered less, it seems, than the enjoyment of a theoretically supreme authority in the universal Church." It was a heavy price to pay, for example the kings right to nominate their own bishops again, but the papacy was willing to pay it for the victory over the conciliarists. The papacy knew the kings saw in the democratic rumblings of the conciliarists a threat to their own growing absolutism so the papacy and royalty became united in opposing the growing power of the nobles and people.

Because the king kept the church money and appointments at home, it meant that after the Constance-Basle Councils, the papacy had to draw its income from the Papal States rather than the Church at large. Consequently the high politics, wars and diplomacy on the italian peninsula occupied the popes up to and during the Reformation. Gregory XI, the pope who left Avignon in 1377, earned a much larger income than did Martin V, the first pope elected after the Great Schism. More significantly, only a quarter of Gregory's income came from the Papal States whereas one half of Martin's did. (24)

Another important consequence of this arrangement was that after the discovery of the New World in 1492 it was the kings who directed the missionary effort because they controlled the bishops and churches in their country and the colonies. Spain and Portugal were outstanding in the numbers of converts they made yet they were often ruthless. They were using the Church as a weapon for the total control and oppression of their newly baptized subjects with very few bishops and religious able to oppose the governments.

* * * * * *

The Church badly needed reform. As Owen Chadwick remarked: "When churchmen spoke of reformation, they were almost always thinking of administrative, legal or moral reformation; hardly ever of doctrinal reformation." (25) The fifth Lateran Council in 1512 had composed a marvellous blueprint; but almost every bishop returned home and virtually changed little. The exception was the spanish church. After the final conquest of what remained of muslim Spain in 1492, Ferdinand and Isabella saw the only way to control what had been up until then separate spanish kingdoms, including extensive areas in the south which contained large numbers of muslims and jews, was to have strong centralized political rule. To accomplish this political unity it was important to have one church only which must support the State in all its endeavours. As the spanish monarchs now almost totally controlled the Church, it was easier for them (compared with other european monarchs who did not have the same control) to purify and prune the Church within their own realms. A royal controlled inquisition which spied on the beliefs of the converted muslims and jews, or any spaniard for that matter who did not follow strict catholic doctrine (those unwilling to convert had to leave Spain, others turned catholic apparently to avoid leaving their homes) was the horrendous price the reformed spanish church had to pay for this. The price paid in personal freedom of conscience has to be weighed against the political unity it created. The reform did produce in Spain regular monasteries, better priests and laity as well as a flowering of learning and mysticism.

Elsewhere in the Church, as Chadwick mentions, everyone desired reform but once it began to affect them in their particular weak spot they turned away from reform. The Alexander VIs and Leo Xs with their banquets, hunting parties and palaces, the absentee bishops enjoying the court life of the pope or king instead of pastoring their flocks back home, the majority of clergy not educated enough, many monasteries full of caretaker monks and nuns, all conspired together to show a crying need for reform but did not possess the leadership seemingly to know where or how to begin this apparently impossible task.

The laity, too, were by now much more distrustful of ecclesiastical authority than at the height of the Middle Ages. Not only had the Babylonian Captivity at Avignon and the Great Schism made them more skeptical of the papacy as the morally strong centre to which they could turn, but more of them were now formally educated. The "re-birth" of the classical writers and philosophers as well as the renaissance of many early christian writings into Western knowledge were utilized by Aquinas and the scholastics. Other thrusts of these studies led, as remarked above, into political theories antedating centralized papal power and a much more critical idea of present Church government contrasted with that which emerged from early christian writings.

The name "Renaissance" or re-birth was tagged to the tremendous flowering of art and letters under the influence of classical models which took place in Italy from the fourteenth to the sixteenth centuries. This Renaissance fairly quickly penetrated to north of the Alps producing scholars of the calibre of Nicholas of Cusa (mentioned previously). It was not only an artistic and literary movement but also one of linguistic and scientific precision based on the classical sources. It also shifted the medieval emphasis on the "other world" (anchored firmly in monastic spirituality) to the practicality of enjoying the beauty of this one without losing a place in the next.

One of the great renaissance scholars, De Valla, proved that the Donation of Constantine was a forgery. As other great scholars such as Erasmus, Dean Colet and St Thomas More researched in greater depth, more and more questions arose regarding the human and cultural evolution of the Church in the previous thousand years. Renaissance scholarship and the invention of printing provided a catalyst to this surging demand for reform; although very rarely, except for small groups already named, no one thought of changing the essential teachings of the Church. Yet it happened.

* * * * * *

Many were provoked into extreme positions by the Church's over-emphasis on power, riches, politics and the constant double standards of so many of its clergy, high and low. Its under-emphasis on Gospel standards particularly the Sermon on the Mount and its lack of sharing authority with all believers (especially in listening attentively to them) was set to drive prophets and other good men and women to an over-reaction. What should have occurred was a balance, a unity long since forgotten. Except for the few who never attained a majority in the corridors of power.

When one uses the term Reformation one usually thinks of Martin Luther's "revolt" on 31 October 1517 in challenging the extremist Dominican Tetzel's teachings on indulgences. Luther's challenge was not questioning any essential doctrine of the Church, rather it was provoked by the superstitious and venal way in which the indulgence was being preached. Most historians see the period 1517-1520 in Luther's life as one in which he considered himself a catholic anxious to reform the Church. "If the Pope only knew what was going on, he would act" seemed to express, perhaps naively, Luther's thought.

What changed the situation was the zealot dominican Eck's challenge to Luther that if he held to what he believed he was like John Hus who was in Eck's mind a heretic. (Many, especially today, would call Hus a schismatic, i.e. not disagreeing with essential catholic teaching). Luther's famous reply: "Here I stand, I can do no other" was based on his convictions from his studies, especially of St Paul's Epistles. The dominican influence in Rome as well as pressure from other quarters precipitated Luther's excommunication by Pope Leo X in 1520. From then on, Luther was pushed into an extreme position. In particular he had to find an ultimate authority now the papacy was not, in his opinion, the ultimate unifier of the Church. The "Faith Alone" and "Scripture Alone" principles became the rallying cry of the Protestant Reformation as the basis for reformation. Despite this, increasing scholarly opinion agrees that nothing in the Lutheran Augsburg Confession or Creed (1529) militates against catholic doctrine.

In the fifth centenary of Luther's birth in 1983, Cardinal Etchegaray, the Archbishop of Marseilles, wrote: "Luther was a Christian straight out of the gospel. His purpose was to have the Church return to the only struggle that is truly its own: to make God's word transparent to a church that is loaded down with excess baggage." (26)

John Calvin (+1564) was among the second generation of Protestant Reformers. His scholarly pursuits led him to the conviction that the presbyteral form of Church government (for him presbyters and elders) had more roots in history than the episcopal and papal ones. Luther kept many traditions not explicitly mentioned in the Scriptures as long as they were not contradicted by them. He based his reforms broadly on the doctrine of the priesthood of the laity. Calvin, while recognizing that doctrine, saw the need for a rightly "called" and "purified" ministry. Thus his insistence on the presbyters and elders whom he claimed existed in the early church. He further taught that no tradition should be accepted unless justified in the Scriptures. (27)

There were the extreme over-reactions usually called the anabaptist movements. Some of the more chapel-type or fundamentalist protestant churches come from this stream or have arisen in the same climate. One wonders if much of the extreme direction some of these movements took (such as John of Leyden's in Munster) was due to the desire for a more simple Gospel provoked by the high living of popes, cardinals and bishops? More deeply one can see that the 'religious' search of so many frustrated and sincere people trying to find a solution grounded in the Gospels led into extreme situations at times by fundamentalist or even fanatical ideologues.

Henry VIII of England (+1547) a catholic king who, incidentally, had not signed the same concordats and received the same concessions to appoint bishops as his royal peers in France and Spain, separated from Rome in 1533-34 over his divorce proceedings. As we see from his actions, especially the Six Articles of 1539, he wanted to establish the english church as an independent catholic church free of Rome, but still with a celibate clergy saying latin masses. He burnt both protestants and roman catholics at the stake. Unfortunately for his plans, his first non-roman Archbishop of Canterbury, Cranmer, was a crypto-lutheran veering towards calvinism who during the reign of young King Edward VI (1547-1553) steered the anglican church more in the direction of other protestant reformers. The Elizabethan settlement that followed was designed to keep both wings, the "catholic" and "evangelical" protestant, in a united church.

Western Christendom was now split in two, roman catholic and protestant, some four to five centuries after the Church had previously begun to drift apart into Eastern and Western. The tragedy is that so much was unnecessary because it concerned inessentials which the Western Catholic Church had not always realized were not essentials. The double tragedy was that provocative life styles, powerbroking and arrogant refusals to reform caused the reactions which ultimately led to over-reacting, the cause of the Western Catholic Church's refusal to compromise.

* * * * * *

It was hard for the roman catholic church to focus its opposition to protestantism and provide a disciplined reform movement. A general council was necessary; but as the last century's papal experience had shown, papal control is necessary, as Emperor Charles V (abdicated 1556) stood for dialogue with the lutherans and wanted them present at the council. The cardinals were divided, one party favouring such dialogue, the other intransigent. Contarini, from the party favouring dialogue, returned to Rome from the Colloquy of Ratisbon with an agreement on Justification by Faith although he was forbidden to negotiate on Transubstantiation (a doctrine in our times seen as not the only explanation of Christ's real presence in the Eucharist). He received an indignant reception being called a "heretic". He reputedly died of a broken heart in 1542.

The intransigents led by Cardinal Caraffa (later Pope Paul IV) represented a party of no compromise with protestants and wanted strict theological definitions and discipline to keep the Church intact. The Caraffa party won the ear of Pope Paul III who warded off the Emperor's demands. "Commit yourself to nothing" a legate warned the pope "until it is agreed that the pope is absolute master of the Council."

The general council finally met at Trent in northern Italy (just inside the Empire to comply with German demands) in 1545. The pope's legates won the day and doctrinal arguments preceded disciplinary discussions. Lutherans were excluded. With long periods between sessions Trent did not conclude until 1563. From one point of view it was eminently successful. It produced dogmatic definitions against protestants. It introduced disciplinary laws for bishops, clergy and laity. One of its greatest achievements was the institution of seminaries where for the first time in Church history almost all, not just some, clergy received education and formation. In many areas of discipline, the council imposed a uniformity down to the minutest detail. Something that many have confused with unity in the following ages.

The liturgist Clifford Howell said Trent put the latin mass into deep freeze until Vatican II (1962-65) changed this. The same could be said of Trent itself, not just concerning the liturgy but of almost every aspect. The main argument winning the often small majorities of the few bishops who attended seemed to hinge on the fact that if changes were made to the mass and celibacy then to the largely uneducated the ceremonies and ministers would look too much like the protestants and they would not be able to differentiate clearly which was the "one, true Church". It sought to create a Church, a perfect society, existing in this "world" but not of it. Its baroque churches and palaces were places where the true Church could triumph, set in the world but free from it. For roman catholicism it was the high water mark of protestant incursions into its territory, for with the help of the newly founded Jesuits especially, the weaker areas of catholicism such as France, Poland, south Germany and parts of Switzerland remained roman catholic.

It would be a long time before this triumphalist Church realized it was responsible for the provocation that produced protestantism. It took centuries before the roman catholic Church could admit the faults were not all on the protestant side. Many commentators now acknowledge as much as Trent preserved the catholic community and kept it in disciplined control, many of the doctrinal statements suffer from an imbalance (understandable in the circumstances) but very much over-reactions to the protestant over-reactions to the sixteenth century church's under emphasis of the gospel.

♣ ♣

Guiseppe Alberigo put it well when he said: "After the medieval Western councils, the Council of Trent suffered, and approved, a drastic narrowing, both qualitative and quantitative, of the Catholic horizon. Rarely had a major council been attended by so small a number of bishops, and by bishops who came almost exclusively from the Latin and Mediterranean world. Despite this limited representation, the council happily succeeded in damming the flood waters that were threatening to destroy Catholicism and in starting a revival. But the price paid for this successful orientation cannot be overlooked; it can be summed up as a drastic isolation of Roman Christianity, now cut off and insulated from any interaction with the other Christian traditions of East and West, condemned to an attitude of defensiveness toward the modern world, and, finally, surrounded by a cordon sanitaire to prevent contamination from alien cultures. Never in the history of Christianity had the "massa damnata" been made to include so much and so many; never had Christianity so extended and exacerbated its own estrangement from the fortunes of the human race." (28)

1. Attwater, Donald. <u>A Dictionary of the Popes.</u> London, The Catholic Book Club. 1939. p. 168
2. Gerest, C. "Spiritual Authority in the 11th and 12th Centuries", p. 87 <u>Concilium Theology in an Age of Renewal</u>
3. McBrien, R P. <u>Catholicism</u>, Vol. I p. 68. East Malvern, Melbourne, Dove, 1980
4. Tierney, Brian. <u>The Crisis of Church and State 1050-1300.</u> Englewood Cliffs, Prentice-Hall. 1964. p. 86
5. Ibid, p. 99
6. Ibid, p. 159
7. Tierney, Brian., "The Idea of Representation on the Medieval Councils of the West", <u>Concilium,</u> "The Ecumencial Council". 1983. p. 27
8. Tierney, Brian. <u>The Crisis of Church and State 1050-1300.</u> p. 98 and p. 159
9. Ibid, p. 167
10. Ibid, p. 175
11. Ibid, p. 182
12. Ibid, p. 182
13. Southern, R W. <u>Western Society and the Church in the Middle Ages.</u> Harmondsworth, Pelican History of the Church, Vol. II. reprint 1976. p. 113
14. Ibid, p. 158
15. Ibid, p. 159
16. Oakley, F. <u>The Western Church in the Later Middle Ages.</u> London, Ithaca Cornell University Press. 1979. pp. 65-66
17. Ibid, p.66
18. Tierney, Brian. "The Idea of Representation on the Medieval Councils of the West", <u>Concilium,</u> "The Ecumencial Council". 1983. p. 29
19. Doyle, Phyllis. <u>A History of Political Thought.</u> London, Jonathan Cape. 1963. pp. 117sq.
20. Tierney, Brian. "The Idea of Representation on the Medieval Councils of the West". p. 28
21. Ibid, p. 29
22. Oakley, F. <u>The Western Church in the Later Middle Ages.</u> p. 71
23. Ibid, p. 73
24. Ibid, p. 74
25. Chadwick, Owen. <u>The Reformation.</u> Harmondsworth, Penguin, reprint with revisions. 1972. p. 13

26. Alberigo G, Jossua J-P, Komanchak Joseph A, Gerault Rene, "The Reception of Ecumenism", p. 55 in "The Reception of Vatican II". Washington DC, Catholic University of America Press, 1987
27. Chadwick, Owen. The Reformation. p. 83
28. Alberigo, Guiseppe. "The Christian Situation after Vatican II" in The Reception of Vatican II. pp. 13-14

CHAPTER NINE

Can a true theology of development restore balance to the Tradition?

There are certain times in history when the human race seems to stay at a moderate pace and even at least superficially stagnate. At other times there are significant developments and on rarer occasions giant leaps ahead from previous positions. During these rare periods the optimists call such development progress and at times revolution. The enemies of this same development call it deterioration, retrogression, demoralisation or even the work of the devil. Such speedy development took place in Western Europe in the 17th and 18th centuries ensuring its world paramountcy at least in the field of technology and thereby enabling it by military and naval superiority to build its world empires during the 19th and 20th centuries. In the churches, particularly the roman catholic, there was an inability to deal effectively with this "Enlightenment" as it was called. Cries of "disaster", "diabolical", "corruption of traditional values" emerged. There was little accommodation with or understanding of what was happening.

The Enlightenment was in a sense a continuation of the movement begun and nurtured by the Renaissance. However, in the 17th to 19th centuries, so many and varied were the channels of enquiry pursued and so pluriform had the religious circumstances and questionings of certainties become that the Church no longer retained its authority to give final answers and was more and more becoming displaced by reason. It was not that the Enlightenment set out to be anti-religious. Many of its chief proponents were church members; but as new certainties proved many of the Church's certainties wrong or doubtful and as the Church positively kept defending these same questioned certainties, then reason became more and more regarded as the ultimate criterion of truth. Because of the churches insistence on the absolute certainties they had "received" from their past Tradition it now drove the disciples of the new sciences to question how the development from the original Gospel idea had gone astray and in turn whether the original Gospel idea itself had to be taken literally. True and false development from the Gospels and early christianity became a central issue especially in the thought of John Henry Newman.

No one event can be said to have ushered in the Enlightenment. However, from the religious and secular point of view the Peace of Westphalia 1648 at the end of the Thirty Years War can serve as a measure of the change in Western Europe. This war, which was said to have reduced the german population by one third, commenced as a roman catholic/protestant conflict which became largely political. Among the peace clauses was the grudging beginning of real tolerance in Europe. As Gerald Cragg, the noted historian of religion, remarks: "It was the end…of religious wars in general…both sides foreswore propaganda by the sword, and henceforth doctrinal disputes were settled within states not between them. Consequently matters of faith ceased to be an important irritant in international affairs." The pope pronounced the clauses affecting catholics "null and void, accursed and without any influence or result for the past, the present or the future." A papacy that had given away its medieval right of nominating bishops to most of the "catholic" rulers and lost most of its centralizing power was largely ignored. As Cragg dryly comments: "…political opinions could now be settled without reference to the opinions of ecclesiastics and theologians…with the international prestige of institutional religion in eclipse." (1)

Much of this had happened arguably because religion had claimed too much certainty. Now it was challenged and where its claims were unsustained, the Enlightenment's ideas grew stronger by the day. Hastening the Church's growing impotence was the way many who thought these claims were baseless argued therefore that its other claims were wrong.

The over-emphasis placed on claims that were not true development from the original christian principle caused an over-reaction against all the Church's claims and the intelligentsia clamoured for the Church to prove its challenged assertions at the bar of reason. Paul Hazard, a modern historian, puts it well when he says: "What men craved to know was what they were to believe, and what they were not to believe. Was tradition still to command their allegiance or was it to go by the board? Were they to continue plodding along the same old road, trusting to the same old guides, or were they to obey new leaders who bade them turn their backs on all these outworn things and follow them to other lands of promise? The champions of reason and the champions of religion were … only fighting desperately for the possession of men's souls, confronting each other in a contest at which the whole of thoughtful Europe was looking on." (2)

The climate in the aftermath of the Peace of Westphalia encouraged challenge and daring. Catholicism was no longer of paramount importance in Western Europe as it had been in the Middle Ages. Prior to the Peace, the scientific revolution had already begun with Francis Bacon divorcing faith from knowledge, reason from revelation, natural religion from revealed religion. At the same time he laid the groundwork for the inductive method of experimentation. (3) Copernicus, a polish priest astronomer working with observation, even earlier than Bacon, had shown that the planets, including the earth, revolve on their own axes and move in orbits around the sun. Copernicus knew this contradicted the literal interpretation of the Scriptures which had the sun rising and setting on the earth as centre of the universe. He wisely left his works to be published posthumously knowing the inquisition could condemn him if he were alive. The same fate was not avoided by Galileo Galilei whom the inquisition forced to repudiate his copernican theories. Giordano Bruno was burnt by the inquisition. He had accused the Church of being the enemy of scientific progress. The Church was giving signals to the Enlightenment that it could condemn, but it was not capable of taking what was positive in many of these scientific findings and melding them into christian tradition as the Church was forced to do from the seventeenth century.

The position adopted at the Council of Trent (noted earlier) was to make the Church as a city under siege refusing to capitulate and an attitude of "deepfreezing" all it saw as positive from the status quo. This then became unquestioned material. The stances of the protestant churches to the Enlightenment, while, not dependent on Trent, were actually not too different from Rome. Individual popes, bishops and clergy showed interest in what was going on but rarely did the institutional Church.

Many of the pioneers of the Enlightenment were practising christians. Such a one was Isaac Newton who considered faith and knowledge were closely related and that the order and beauty of nature was a proof of God's existence. John Locke wrote on the reasonableness of religion helping to produce a morality where reason was the criterion of good religion. He went on to assert the natural and inalienable rights of the individual, denying the divine right of kings or popes to oppose the sovereignty of the people. But even the people's sovereignty should not, he maintained, override the rights of the individual. Rene Descartes, a pupil of the Jesuits, posited that the initial reaction to all questions should be one of doubt. This was the essential ingredient for building true thought.

Tarnas, a modern religious philosopher, summarizes the period well when he states: "And so between the 15th and 17th centuries, the West saw the emergence of a newly self-conscious and autonomous human being - curious about the world, confident in his own judgements, skeptical of orthodoxies, rebellious against authority, responsible for his own beliefs and actions, enamoured of the classical past but even more committed to a greater future, proud of his humanity, conscious of his distinctness from nature, aware of his artistic powers as individual creator, assured of his intellectual capacity to comprehend and control nature, and altogether less dependent on an omnipotent God. This emergence of the modern mind, rooted in the rebellion against the medieval Church and the ancient authorities and yet dependent upon and developing from both these matrices, took the three distinct and dialectically related forms of the Renaissance, the Reformation and the Scientific Revolution. These collectively ended the cultural hegemony of the Catholic Church in Europe…" (4)

Western Europe's peripheral contacts with Islam and journeys by men such as Marco Polo made europeans aware of other religions. This was accentuated by the spanish and portuguese contacts and conquests of the 15th and 16th centuries and there began a scientific study of what we call today comparative religion. This in turn caused some to question the originality and uniqueness of christianity and its base of judean religion. While christianity clung on to many pretensions and was often unable to distinguish within itself the difference between religious creed, code and cult from the uniqueness of the Gospel message, the task was made more difficult for the Church to avoid the counter-claim of the Enlightenment that it was just one more religion basically the same as any other.

The Church particularly was unable to extricate itself from its hellenistic european background. Some of its outstanding missionaries, such as Matteo Ricci in China (who lived the life of a mandarin and mathematician at the court of the Emperor) and Roberto de Nobili who became a hindu holy man to show the Gospel could take root in any soil, had their experiments suppressed as being "pagan". Twentieth century missiology was to commend the general thrust of their principles.

This inability of christianity in general to do other than condemn criticism of itself or work positively with the new knowledge based on using reason as supreme arbiter did little to help its cause. Reason reinforced newly discovered physical laws by concluding that there was a supreme mover of all these intricate mechanisms built into nature. When these findings were combined with comparative religion purporting to show the relativity of the christian revelation then deism (the belief that God was the inventor of the great clock of creation which he wound up and let go) became a popular form of conviction, among intellectuals especially, making christianity seem less and less relevant.

"I believe in God" said Voltaire "not the God of the mystics and theologians, but the God of nature, the great geometrician, the architect of the universe, the prime mover, unalterable, transcendentally everlasting." (5)

The churches still kept the adherence of most of the rural populations and many of the urban dwellers. Pietism and methodism among protestants and jansenism, quietism and popular "missions" given by jesuits, redemptorists and others kept a lively faith going among sections of the population even though in general pulpit oratory became stylized and often long and boring. Ceremonies were often pompous and ritualistic.

A more formidable attack on what the Church held as unquestionable was being prepared by scripture scholars such as the catholic Richard Simon and the protestant Reimarus who began to apply the same literary criticism to the Bible as was being applied to all other historical documents. The criticism grew into a questioning of all the doctrines the churches had built on literal or allegorical interpretations.

As the 18th century wore on, through people like Voltaire and groups such as the encyclopedists, the Enlightenment permeated not only the intellectuals and aristocracy but large numbers of the educated bourgeoisie or middle class. The thought of Locke and other encyclopedists was drawn on by the framers of the American Constitution and the leaders of the French Revolution which started off originally as a bourgeoisie revolt claiming a power sharing for the middle and mercantile classes with the aristocracy. As the French Revolution degenerated into mob rule and whilst Reason was enthroned as a goddess on the high altar of Notre Dame, the bloody terror and lawlessness caused reasonable people to over-react. Whatever good the enlightenment ideas contained, and they were many, they were seen as dangerous. Enlightenment thought was often blamed for the excesses of the Revolution.

The first over-reaction was seen in the law and order Napoleon imposed, carrying out the Revolution in principle but in a guided populist way. Napoleon saw the value of religion as a cement binding society together and its supportive role in reinforcing authority. "What is it that makes the poor man take it for granted" he asks "that ten chimneys smoke in my palace while he dies of cold - that I have ten changes of raiment in my wardrobe while he is naked - that on my table at each meal there is enough to sustain a family for a week? It is religion which says to him that in another life I shall be his equal, indeed that he has a better chance of being happy than I have." (6) He therefore brought the divided Church in France together and both used and appeased the papacy until an exasperated Pius VII excommunicated him.

When his great Empire fell, an even greater over-reaction set in. Many argued what had happened - the reign of terror, the slaughter of so many in the Napoleonic Wars - was because the established order had been upset and a return, as far as possible, to restoring the status quo alone would give Europe stability. A return to tradition for tradition's sake was the cry. Books such as Chateaubriand's "The Genius of Christianity" caught the imagination of a war weary generation upset by constant change and provided the background to the Congress of Vienna that met after Napoleon's defeat.

What was forgotten by the apostles of this "Restoration" was that the writings of the previous century and the spirit engendered by them were now permanently etched in the Western mind, particularly by those who continued to be repressed under the restored monarchies. The revolutions and rise of liberalism, socialism and even communism in the 19th century endorsed that. The Church in backing the Restoration (which largely coincided with its own policies since Trent) was really backing the wrong horse. This helped to estrange both the working classes, more and more brutalized by the industrial revolution, and the intelligentsia in the century that was to follow.

The atmosphere of the Congress of Vienna and the Restoration as it was called was exploited to the full by the "restored" papacy. Pius VII's benevolence and dignity as a prisoner under Napoleon impressed the world but especially won the affection of his catholic people. At least once before (in the 11th and 12th centuries) the bishops of the catholic world weighed down by the interference of their civil rulers in the local church looked to a centralized papacy to protect them from such interference. The ensuing papacy in its turn had become an over-lord often more powerful than the ruler. This aspect became forgotten. Local churches then began to look more and more to a centralized papacy as the restorer of Europe as they recalled the collapse of their own monarchies under the onslaught of the french revolutionary armies. Looking across the Alps to Rome gave this popular movement within the Church the latin name Ultramontane.

Pius VII's secretary of state, Cardinal Consalvi, was the genius of the papal restoration. At the Congress of Vienna he drew on the respect both protestant and catholic states of Europe now held for Pius VII and the realization they had that religion was a supportive and stablilizing element in restoring the monarchies. The boundaries of the Papal States were extended. More importantly Consalvi saw how papal control over the Church could be restored by the same means the medieval papacy had used - the centralized appointment of bishops.

Before the French Revolution, Rome interfered only in episcopal appointments already made by the "catholic" kings when there was a suspicion of heresy in the appointee and this was rare. It, therefore, controlled episcopal appointments only in its own Papal States and a few other territories (mainly bishoprics in protestant countries and vicars apostolic or missionary bishops in lands under the Propagation of the Faith congregation founded in 1622 for missionary territories not under the "catholic" kings).

Napoleon had opened the way to new concordats with the "catholic" kings by giving power to the papacy in regard to appointing bishops because he knew the only authority the two contending parties would look up to in healing the schism in the french Church in 1801 was the pope. The power he gave the pope would never have been given by the former "catholic" kings; but once it was a fact, it persisted.

With the revolution of the former colonies against "catholic" kings in Latin America, new concordats could be arranged by Consalvi where more papal control of bishoprics could be extended and new dioceses established in South and Central America. With the huge expansion of colonial powers in the 19th century and the revival of the jesuits and flourishing new religious congregations particularly in France, Italy, Spain, Germany, Holland, Belgium and Ireland a vast stream of catholic missionaries arose to follow the european colonisers with their superior technology to their remotest outposts. Although not always expressed, the colonisers often saw the missionaries as a help in expansion because they "tamed" the natives and made them more open to european colonization. Therefore even under protestant flags, catholic missionaries could find protection and sometimes encouragement.

All of these new and speedily expanding missions were given missionary bishops from the Propagation of the Faith appointed by a centralized papacy. These missions proliferated into hundreds of bishoprics which together with the large number created by the population expansions taking place in the former european colonies such as the United States of America and Latin America, and the existing colonies in Canada, Australia, New Zealand and elsewhere gave Rome almost complete control over their appointments.

The 19th century catholic mood was for a centralized papacy under a pope, head and shoulders above any other european leader, governing a Church expanding to the four corners of the world. The fact that the 19th century Church was fast losing many of its urban proletariat and intelligentsia was barely noticed. Ultramontanism had a left wing until de Lammenais' newspaper was suppressed by Rome. It then became a largely conservative movement growing in volume and numbers right into the 20th century. Even though the revolutions of 1830 and 1848 stirred and changed much of Europe, the papacy condemned them and kept the Papal States under a strong theocratic regime until their capture and collapse in 1870.

* * * * * *

The atmosphere described above nurtured in Rome a theology of the Church which has persisted until today. The neo-platonism that undergirded much of catholic theology in the Middle Ages had been revived in a newer form by the jesuits at the Gregorian University - truth was eternal, fixed, immutable and always stayed the same once the Church had defined it exactly. Even though scholastic thomism and aristoteleanism were not officially adopted in the Gregorian University (until after Leo XIII's letter reinstating them as neo-scholasticism in 1879) the same neo-platonic ideas shared many theories in common with the schools of the Middle Ages.

Whereas the scholastics, particularly Thomas Aquinas, had a much more flexible idea of the magisterium (or teaching charism and its authority reinforced by the apostolic authority in the Church) in that it came from both the bishop's chair and the teacher's or theologian's chair (p. 115), the new Gregorian school taught the magisterium was narrowed down to the first chair only, and constituted by the pope and bishops and official teaching. The weight of that magisterium was heavily loaded towards papal authority supported by the universal episcopate. (7) In this it differed from most medieval theology and the early church's teachings. While Tradition was always an essential element, the papal component was now markedly increased and given priority over General Councils. Yet magisterium as an official term had a low profile and was not even mentioned in the Council of Trent. It was now given a specific meaning in roman theology. This holds until today.

There were many great minds such as Perrone in the new roman jesuit school. With Perrone and his colleagues there was a lack of an appreciation of the historical and contextual evolution of the Church's teaching. It had come to a point where as Congar remarks "it was inevitable that Tradition should be identified with the magisterium." (8)

This theology became not only official in Rome but carried an importance far out of proportion to its roman backing. Many seminaries in Western Europe had been forced to close during the French Revolution as well as in the subsequent period of Napoleon's Empire and even the royal restoration period. A large number of european local churches built or re-established seminaries in Rome. Many of the new religious congregations founded in the wake of the French Revolution were encouraged by the pope to create seminaries in Rome also. Their students more often than not attended the Gregorian University. (9) Among the seminarians were many of the future bishops of the Church. They were trained in one mould and observed closely for their loyalty to the Holy See by the Curia whose increasing power included nominating bishops. Consequently a whole future episcopate and many professorial staff for seminaries all over the world were shaped in an "official" theology. This imbalanced theology in that it gave an over-emphasis to papal teaching and a differently nuanced definition of the magisterium. From 1830 until 1959 the official theology of the Gregorian University left its stamp on the Church, shaped its leaders and gave a respectability to ultramontanism that even popular piety and adulation for the papacy had not done as successfully.

* * * * * *

It is no wonder (given Perrone's ideas) that when the newly converted John Henry Newman arrived in Rome in 1847 and presented his ideas to him for evaluation, Perrone was respectful but puzzled. Newman had wrestled with his prior anglican position and in his agony at Littlemore wrote his "Essay on the Development of Christian Doctrine". It clarified in his own mind the necessity of conversion to roman catholicism in which he now saw the true development of original christianity. In his search, he had studied the "Fathers" or the early christian writers, particularly of the 3rd, 4th and 5th centuries.

His essay attempted to show there was a "true" as opposed to a "false" development of the original Gospel message. He argued that this theological development had criteria which ensured it was a "true" growth. His essay was written to show these true criteria. Up until this time the 5th century Vincent of Lerins' comment on catholic teaching that it is found 'in every place, at all time and believed by all' was being taken literally. Even as great an apologist as Bossuet, the notable french bishop in the 17th century, held that nothing new had been added to Tradition. When the Church defined a doctrine, according to Bossuet, she was applying her mind to the particular question. 'She only declares what she has always believed - explicitly, consciously and continually believed.' (10)

Newman went more deeply into Tradition. He said things did change and develop. So can development then assess the degree to which doctrine within Tradition has changed and whether the changes within it have been genuine or mixed with 'parasite ideas' or been distorted even though it still perdures? Newman tried to grapple with this problem and succeeded in posing the right questions and answers as regards the genuine development of Tradition. However he did not come to grips with the problem of the Church's teaching when it was not sufficiently grounded and needed redefinition. Newman seemed to conclude it would either die out or a future council would fix it.

Newman's ideas on development of christian doctrine have been both praised and harshly criticized. They are too complex to be gone into here, but they group around the first criterion that identity in change preserves its substantial form throughout all the changes. His other criteria are that this same identity is continuously dynamic and that at any moment is present with vigour: that the identity organically assimilates new elements and that new principles can be drawn from it and are in fact the result of clinging faithfully to the original principles thrust into new contexts and rendered imperative by their new growth: that careful investigation already shows an anticipation of later developments at much earlier stages. The essay was read widely and caused a stream of conversions to Rome. The clarity it gave Newman during its writing had resulted in his own conversion in 1845.

When Newman decided to go on for priesthood and went to Rome in 1847, Perrone, though friendly, could not agree with Newman's concept of the evolution of doctrine and often seemed at times to misunderstand Newman's position. He came from a stance of immutable and unchangeable criteria and could see no need for Newman's organic evolutionary perspective. For instance, at one point in his submissions to Perrone, Newman said "until the Church understands this or that part of the deposit of revelation in dogmatic form, it could happen that the Church itself is not yet fully aware of its view on the matter." Perrone wrote beside the remark: "New dogmas do not arise, but old truths are presented explicitly for belief in new definitions." Perrone did not condemn Newman's ideas even though many north american bishops had done so. (11) He had read and at times welcomed the theology of the german school of Tubingen which had similar ideas to Newman's on organic growth of doctrine.

Perrone must have felt a degree of unease at certain ideas, explicit or implicit in Newman's works. Newman's central idea of the consensus fidelium which unlike Perrone's more passive assent of the faithful to what the hierarchy or magisterium taught was, in contrast, an active participation of all baptized people right up to the build-up to the decision and doctrine making of the Church. Moreover, Newman asserted, when many of the bishops taught wrong doctrine at the time of arianism, it was often the laity who kept the faith!

When Newman, a decade or so later, not only repeated the same assertion but entitled his article "On Consulting the Faithful on Matters of Doctrine", a shadow was cast on his ecclesiastical career and orthodoxy in many official circles. Fortunately he was protected by his strong and acceptably orthodox bishop. Newman was merely proclaiming what we have seen was from the earliest times the synodal principle enunciated by Nicholas of Cusa and the more balanced conciliarists. This was the basis of the Church's teaching from the first centuries and remains the Eastern Orthodox Churches' position. It was the task of Perrone to prove the valid continuity of his own teaching rooted in what had gone before.

Owen O'Sullivan has put it well when he said: "The process of reception involves the whole church. Vatican II expressed this as follows: 'The whole body of the faithful cannot err in matters of belief. This characteristic is shown in the supernatural appreciation of the faith of the whole people, when, from the bishops to the last of the faithful, they manifest a universal consent in matters of faith and morals.' (Lumen Gentium Art 12). This process, therefore, involves bishops and people together, not in a merely juridical decision, or in a public opinion poll, but in a common effort to articulate what is the Christian faith, with confidence in God's abiding presence in his people." (12).

Another upset for Perrone and his roman colleagues was Newman's use of what we would now call the "critical historical method" of doing theology. Evolution implied a growing organism tracing its growth in history and examining how certain doctrines had been affected and often limited by the impact of historical context, contemporary cultures and thinking. This process ran counter to the immutable, ahistorical essences and definitions of the revived Roman and later neo-scholastic theology where history was used as a proof of the truth of this immutability often with a very strained selective interpretation.

Another aspect of Newman's teaching which caused suspicion in Rome and its own developing teaching on the magisterium confined to the hierarchy was Newman's high regard for the prophetic and teaching offices in the Church. In this we see the application of the synodal principle of balancing these charisms with those of leadership.

During his anglican days, Newman had written many of his ideas. He had written concerning the prophetical office of the Church in 1837 asking the question how should the Church sift the fundamental tradition of the faith from the non-dogmatic convictions and the theological opinions which have grown out of it? He drew an important distinction between the episcopal and the prophetic tradition. "The first is a uniform and strictly doctrinal teaching, handed down from bishop to bishop in creed and ceremonial; the second is a product of those interpreters of revelation whom St Paul calls 'prophets' and 'doctors'. (13) For Newman, more than perhaps many other interpreters of the charism of prophecy in the Church, the distinction between prophet and teacher (doctor) was not as great. Often he seems to equate the two. Walgrave, the noted Newman scholar, explaining Newman, says that just as the episcopal office has its dangers, so also does the prophetical. "The first is exposed to a rigid conservatism, a worship of the letter to the exclusion of the spirit and life, a timorous immobility. The second under the influence of various forces, among others the subtle, hidden tendencies in man weakened by sin, is continually drawn to deviate from the faith of antiquity. The two are divergent and complementary and serve to hold each other in equipoise. The bishops have to keep continual watch over the "prophets", but the latter have to prevent assent to doctrinal propositions from degenerating into sterile conformity." (14)

The final aspect of Newman's teaching that disturbed Perrone and his colleagues was his belief in the liberty of conscience in every person's life. As recently as 1832 Pope Gregory XVI had condemned in his encyclical "Mirari Vos" liberty of conscience as a "sheer madness". (15) Newman meant what today we would call an "informed" conscience which arrived at its decision after prayer, competent advice and study. He picked up Gladstone's famous quip in his letter to the Duke of Norfolk (1875) writing: "Certainly, if I am obliged to bring religion into after- dinner toasts (which indeed does not seem quite the thing) I shall drink - to the Pope, if you please - still to Conscience first, and the Pope afterwards." (16)

From 1859 when he wrote his "On Consulting the Faithful" until Pope Leo XIII created him a cardinal twenty years later, Newman was under a cloud and ostracized by many catholics including Cardinal Manning, the leader of the english catholics. Even after 1879 until his death in 1890, many viewed him with suspicion. Yet of all the 19th century roman catholic theologians, Newman's thought has persisted and eclipsed his contemporaries. So his theology remains fresh and seminal right into this century.

Newman's life-span (1801-1890) corresponded almost exactly with that of the famous catholic historian Ignaz Dollinger (1799-1890). Their differing attitudes portray, in Newman's case, the brilliant theologian who was also an excellent historian and, in Dollinger's case, the brilliant historian who was also an excellent theologian. Both suffered much from the Church they loved and reacted strongly against the naked use of power by those in authority. Yet the one died a cardinal of the roman church, the other an excommunicate.

Given the long history of the Church and its absolute use of authority, such solutions seemed inevitable. This book asks the question in the final chapter: Is the only way to arrive at truth the battering and polarizing of the personalities involved as well as provoking them to extreme attitudes? This question is particularly pertinent when much of what was condemned in what they wrote is subsequently vindicated. Whilst it may be argued that suffering made Newman a saint, it also left Dollinger a bitter man. It is a strange perversion of christianity verging on masochism to wish suffering on any creature when reconciliation and charity suggest alternatives.

Ignaz Dollinger was a catholic priest, and professor at the newly established University of Munich. His earlier writing was coloured by the ultramontanism of the day; but as his historical studies led him further into Church History, particularly that of the early church, he became more critical of the claims to total authority and infallibility being claimed for the papal office. Even without access to much of the documentation and study used in the first chapters of this book, Dollinger had come to similar conclusions.

After a visit to Rome in 1857 he became convinced of the curial lack of interest in historical studies. Their absorption was in preserving the temporal power of the papacy. His attitudes began to change. In the famous Odeon Munich lectures in 1861, he kept the trust Rome had given him by showing that a Church which energetically preserves the principle of unity (the papacy) has a vast superiority over the churches devoid of it and would therefore prevail. However Rome's suspicions were raised by his suggestions that this great asset could be lost by its discrediting failure in governing the Papal States. He also showed the faults of the papal government through many centuries and the hopelessness of all efforts to save it, unless it was reformed. (17)

His indignation (amounting to almost obsession) continued during the 1860s as he witnessed the manoeuvring especially from the extreme ultramontanes to have the pope declared infallible. Ultramontanism since de Lammenias' excommunication in 1832 had fallen more and more under the thraldom of conservative elements. Pius IX's exile in disguise from Rome in 1848 had not only made him more conservative on his return but had enthroned him in many catholics' minds as a martyr.

The whole saga of Pius VII and Napoleon was re-enacted. When the Papal States were again threatened, many dedicated young men from a number of nationalities volunteered as soldiers to defend the pope.

The adulation during the 60s rose to a deafening chorus in the "Civilta Catholica". "When the pope meditates, it is God who thinks in him" the journal wrote. The bishop of Geneva spoke of the threefold incarnation of the Son of God: - in the Virgin's womb, in the Eucharist, and in the old man of the Vatican. St John Bosco spoke of the pope as "God on earth" and continued: "Jesus had placed the pope higher than the prophets, than the precursor John the Baptist, than the angels. Jesus has put the pope on the same level as God." (18)

Dollinger was appalled. This was not just popular piety. Serious assertions were also being made by competent bishops and priests. As the papal and curial manoeuvring grew, so did Dollinger's opposition. He rallied many catholic intellectuals to his side. His historical research had shown how the rise of the papacy had taken place in cultural and historical conditions peculiar to their times and thus were not necessarily a valid development. His studies had shown also how the papacy, while often acting as the means of unity and doctrinal orthodoxy in the Church, had again and again misled good people by using false teaching or expedient actions in order to retain power. His warnings to the catholic world became more earnest especially when the pope called for a council summoned for 8 December 1869 we now call Vatican I.

Dollinger's book "The Pope and the Council" written on the eve of Vatican I and published under the pseudonym "Janus" was promptly put on the Index of Forbidden Books. In it, he showed the many cases in history where popes had subsequently been proven wrong or contradicted each other's important doctrinal statements or even declared their predecessors' decisions were not infallible or irreversible.

Dollinger's examples of papal fallibility in "The Pope and the Council" were many. The most important of these were Liberius (352-366) who had signed a semi-arian confession of faith (under duress probably) and Honorius I (625-638) who tolerated the heresy of monotheletism and was condemned as a heretic by two subsequent General Councils. The infallibilists argued that Honorius had taught as a private theologian not imposing the heresy on all the Church. Dollinger went on to use Pope Virgilius (537-555) as another example. Under pressure from the Emperor, he disavowed the decrees of the General Council of Chalcedon. More examples were cited, such as popes granting divorces in the first thousand years of the Church, or Stephen II who allowed a freeman's marriage with a slave girl to be dissolved contrary to many predecessors' decisions. (19)

Brocard Sewell, writing in the last century, mentions more misleading or wrong papal decisions among which he mentions:

Gregory XI (1370-1378) approved slavery when in a dispute with the City of Florence, he decreed that any florentine, wherever he might be found, should become the slave of his captor.

Urban V (1309-1370) dissolved the marriage - consummated marriage - of Duke Barnabo Visconti of Milan in 1363 on the grounds of the Duke's heresy and unbelief.

Urban III, in 1185, affirming the standard teaching on the ethics of interest in his letter "Consuluit nos", taught that merchants who charged a higher price for goods sold on credit than for those purchased with cash were guilty of the sin of usury and must make restitution.

Boniface VIII, in the famous 1302 bull "Unam Sanctam" said: "We declare, pronounce, and define, that it is absolutely necessary for salvation that every human creature be subject to the Roman Pontiff." What theologian today would care to defend this proposition?

Pius IX in his 1860 letter "Cum Catholica Ecclesia" said that the papal monarchy had been "most wisely determined by God himself", and spoke of "the civil principality with which God has willed that the see of blessed Peter be provided." This was virtually to make God responsible for the False Decretals and the Donation of Constantine.

Pius XI in "Divini illius Magistri" (1929) condemned co-education as fallacious, and repugnant to christianity. This is barely relevant today.

The same pope taught in "Quadragesimo Anno" (1931) that even a mitigated form of socialism was incompatible with christianity. It was a contradiction in terms to speak of a religious or christian socialism. "No one can be at the same time a genuine Catholic and a true Socialist."

Pius XII in "Humani Generis" (1950) affirmed that christians are obliged to believe in the existence of an individual man called Adam as the founder of the human race, and may not hold that "Adam was the name given to some group of our primordial ancestors". Today not only does it seem biologically more probable that humankind had a polygenistic origin, but it is a commonplace for theologians to admit it.

Pius XII taught in "Mystici Corporis" (1943) that the mystical body of Christ and the roman catholic church are the same, and he re-affirmed this in "Humani Generis". This doctrine has been discarded by Vatican II.

In "Humani Generis" the same pope taught that it is not to be supposed that "a position advanced in an encyclical letter does not ipso facto command assent", because such statements are covered by Christ's promise "He that heareth you heareth me." (Luke 10: 16). It must be clear, the pope goes on to say, that even though popes are not exercising their authority to the full in encyclical letters, the matters dealt with "can no longer be regarded as a matter of free debate among theologians." Brocard Sewell adds "This is simply an assertion of the "oracular" idea of papal authority, which today lies in ruins as a result of 'Humanae Vitae'". (20) Here, of course, Sewell is referring to the encyclical still defining artificial birth control as a moral evil.

The actual decree on papal infallibility when passed laid down strict criteria for the papal exercise of this authority - the pope must speak solemnly intending to bind the whole Church on faith or morals and speaking from his position "ex cathedra" or using his full office as bishop of Rome and head of the Church. The fact, however, still remains that when the earlier erroneous papal decrees mentioned above were promulgated, hundreds of thousands, even millions, believed them as true and acted upon them with certainty just because they came from the pope. It was the damage done in the past to untold millions that hurt and upset Dollinger.

When the Church wants to, it can discard the teachings it currently knows to be wrong often without any apology or public admission that it maintained those teachings stubbornly for centuries. Its followers are expected to wait for the Church to do the discarding (often again decades or centuries after others have tried to tell the Church this belief is obviously obsolete). It is sometimes reinforced, as mentioned above, by compilers of official documents such as Denzinger, who often fail to include documents detrimental to these subsequently abandoned beliefs.

* * * * * *

The well stage-managed Council, manoeuvred by committees over which the ultramontanists had succeeded in getting full control, moved from the discussion on faith to the question of infallibility. The agenda had proposed first to look at the Church's infallibility and in that context proceed to papal infallibility. The threatened Franco-Prussian War pushed this agenda aside and papal infallibility became the topic which, amidst much drama, was finally passed and solemnly promulgated by Pius IX. The Council never reconvened because Garabaldi's troops entered Rome in the summer recess invading the Papal States to make them the last piece to add to the map of modern Italy. The pope became the "prisoner of the Vatican."

At the time several of the bishops wrote home intimating that the moral pressure and manipulation at the Council was so great that its freedom could be questioned. In the last decade or so a strong case for this was made by Bernhard Hasler in his book "How the Pope Became Infallible." An introduction to Hasler's book by Hans Kung earned Kung a condemnation from Rome forbidding him to teach as a catholic teacher. Hasler's thesis is well founded; but I think one has to go deeper to see the power brought to bear on the Council's participants.

Vatican I may well have been the first General Council of the church (remember orthodox and protestants were not present or participating) where the pope had appointed most of the bishops present and, in Pius IX's case, had been pope so long there was a not unfounded suspicion he appointed as bishops those who favoured ultramontanism, for example, Manning. The synodal principle of the earlier General Councils where the bishop emerged from his own local church representing its faith and attitudes was seriously impaired. This to me seems a far more serious flaw than the argument of moral pressure. In other words, how representative of the local churches in communion with Rome were the participants of the Council?

The proportionality existing among the local churches was very seriously impaired. Bishops of small italian sees with barely 10,000 people, curial bishops, missionary bishops from Burma or the Pacific or Africa with a handful of recently converted catholics (where there had been no time for a local theology to be formed and no local priest long enough ordained to be bishop) had one vote, equal to that of Archbishops of some European sees representing millions of catholics who had a thousand or more years of catholic tradition.

Given the strength of contemporary belief that the bishop alone was the representative of his local church it was not so strange. Given the strength, however, of the synodal principle, these churches with such a wealth of tradition often representing millions of catholics - a tradition that upheld the supremacy of the pope in the Church but often lacking in a tradition of his infallibility were despite the size and antiquity of their churches, given scant attention. They lacked and lacked a proportional say in the universal church. Many of these "minority" bishops were cardinals, archbishops and bishops from such sees. They absented themselves from the final voting by going home early. One such bishop, Lecourtier of Montpellier in France, who was later forced to resign, wrote: "Our weakness at this moment comes neither from Scripture nor the tradition of the Fathers nor the witness of the General Councils nor the evidence of history. It comes from our lack of freedom, which is radical. An imposing minority, representing the faith of more than one hundred million Catholics, that is, almost half of the entire Church, is crushed beneath the yoke of a restrictive agenda, which contradicts conciliar traditions." (21)

Whatever the coercion, there still seems to me a deeper problem. The moral consensus (not majority force) needed for a General Council seemed to be lacking. The almost hundred bishops often of the most important sees who had avoided the final vote were pursued fairly relentlessly after the Council until each had written in his final submission. Here taken to an extreme degree was the belief that a bishop as an appraiser was absolute in a General Council, even if divorced from the synodal principle of 'episkope' he was supposed to be representing.

When the pope had inserted in the final definition that he did not need the consent of the Church even before pronouncing an infallible statement, Dollinger was amazed. This insertion was made days before the decree was finally voted on and not even debated. The Council of Constance had decreed a General Council was superior to a pope in certain instances. Pius IX's insertion of course was put in to nullify this decree of Constance - another General Council. Dollinger could not submit to the Vatican I decree on the pope's infallibility, was excommunicated, and died twenty years later a rather bitter priest who had never joined another church but had not reconciled finally with his own.

* * * * * *

It is fruitful to compare Newman and Dollinger. Strangely enough although both respected the other, they did not correspond though they knew each other's thoughts particularly through Alfred Plummer, a mutual anglican friend. He often spoke and corresponded with them both. After their deaths Plummer summarized the differences as he saw them: "The one (Dollinger) took his stand upon historical facts, which for every competent student of history are indisputable, and which admit of only one reasonable interpretation. The other (Newman) staked everything upon the inerrancy of a divinely guided authority; and for him the fact that this authority had given a decision that once made well attested historical facts disputable, or made what would otherwise have been strained and improbable interpretations of them reasonable." (22) Plummer was a scripture scholar and deacon who well realized the theological and historical stances of both famous men. However, being an anglican, he did not fully realize Newman's deep conviction, not so much because of the "inerrancy of a divinely guided authority" to which, of course, Newman subscribed, but the highly nuanced way Newman interpreted this.

For Newman, as Dollinger, the First Vatican Council was unfortunate; but, given his conviction that the Council was just one more step in a saga of development which the Holy Spirit in time could adjust, his faith in the continuing right direction the Church was taking was not shaken. "Why is it, if I believe in the Pope's infallibility, I do not wish it defined? Is not truth a gain? I answer, because it can't be so defined as not to raise more questions than it solves." (23) So Newman wrote on the eve of the Council and it expressed his deepest convictions.

While he regretted that the infallibility of the Church was not defined first thus putting into proportion the pope's infallibility, it was perhaps better, many agreed, that the discussion on the Church was put off to a later time, given the roman theology of the day. After the doctrine of Papal Infallibility was defined, Newman wrote: "This does not justify the way it has been carried at Rome - but God overrules evil for good. A heavy retribution may still await the perpetrators of the act." (24)

The above quotations from Newman's private correspondence and diaries highlight his convictions about the First Vatican Council's hastiness and power struggle. Yet, unlike Dollinger (who never recovered from the shock of seeing his beloved Church go through such contortions) Newman in a sense was the better theologian. He saw that in the process of time, adjustment would occur. Imbalance would be corrected by historical process and development.

This deep conviction of Newman's described by Plummer as "staking everything upon the inerrancy of a divinely guided authority" was not a blindness to a present situation but a deep conviction that the Holy Spirit would still guide the Church essentially into truth, though time may be needed to redress the imbalance that had forced the Church into a certain line of action. "The Church moves as a whole;" Newman wrote to a jesuit friend in Rome, "it is not a mere philosophy, it is a communion." (25) The balance will in time be effected: "Pius is not the last of the Popes - the fourth Council modified the third, the fifth the fourth...the late definition does not so much need to be undone as to be completed...I know that a violent reckless party, if it had its will, would at this moment define that the Pope's powers need no safeguards, no explanations - but there is a limit to the triumph of the tyrannical - let us be patient, let us have faith, and a new Pope, and a re-assembled Council may trim the boat." (26)

The ultramontanes wished to give the definition its maximum application to use what is still called, and even currently has relevance, "creeping infallibility". Fortunately Pius IX's approval of the german bishops' explanation of the definition showed a more open interpretation was possible. The minimalist line was the one Newman took in his famous and well received letter to the Duke of Norfolk in answer to Gladstone's charges (1875).

It is possible to discern in Newman's attitude helpful arguments supporting what this book is endeavouring to say. Newman's belief in the synodal principle (although, of course, he does not call it that) and his suffering for it is beyond question. He was less sure how it should or could be applied. He saw the need for balance and believed historical development had effected such balance even though centuries may have been needed for its completion. Too facilely, later minds used his doctrine of development as merely showing how any present belief could be justified by finding some historical proof of it ignoring the context of that proof, what Dollinger was later to compare to a person on a riverbank casting a line as a trajectory to some similar point in early christian history often ignoring the context. Newman's theory was far more nuanced than that.

Vatican I had made Newman aware of how a powerful element in the Church could (temporarily) tilt the Church's balance. We have already seen how as an anglican he had written in 1837 his Lectures on the Prophetical Office where he drew an important distinction between the episcopal and prophetic tradition. As a catholic some forty years later, having seen the power play at Vatican I, he wrote a preface to the third edition of the "Via Media" expanding on his original ideas on prophecy written in 1837.

Newman in his preface-essay expanded the distinction between "episcopal" and "prophetical" tradition into a threefold distinction of the Church as a community for teaching, worship and ministry. The entire community of the Church shared in the threefold office of Christ as priest, prophet and king. Christianity for Newman "is at once a philosophy, a political power, and a religious rite...as a religion (priest), its special centre of action is pastor and flock; as a philosophy (prophet), the Schools; as a King, the Papacy and its Curia.

"Each of these three offices has its own thrust. If any one of them is allowed to flourish at the expense of the other two, the result will inevitably be a distortion" or an imbalance.

"Truth is the guiding principle of theology and theological inquiries; devotion and edification, of worship; and of government, expedience. The instrument of theology is reasoning; of worship, our emotional nature; of rule, command and coercion. Further, in man as he is, reasoning tends to rationalism; devotion to superstition and enthusiasm; and power to ambition and tyranny." (27)

Tension is therefore very necessary as each office pulls its own way. The balance is achieved by keeping these various thrusts in equipoise. Each thrust has a shadow side as well as the Spirit filled action necessary for building the whole Church. We will have occasion to examine this balance again in the last chapters.

* * * * * *

Newman's heart went out to Dollinger. He wrote to Plummer: "...I will say I can hardly restrain my indignation at the reckless hard-heartedness with which he and so many others have been treated by those who should have been their true brethren and of whom the least that can be said is that they know not what they do...I must say on the other hand I neither can take Dr Dollinger's view of it, nor do I enter into the reasons which are contained, as you report them, in his Reply...I never should have been a Catholic, had I not received the doctrine of the development of dogmas..." (28) Newman in his old age after receiving his cardinal's hat in Rome in 1879 intended to visit Dollinger in Munich on his way home to England; unfortunately ill health prevented him. (29)

Both Newman and Dollinger were not men of a single, but of two disciplines – history and theology. Both were good theologians and good historians. Newman was probably the better theologian, Dollinger the better historian. Newman was well versed, as one can see, in those early church histories - such as Eusebius and Sozoman - as well as being immersed in the early Fathers or writers of the Church and all the classical pagan authors. However, he did not have the deep scientific knowledge regarding the first two centuries that Dollinger undoubtedly had. Nor had he at his disposal many of the fruits of study (referred to in the first chapters of this book). However, in Newman there was a distinct tendency to look at the first christian century or two through the prism of fourth and fifth century history as though the more advanced structures of those centuries were present almost in their precise form in earlier christian times.

151

As we have seen Apostolic Authority carried on in diverse ways, even democratically, in the Johannine communities. If he had known this, Newman may well have used these arguments to show the necessity of lay consultation and sharing even in doctrine rather than the arguments he actually used.

Newman's basic intuition of faith that decision making in the Church is a shared consensus even though those who possessed Apostolic Authority did have the last say was a very valid one and an implicit corrective of the direction roman theology was taking. It confirms the synodal principle enunciated throughout this book.

While Dollinger held Newman in great regard, he did not hesitate to criticize his theory of historical development as darwinism transplanted to religion with one difference: for Darwin the ape evolved to man while for Newman man degenerated to ape! He also saw how already Newman's theory was being used by some to validate stances in the Church as a person standing on a riverbank to cast a line as a trajectory to some similar point in early christian history to justify any present development. He never seemed to have understood that Newman saw his theory of development as explaining to himself and hopefully to others the Holy Spirit's working organically through change which is the concomitant of development: preserving what is essential from what is circumstantial despite the sins and frailties in the all too human story.

Three years after the Council, Plummer read to Dollinger from Newman's letter: "When you see Dr Dollinger say everything that is kindest to him from me. Of course, I cannot overcome the sad feeling that he should have felt it right to place himself in such antagonism to men, who, though his inferiors in moral worth and unscrupulous in their proceedings have, as I think, the right on their side." After laughing assent as Plummer read "unscrupulous in their proceedings" Dollinger added after a pause, "If Newman knew the history of the 5th and 6th centuries and also modern Church history better, he would not think it possible that those men can have the right on their side. I suppose that he has not been in the way of studying all the falsifications and frauds of those times. The matter has scarcely been sufficiently investigated and exposed yet, and cannot be studied in convenient books, as it deserved to be." Dollinger was voicing a concern raised in chapter six and to be investigated again in the chapter twelve about how forgeries can influence future authoritative teaching and the "consent of the faithful" in certain areas when these have been passed down as true documents modifying the certainty arising from such assent. On another occasion Dollinger said of Newman: "It is very strange that a man who has written a history of the Arians should believe in the Pope's infallibility. No one asked a Pope to give an infallible judgement on that great question...I suspect that Newman would have been a very different man, if he had been well read in medieval history. But that, I fancy, is a field in which he has not even touched the precincts." (30)

Reading Newman, one suspects Dollinger's appraisal was reasonably accurate. What he failed to see was the deep faith that Newman brought to the facts of history that despite them and through them the Holy Spirit was still working, re-adjusting and balancing even though it may have been the work of centuries. Boudens is probably correct when he summarizes Dollinger's weakness: "But he seems to have lacked the openness to surmount his historical objections, to view the total event in a broader context, and to interpret it from within a viewpoint grounded in deeper faith." (31)

As the last chapter twelve will, I hope, show both Dollinger's deep fears about the influence of forgeries and distorted tradition on present teaching as well as Newman's conviction that in time balance in the development of traditional teaching and that the Holy Spirit never deserts his Church are not mutually exclusive ideas. Both, taken together, can contribute much to a fuller understanding of how Tradition develops in the Church but asking the question: Is Newman's answer of waiting on the Holy Spirit to balance out decisions decades or centuries later the only way the Church can operate despite, during the waiting, the damage done to so many perhaps millions of souls and the alienation caused to many millions seeking Jesus Christ and the "true" Church?

Those two great men whose lives spanned the 19th century died within months of each other in 1890. The problems they endeavoured to address would continue to be the underlying problems of the Church into the subsequent centuries.

♣ ♣

If there is development in the Church's teaching, is it possible to have an independent, scholarly body to advise the bishops continually?

1. Cragg, Gerald. The Church and the Age of Reason 1648-1789. Harmondsworth, Pelican Books. reprint, 1977. p. 9
2. Hazard, Paul. The European Mind 1680-1715. Harmondsworth, Penguin. 1964. pp. 8-9
3. Holmes, J Derek & Bickers, B. A Short History of the Catholic Church. Tunbridge Wells, Burns Oates, 1983. pp. 189-190
4. Tarnas, Richard. The Passion of the Western Mind. New York, Ballantine Books. 1993. p. 282
5. Cragg, Gerard. The Church and the Age of Reason 1648-1789. p. 237
6. Vidler, Alex R. The Church in an Age of Revolution. Harmondsworth, Pelican. reprinted 1976. p. 19
7. Sanks, T Howland. Authority in the Church, a Study in Changing Paradigms, Dissertation series, Number two, published by the American Academy of Religion. pp. 20 sq. Missoula, Mont. 1974.
8. Ibid, p. 17
9. Ibid, pp. 3 and 9. Also Caraman, P. University Of the Nations. New York, Ramsey, Paulist Press. 1981. pp. 91-92
10. Chadwick, O. From Bossuet to Newman. Cambridge University Press. 1987. p. 19
11. Caraman, P. University of the Nations, pp. 95-96
12. O'Sullivan, O. OFM Cap. The Silent Schism. Dublin, Gill and Macmillan 1997, p. 68
13. Walgrave, J H. Newman, The Theologian. London, Geoffrey Chapman. 1960. pp. 45 and 46
14. Ibid, p. 46
15. Bokenkotter, T. A Concise History of the Catholic Church. Garden City, New York, Image Books. 1979. p. 309
16. Trevor, Meriol. Prophets and Guardians. London, Hollis and Carter. 1969. p. 129
17. Plummer, Alfred. Conversations with Dr Dollinger 1870-1890 Ed Robrecht Boudens. Leuven, University Press. 1985. p. 259
18. Hasler, August Bernhard. How the Pope became Infallible (Introduction by Kung, Hans) transl. by Heinegg, Peter. Garden City, New York, Doubleday and Co. 1981. p. 48
19. Ibid, p. 165
20. Sewell, Brocard. The Vatican Oracle. London, Gerald Duckworth and Co. 1970. pp. 77-79
21. Hasler, August Bernhard. How the Pope became Infallible. pp. 131-132

22. Plummer, Alfred. <u>Conversations with Dr Dollinger 1870-1890.</u> p. 264
23. Trevor, Meriol. <u>Prophets and Guardians.</u> p. 115
24. Ibid. p. 120
25. Ibid. p. 118
26. Ibid, p. 120.
27. Quoted in Lash, Nicholas. <u>Change in Focus.</u> London, Sheed and Ward. 1973. p. 101
28. Plummer, Alfred. <u>Conversations with Dr Dollinger 1870-1890.</u> p. 18
29. Trevor, Meriol. <u>Prophets and Guardians.</u> p. 127
30. Plummer, Alfred. <u>Conversations with Dr Dollinger 1870-1890.</u> pp. 66 and 67
31. Ibid, p. XXXV

CHAPTER TEN

Vatican II and Attempts to Restore Balance

Newman's contention that there would be "another pope, another council" came true when Pope John XXIII, beloved not only in the Church but by the world, opened the Second Vatican Council on 11 October 1962. It was to last a little over three years and to take an outward direction where Vatican I had looked inward. The Church came out of the "deep-freeze" and a great thaw commenced. As many remarked, the spirit of Newman seemed to hover over much of the Council's proceedings and documents.

It was not an easy road from Vatican I to Vatican II. Pope Leo XIII (1878-1903), the successor of Pius IX, tried to open the Church out to the scholarly world. Even though he perceived neo-scholasticism as the main instrument of the Church's thought, he was open to other trends when he saw they did not conflict with the Church's teachings. His encyclicals on biblical studies and social justice especially as applied to manual workers were a big breakthrough in the catholic church of his day. His creating Newman a cardinal was a generally popular move and vindicated that scholar in the eyes of his enemies.

The cautious thaw in the Church's policy allowed a number of catholic scholars to emerge, some of whom became the leaders in what was to be called "modernism". One of these, Alfred Loisy, wrote a defence of the Church which was applauded for its creativity. Harnack had claimed in a famous series of lectures that the essence of christianity was the fatherhood of God and the brotherhood of man. "Traditional Christianity, with the institutional Church, the christological and other dogmas, and the Catholic cultus, was a perversion of the simple, original gospel. The Reformation had been an attempt to recover it, but only a partially successful one. It had not made a clean sweep of ecclesiasticism. The time had now come to reduce Christianity to its true essence, filial and individual trust in the divine fatherhood." (1)

Loisy attacked Harnack for a simplistic explanation. Historical religion must be considered as a whole in its organic development. Jesus foretold the Kingdom and it was the Church that came with its hierarchy, its dogma and its cults that embodied the Gospel. These were necessary because every religion must be embodied in social and symbolic forms. Catholicism was this continuation. The acclaim Loisy received came from many quarters, but not from Rome. The upholding of the immutability of orthodox dogmas did not seem sufficient to the authorities nor the suggestion among others that Jesus came to bring the Kingdom from which the Church proceeded.

The condemnation of Loisy and many other prominent catholics as "modernists", not without some foundation, highlighted the Church's seeming inability to come to terms with modern scholarship. For the remainder of Pius X's reign (he died in 1914) a witchhunt went on in seminaries, chanceries and elsewhere against anyone suspected of being influenced by many contemporary ideas. Much reporting was done secretly with even one future pope being accused. The most typical example of the era was the Biblical Commission, full of conservative scholars, which forbade catholics to question the Mosaic authorship of the first five books of the Bible, to question if Matthew was the first of the Gospels or whether St Paul wrote the Epistle to the Hebrews, all of which are open questions today.

Under Pius X's successors there was a gradual reaching out to the world especially in papal social teaching on Justice. Scholars had to act with great caution and at times some of those who were to be the great theologians at the Second Vatican Council were silenced or placed under a cloud.

Perhaps it was the two world wars that raised in the minds of many christians questions about ecclesiastical and doctrinal divisions. Particularly in the concentration camps of World War II the appalling genocide going on forced prisoners to share basic faith and hope. After World War II, many noted the loss of interest in institutional christianity and asked just where were the churches going?

One man, a chaplain in World War I and a diplomat in World War II, saw positive advantages in the way the modern world was going. Angelo Roncalli, an italian priest, was not blind to the defects of the world. He combined his peasant beginnings with a moderate education which predisposed him to history. As Church History opened before him it gave him a love of Church yet an awareness of the human failings of its members. He developed a compassion and a tolerance quite extraordinary for one of his background, particularly when as a papal diplomat he made contact with the orthodox churches and islam. Yet as his writings show, he still kept a fairly traditional but deep spirituality.

When quite unexpectedly he was elected pope in 1958 as an old man, many thought of him as a "caretaker" after his brilliant predecessor. His simplicity and goodness won the hearts of all - or almost all.

When he announced to his Secretary of State, Cardinal Tardini, in 1959 that he was going to call a Council, the reply, not unexpectedly, was "But why, Holy Father, you are infallible." Tardini was one of the more open members of the roman curia, but his answer was significant - what more could be added to an infallible pope by a council?

John had observed the world. Deep down he knew the Church did not have all the answers and that it came across to many people as negative. He did not profess to know the answers, but he was both humble enough to know he needed help and shrewd enough to see the roman curia would never reform itself nor would even see the need to do so. His faith told him to call on the bishops of the world in a General Council. They would surface the real problems and find answers for them. This would be a pastoral council not condemning heretics or proclaiming dogmas as usually happened.

* * * * * *

In his address at the opening of Vatican II, Pope John XXIII sounded a positive note when he spoke of having to listen "much to our regret to voices of persons who, though burning with zeal, are not endowed with too much sense of discretion or measure. In these modern times they can see nothing but prevarication and ruin. They say that our era, in comparison with past eras, is getting worse, and they behave as though they had learned nothing from history, which is, none the less, the teacher of life...we feel we must disagree with those prophets of gloom, who are always forecasting disaster, as though the end of the world were at hand." (2)

He then went on thoughtfully to show how Divine Providence was leading human beings to "a new order of human relations...and everything, even human differences, leads to the greater good of the Church." This could be done not by renouncing the patrimony of the Church, but this should be "studied and expounded through the methods of research and through the literary forms of modern thought. The substance of the ancient doctrine of the deposit of faith is one thing, and the way in which it is presented is another. And it is the latter which must be taken into great consideration with patience if necessary, everything being measured in the forms and proportions ("balance" is my interpretation and fits well with the Hierarchy of Truths in the chapter twelve) of a magisterium which is predominantly pastoral in character." (3)

When he had convoked the Council a year before its opening, he had urged the bishops to read the "signs of the times" (4), a phrase which became a byword at the Council. Now as he concluded his address to the two thousand or more bishops, he recommended them to "make use of the medicine of mercy rather than that of severity." (5) The gentle optimism of the aged pope who died within a year of the Council's opening pervaded all the subsequent sessions.

After the bishops had rejected most of the prepared documents drawn up in terms of roman theology and took control over their own Council, they began the massive task of opening the Church out to the world while planning for its inner renewal. One of the Council's most extraordinary features was that the bishops did their homework in between and during the sessions by attending lectures and discussions and updating themselves with the help of some of the foremost theologians, many of whom had been suspect in bygone days. The episcopal magisterium consulted and learnt from the teaching magisterium!

Volumes have been written on the 2nd Vatican Council and its aftermath. Suffice it is to point out here some of the more important emphases or actual changes of teaching that came from this Council. I am grateful here to Thomas Bokenkotter whose summary of the Vatican II Decrees I have largely followed. (6) It also served to demolish the idea that the universal latin mass, no meat on Friday (which was also changed) showed the unity of Catholics. In reality, this was uniformity posing as unity. These changes unsettled and continues to unsettle many catholics formed in that mould.

Summary of changes

(1) The most obvious change to the average catholic was the return to the vernacular in the liturgy, so that all could participate more fully in the Eucharist and the sacraments. This was a reminder to all present of the priesthood of all the faithful.

(2) The change in the Church's self-image. When the revised document for the constitution on the Church was presented it gave many traditional bishops thinking in terms of a hierarchical Church a shock to find after the introductory chapter, a second chapter on the whole people of God before the hierarchical structure of the Church was discussed in chapter three onwards. The arrangement was deliberate to show how pope, bishop or peasant woman were all by baptism members of the people of God before they had special offices or ministry. The barriers between clergy and laity began to diminish. More and more the word "communion" was used for the people of God rather than the phrase "the perfect society" used by canonists and theologians during the previous thousand years.

(3) A change in relationships with other christians became evident. The Council's document on ecumenism put relations with other churches or ecclesial bodies in perspective. The ultimate goal of ecumenism was no longer seen as the conversion of non-catholics to the one, true Church. It

was now seen as more important to dialogue with the other christian bodies, to pray and work together where possible. While doctrinal differences were not to be glossed over, admission by the catholic church that other christians in varying degrees participate in the fullness of Christ's revelation and that the separation was also partly the catholic church's fault were signs of hope to other churches. Special documents on the Eastern Churches so close to the Western Church in doctrine and practice and non-christians were passed by the bishops showing their good-will.

(4) The Council used historical theology more than the scholastic non-historical theology. This gave importance to ideas in the context of time and space. The unchanging ideas bore the influence of platonism especially on medieval theology and especially revived under Leo XIII. Vatican II carefully placed its ideas not only in the context of sacred history but also human history. Once again Newman's stress on historical development foreshadowed the importance of seeing how doctrines became part of tradition just as reading the "signs of the times" was understanding the world of the day in its own context before judging which way the "pilgrim" church was to travel. The Church by its acceptance of historical methodology began to come to terms with many of the movements triggered by the Enlightenment.

(5) The acceptance of the modern world and all that was positive in it. This was avoided by Trent and Vatican I. It was a huge advance especially when the Church placed itself humbly at the service of humanity and to work with any people of good-will where there was a common ground.

(6) The document on religious freedom. This caused much debate among the bishops, especially as seminaries even in my time were justifying the moral adage "Error has no right to exist". This was adduced to keep protestant missionaries out of Spain and South America but led to church protest when catholic missionaries were excluded from protestant or non-christian countries. Newman with his toast to "conscience first then the pope" would have been pleased with this document.

(7) Redressing the imbalance in the Church's structures by a return to the older teaching on the bishops as successors of the apostles constituting with the pope as the centre of unity a college in which every bishop was responsible for his own local church and with all his brother bishops for the whole Church. Also stressed was the local church or diocese being the catholic church in a geographical area and the bishop by right being its leader and not just a branch manager for Rome. This was a healthy reaction to much of the centralization and ultramontanism surrounding Vatican I. There would still need to be the further balancing of pope and bishops with teachers, prophets, priests and lay people to achieve the equilibrium needed

for the synodal principle. But as Newman would have said: "Another Pope, another Council."

Democracy, as has been said, is not a one person one vote situation in the Catholic Church; but a certain democracy, as we have seen, is its partly forgotten Tradition. In 1931 in his famous social encyclical "Quadragesimo Anno" Pope Pius XI enunciated the principle of subsidiarity to the modern States of the world. In the light of modern historical research of our own past the same principle could well apply to the structures of the Church as well.

"Just as it is wrong to take away from individuals what by their own ability and effort" he stated "they can accomplish and commit it to the community, so it is an injury and at the same time both a serious evil and a pertubation of right order to assign to a larger and higher society what can be performed successfully by smaller and lower communities. This is a fixed and unchangeable principle most basic in social philosophy, immovable and unalterable. The reason is that all social activity of its very power and nature, should supply help to the members of the social body, but never may destroy or absorb them." The centrism of Rome could well reflect on these papal words and apply them to their actions of the last nine hundred years, particularly since the renewed centrism of the last two hundred years.

Pius XI goes on to say: "...let those in power, therefore, be convinced that the more faithfully this principle of 'subsidiary function' is followed, and a graded hierarchical order exists between the various associations, the greater also will be both social authority and social efficiency. The happier too, and more prosperous will be the condition of the commonwealth." (7) The same stress on the Principle of Subsidiarity was made by Pope John XXIII in his encyclical "Mater et Magistra" (8) and Pope Paul VI in his "Progressio Populorum" when he invokes the principle of subsidiarity to avoid "total collectivization...which might threaten human liberty and might obstruct the exercise of a person's basic human rights." (9)

In a famous interview after the Council, Cardinal Suenens gave the fundamental shift of paradigm. Before Vatican II the Church was like a pyramid with the pope on top and the Holy Spirit percolating down through him to the bishops and clergy with the laity at the pyramid's base. Now the Holy Spirit was seen to be entering into all levels of the pyramid and the pope's position and the bishops was to sift the Holy Spirit's action coming from below. (10)

* * * * * *

161

The euphoria experienced after the Council in most parts of the catholic church seemed to blend in well with the contemporary Age of Aquarius, the Kennedy era and the liberal "sixties". As they faded into the cautious "seventies" and the neo-conservative "eighties", so did the mood of the Church, as we have seen frequently, match the mood of the times. Some people did go "overboard" with the "new-found" freedom just as often a repressed child will at first over-react when given sudden freedom. The majority of catholics, however, reacted soberly and thoughtfully to Vatican II as the full implications were absorbed. "Humanae Vitae" Paul VI's (the successor of John XXIII) encyclical on human life, taught that each and every marriage act must remain open to the transmission of life. In rejecting the legitimacy of contraception for catholics, the pope was also rejecting the majority report of the special commission of bishops and theologians he had set up to advise him on the issue of birth control after forbidding its discussion on the floor of Vatican II. It brought many catholics face to face with the issue of personal freedom of conscience and raised the question in many people's minds of unilateral decisions of the papacy which, of course, again connects with the synodal principle constantly raised by this book.

As the disobedience of catholics to the norms of the Encyclical (which was not regarded as infallible) became apparent and instances of liberal over-reaction became reported, accurately or not, a number of catholics grew fearful of the extremes the Council seemed to have inspired and pressed for a stricter interpretation. In this they were aided by the documents themselves.

At Vatican I the minority group represented a far larger group of the Church percentage-wise than the minority at Vatican II. As indicated above, the minority bishops at Vatican I may well have represented half the Church and had seemingly with the help of a number of moderate majority bishops prevented the doctrine of papal infallibility from being formulated in its ultramontane form. In Vatican II the many fought-over ideas were often not synthesised into one text, but the new idea was expressed side by side with the minority conservative opinion unless it obviously contradicted it. The majority of bishops seemed quite happy, perhaps not seeing the long-term effects, when having made their points, the minority then insisted on the inclusion of its points. The majority for diplomacy's sake allowed them to do so. While the main thrust of the document was quite clear, if however one chose to be selective in picking out texts that suited one's arguments then often two quite different interpretations could emerge.

As an example take these texts from the Vatican II documents:

1	2

Priests

1	2
Priests 'have as their primary duty the proclamation of the gospel of God to all.' (Ministry and Life of Priests chapter 1, section 4) (11)	'Priests fulfil their chief duty in the mystery of the Eucharistic Sacrifice.' (Ministry and Life of Priests, chapter 3, section 13) (12)

Laity and Church

1	2
'In matters of faith and morals, the bishops speak in the name of Christ and the faithful are to accept their teaching and adhere to it with a religious assent of soul. This religious submission of will and mind must be shown in a special way to the authentic teaching authority of the Roman Pontiff, even when he is not speaking ex-Cathedra.' (Lumen Gentium on the Church, chapter 3, section 25) (13)	'An individual layman by reason of the knowledge, competence or outstanding ability which he may enjoy, is permitted and sometimes even obliged to express his opinion on things which concern the good of the Church.' (Also Lunem Gentium on the Church, section 37) (14) 'In order that such persons may fulfil their proper functions, let it be recognised that all the faithful, clerical and lay, possess a lawful freedom of inquiry and of thought and the freedom to express their minds humbly and courageously about those matters in which they enjoy competence.' (Church in the Modern World, chapter 2, section 63). (15) 'Hence every man has the duty and therefore the right, to seek the truth in matters religious, in order that he may with prudence form for himself right and true judgements of conscience, with the use of all suitable means…in all his activity a man is bound to follow his conscience faithfully, in order that he may come to God, for whom he was created. It follows that he is not to be forced to act in a manner contrary to his conscience.' (Declaration on Religious Freedom, chapter 1, section 3) (16)

Much ink has flowed in the letters to the editors' columns of catholic newspapers by both sides pressing their own theology of what a priest should be. The passages need not be contradictory but at face value can be.

The quotations in column 2 seem to contradict the 'Mirari Vos' of Gregory XVI (1832). But they need not be contradictory and can be married. Many would say the second lot of quotations about freedom are discussing freedom from governments not within the Church; but has the Church with its often shadowy classification of what is Tradition got the authority to bind Catholics against their consciences in non-infallible areas? Those and other issues with two different thrusts within the documents of Vatican II have caused and will cause controversy until the issue of what is really Tradition as opposed to traditions is clarified. The result has been at least two contrary interpretations in some of the more controversial texts. When as, at present, those who are more disposed to a minority and stricter interpretation of texts, often ignoring the main thrust of a document, hold power and also appoint the bishops of the catholic church, there is no real redress or balance in the present structures.

The old story of one group claiming too much absolute power putting down another group which has a very legitimate basis in the Gospel and seemingly a more valid interpretation of the thrust of Vatican II is a splendid example of what has gone on throughout history. But need it? The provocation grows, many are upset and internal dissension within the Church gets greater. Other churches witnessing this do not see the hardening of one power group even if it controls the central machine as giving any real hope for ecumenism. We seem to be at a terrible impasse. When the Curia insisted recently that definitive theological statements must be believed and adhered to with in effect the same obedience as infallible statements, this seemed to many to be the last straw, besides not being based on Tradition.

We have seen the answer Newman would give - the Holy Spirit will balance the situation in time. The Church has that essential thrust to truth which will always be there. Leo XIII would succeed Pius IX, John XXIII would succeed Pius XII, Vatican I would succeed Vatican II. The Holy Spirit's relentless guidance would bring the Church to a more balanced appreciation of her mission.

Where I think Newman's answer fails to find the echo in the 20th and 21st centuries that it may well have found in the 19th is that the 20th and 21st centuries have in personal freedom, technology and general education among many other factors advanced at such a rate that slow and leisurely changes seem no longer viable options for this generation or even for those that have gone immediately before it or those that will come after it. While "Festina lente" (hasten slowly) must always be a counsel of prudence and wisdom, especially for a huge organization like the Church, so often as history shows us it has been indolence, arrogance, pride, lust for power and stubbornness that have slowed change down until the Church is often forced to face it. Moreover when slowness arising from sin makes tens of thousands suffer unnecessarily whenever law is hindering their growth or fullness of life and experience of Christ then the Church, which is the Body of Christ, becomes a hindrance to the work of Christ who had "compassion on the multitudes".

Quite apart from the damage the Church can do and has done to probably hundreds of thousands or millions in history by a refusal to change then later effecting change when it suits itself, and despite Newman's deep faith that saw the Holy Spirit finally breaking the barriers and balance restored, as implied above, this generation has not that sort of patience and the question could further be asked "why should it?"

People of this generation expect ready replies to legitimate queries without having to reverentially touch forelocks and wait in unquestioning awe for authoritative answers however long they may take. They also have little tolerance for being ignored or put down by an authority that, as one recent catholic body puts it, "hears but does not listen". They are less and less responsive to an authority which calls for their participation but stifles their honest attempts at appeal. In Newman's day deference to authority, whether ecclesiastical or secular, was part of life. Today's authority in Europe, North America, Australasia and increasingly in other continents has to earn its following by its service to the name of Christ, its example and its compassion. Nor does the adding of law upon law add credibility to a generation seeking for a simpler vision of the Gospel. Nor does pontificating on subjects and closure of debate on them unilaterally satisfy millions of educated people, who neither see the need for definitive attitudes nor their roots in logic or history.

Dollinger's criticism of Newman had a point in that his identification of the early Church with the Church of the 3rd, 4th and 5th centuries by which time mono-episcopacy was unquestioned and his lack of detailed scientific knowledge of the later medieval Church made him fail to appreciate the great damage done to souls through say the inquisition, the crusades, torture, slavery or even papal wars. Newman's readings too of the first and second centuries was prior to much of the nuanced findings of Raymond Brown and other scholars of the Didache and the letter of Clement.

Peter de Rosa's recent book "The Dark Side of the Papacy" was regarded as scurrilous in some quarters; but this popular account by a learned and perceptive scholar of the number of souls that suffered through a lack of proper leadership, persecuted for unchristian reasons often by inept theology and the use of forged documents, who were led into bloody crusades and wars, served as a reminder of the millions of souls the Church did not help to the fullness of their spiritual and human growth and often adversely led into bitterness, frustration and alienation. Dollinger in his writings was moved by the damage to truth and the unnecessary suffering caused to millions of christians inside and outside the Church and to those who were not christians that often reduced the Church to a travesty of the Gospel, so repelling people not drawing them to Christ.

Suffering as part of a christian's purification was always to the forefront of Newman's vision as it was in his personal life. A Dollinger or a de Rosa went further as they uncovered the unnecessary suffering caused by misguided leadership and example.

I think that Newman's intuition and conviction was that the Holy Spirit's omnipresent guidance of the Church would ultimately effect a change. I also think Dollinger's realization of the unnecessary suffering the Church had caused millions in history by arguing that it changed the teaching or corrected the human weakness later on without often an apology is not good enough for the conduct of the Body of Christ on earth. Only when time, social pressure, expediency or a very obvious intellectual movement showing the contrary forced the Church to change should not be the only pressures the Holy Spirit brings to bear on a given situation before change is possible. Tough luck for those who get caught in the historical process!

What Dollinger, de Rosa and many others have tried to say is "why keep on repeating that process not learning from what can be corrected in our past?" In every century of Church History, naked power in the name of God's authority provides so many shameful examples of abuse even while millions of other church members were doing much good for their neighbour. Does the power, however, have to be naked, unchecked, untrammelled and largely unaccountable except to God Himself? I think lessons of our two millennia of christian history are pointing out to us that this need not be so.

♣ ♣

There is an Apostolic Authority in the Church. That it must be unchecked, untrammelled and unaccountable except to itself is, I believe, not borne out by our previous history, certainly as the early Church saw it, with its flexibility of shared authority and diversity in unity and its accountability to Scripture not just selected portions of it which has been slowly lost in the mists of time. Until that balance is restored that keeps all these fine elements alive in the early church with its balance of charisms then we seem condemned to go on repeating our same mistakes.

1. Vidler, Alec R., Summarized in <u>The Church in an Age of Revolution.</u> Harmondsworth, Pelican History of the Church. reprint 1976. p. 183
2. Abbott, W M, S.J. (Ed). <u>The Documents of Vatican II.</u> London, Geoffrey Chapman. 1966. p. 712
3. Ibid, p. 715
4. Ibid, p. 704
5. Ibid, p. 716
6. Bokenkotter, T. <u>A Concise History of the Catholic Church</u>. New York, Image Books. 1979. pp. 421-424.
7. Husslein, J. <u>Social Wellsprings Vol. II Pius XI</u>. Milwaukee, Bruce. 1942. pp. 206- 207 nn 79 and 80 of Quadragesimo Anno
8. Calvez, Jean Yves. <u>The Social Thought of John XXIII.</u> Chicago, Henry Regnery Co. 1964. pp. 48 and 51
9. <u>Proclaiming Justice and Peace</u> (Ed. Michael Walsh and Brian Davies). Mystic, CT, Twenty Third Publications. 1991. pp. 230-231
10. De Broucker, Jose. <u>The Suenens Dossier - the Case for Colligiality.</u> Dublin, Gill and Macmillan. 1970. pp. 14-16
11. Abbott, W M, S.J. (Ed) <u>The Documents of Vatican II</u>, London, Geoffrey Chapman. 1966. pp. 538-539
12. Ibid. p. 560
13. Ibid. p. 48
14. Ibid. p. 64
15. Ibid. p. 270
16. Ibid. p. 681

CHAPTER ELEVEN

Restoring the Laity's Rights

While Vatican II restored the laity's role to its more traditional balance, the subsequent years however have revealed a much more subtle twist than the Council seemed to indicate. The ideas began to emerge after the Council saying:- "You as laity are placed by God in the world in your various jobs and professions to carry the Word of God to your surroundings. Our job as Apostolic Authority is to form you for this, your vocation. But as for bringing you into helping in framing doctrine or running the institutional Church's structures, that is not your job - it is ours".

Far more democratic structures were recommended in parishes and dioceses to assist in their running. Often these pastoral councils became caught up in the material running of the parish or its social life. These ideas as expressed above became incorporated in the new canon law and catechism that were published some two decades after Vatican II.

The present catechism particularly Questions 897 to 913 which treat of the laity, use rights always within the area described above of working for the salvation of all people (Q. 900). So that even when giving their opinions the right "to manifest to the sacred pastors their opinion on matters which pertain to the good of the church" is balanced "with due regard to the integrity of faith and morals and reverence towards their pastors" (Q. 907). They can "feel called, or be in fact called, to co-operate with their pastors in the service of the ecclesial community" (Q. 910). Always the return to the Pre-Vatican II situation of being asked by those above.

Canon law also follows more or less the same course of the catechism using the same phrases. Commencing with the canons 204-231 there is a hopeful passage in canon 208 which states:- "Flowing from their rebirth in Christ, there is genuine equality of dignity and action among all of Christ's faithful." (1) However when the subsequent canons spell out the duties and rights the theme recurs of "the right to strive so that the divine message of salvation may more and more reach all people of all times and places." (canon 211) Obedience is stressed to the "sacred pastors" with the right to manifest their views but as stated in the catechism in order to respect "the integrity of faith and morals, show due reverence to the pastors and take into account both the common good and the dignity of the individuals." This of course can mean as so determined by the hierarchical powers. It would seem to remove their basic right for a say in things and their views to be listened to properly as determinants in whatever ultimate authority finally decides.

The canons add – a right to be assisted by their pastors from the spiritual riches of the Church (canon 213): a right to worship God (canon 214): a right to freely establish and direct associations, hold meetings and share in the Church's mission but "No initiative, however can lay claim to the title 'catholic' without the consent of the competent ecclesiastical authority" the 'rights' to go on as summarized above to carry the Gospel outside, educate their children, go to theological institutes but "don't tell how to run things especially theological or structural. That's our business" (my own interpretation). There has been ample evidence of the token application of many of these canons with one important group of laity saying sincerely, "Don't just let us speak to you, listen."

This book had been written very conscious of the fact that this was not the situation in the first few centuries. The laity's role and unquestioned rights were inextricably woven into the evolving consciousness of who had the right to authority in the Church and who had the ultimate authority to finally say 'Yes' or 'No'. There was never any doubt that those members of the priestly people (2 Peter) exercised their rights to elect the ones who exercised ultimate authority among these priestly people, to give opinions which were taken into account by their locally elected bishop who must have been elected not just for his leadership qualities but because of his theological outlook. The evolution and practice of this shared authority form the early part of this book.

However as history proceeds, we notice the seeds of a more authoritarian episcopal status evolving even in the third century with Cyprian and Hippolytus and a growing centralism of Roman authority which did not have the full consensus of the Faithful partly because of the growing isolation of the Eastern and Western Empires and the barbarian invasions of the fourth century onwards.

The result was in the West when totally different cultures dominated the newly converted barbarian kingdoms: when a barbarian chief/king/warrior and serf situation evolved into feudalism, the role of a participating laity disappeared except for laity with power. The various factors in that disappearance are traced whether they be political, spiritual, liturgical or other causes. The result was the loss to the laity of being in any way appraisers of their Tradition, becoming merely passive recipients of what those who claimed to be the sole appraisers of the Tradition taught.

Yet the powerful laity began to trespass on the rights of those who had ultimate authority by Holy Orders and to wrest from them the rights they had acquired over their local churches. The practical answer to this imbalance was found in centralizing the Church under the pope who had ultimate authority in defined but limited spheres.

The strong influence of this centrism is set out in earlier chapters. What was seen as a positive solution for a certain time e.g. in wresting back for the Church the lost authority and power became the benchmark. It was canonized in Theology and Law for the next centuries on down to today.

Canon Law now codified the laity's passive role; but every now and then the powerful laity had to intervene to help the unity of the Church which disintegrated papal centrism seemed unable to control in 1046 and 1417.

Trent in answer to a more democratic approach from many of the protestant reformers made the laity more dependent on their ecclesiastical superiors.

The fears the French Revolution left behind of the total collapse of all the values many people treasured gave rise to a conservative reaction within the Church which very much kept lay people as lower citizens in the City of God until the many more democratic elements within the Church converged in Vatican II.

This new impetus began restoring their rights to the laity. "Began" is the operative word; but we have seen how the impetus was channelled into an ideology behind canon law and the catechism which blocked out more advances in the laity's position.

At the time of the french edition of the catechism's publication, Paul Valadier, an eminent french Jesuit wrote:-"And indeed nothing is omitted: no point of dogma (first part: the Creed), of sacramental practice (second part) of moral teaching (third part) or of Christian prayer (fourth part) is neglected. The presentation is moreover restrained, reminding the reader of what every good Catholic has known for a long time. Notably in the section on morals it puts forward the courageous teachings of the Church on social justice and international solidarity as well as those, unchanged, on sexual ethics; but here as elsewhere there is clearly visible a willingness to put the teaching forward without overemphasis or aggressiveness: there are even some gentle movements towards openness. With regard to marriage, for example, while it always talks of the double end of marriage, it reverses the usual order and priority by citing the "good of the spouses themselves" before "the transmission of life" (S2363).

"Despite the evident concern to avoid overemphasis, what is surprising is the desire to say everything and to put everything forward without really drawing a distinction between truths and assertions.

"This is noticeable in the fact that all the quotations with which the text is teeming are juxtaposed as if they all had the same value. Thus the various sections place end to end quotations from the Scriptures, references to ecumenical councils, texts from theologians, and passages from papal speeches, as if each text bore the same weight in proving the proposition in question. This approach is all the odder in that in sound Catholic teaching the off-the-cuff remark of a saint (as with Joan of Arc in S2005) cannot have the same weight in determining a point of doctrine as the conclusion reached by an ecumenical council or a passage from Scripture.

"The aim seems to have been to convince the reader that everything converges in harmony to demonstrate what one wants but this to some extent sacrifices the authentic approach to understanding the faith, since one does not succeed in knowing what one is really depending on to reach this kind of conclusion."

Valadier goes on to analyse the attitude of the authors of the catechism:- "The business of putting all quotations on the same level reveals a characteristic of the theological perspective adopted by the book's authors. They wanted to say everything and explain everything so as not to leave anything in obscurity. The first result is to emphasise the bulk mentioned above, but the effect above all is that the reader is unable to know what really matters, because everything seems to have the same importance (acknowledging one God in three persons, indulgences, the existence of angels). Because everything is on the same level, everything is neutralised and flattened. Against their will the authors thus give the impression that, because every detail of Catholic teaching is essential; nothing really is. Thus a concern for integralism gives an impression of relativism. The authors no doubt forgot that the Second Vatican Council asked us to have regard to the 'hierarchy of truths' without which christians no longer find themselves introduced step by step into the mystery of God revealed by Jesus Christ, but are faced with a system of axioms in which every proposition depends on every other proposition. But the faith is "a way" as the Acts of the Apostles puts it, in a pilgrimage, not a fortified cathedral in which one shuts oneself up once and for all." (2)

This ideology behind the catechism and canon law which seems to display a theological intransigence about altering anything about the present Theology or structures has brought about the impasse in the Church at the moment. This applies not just concerning the laity being kept in their supposed place but also Theology becomes a science explaining the present situation in the Church and elaborating on it but never daring to challenge it. The amount of frustration building up in the Church among those left to challenge has become quite explosive as many bishops are appointed on the basis of fitting in with this ideology: as bishops who want to change things constructively are neutralized by participating in assemblies where thrusts are neutralized by small groups larded with sympathisers of that same ideology who in turn pass beautifully worded but bland statements of where the Church is at. Things really do need the common sense of lay participation in the councils of power and their traditional right to elect their own bishops to reflect the sensus fidelium of the whole Church. This is of course only one but an important change to relieve the tension and break the present deadlock.

Some would suggest a married clergy, women priests, decentralization of the Roman Curia and so on to alleviate the present ills of the Church. All of these may or may not be improvements on present Church structures. However I do think long-term solutions have to be put in place as these last two chapters endeavour to show. All the above solutions are piecemeal. Once genuine lay involvement is put in place the above suggestions could well follow. Without the long term solution of putting genuine lay involvement in place, all the above suggestions might do is precipitate fight after fight between an entrenched oligarchy and an increasingly enraged laity with even more bitterness and schisms. First is the need to restore the laity's place.

When one looks back at the account of the impasse in the present day Church set out in chapter one, the first point was the polarization of the right and left wing elements in the Church. Avery Dulles analyses the two camps well when he portrays the right wing camp as the "neo-Augustinian" and the left wing as the "communitarian" camp. The neo-Augustinians put their accent on worship and holiness, want a church more separate from the world, more manifestly united in itself, more taken up with the cultivation of a direct relationship with God. The "communitarian" school wants the Church to become more involved in the promotion of peace, justice and reconciliation. For the first group "mystery" becomes a code word. It is more "eschatological" (or emphasising the future life) and other-worldly. The second group uses "community" as its code word. It is more incarnational and this-worldly. (3)

The neo-Augustinians argue that the "eighties" and "nineties' are different from the "sixties" where even the secular atmosphere was euphoric. Since then "the signs of the times" indicate greater misery, division and violence, the power of the Evil One. They argue that many catholics who have become friends of the world have become victims of materialism, consumerism and indifference. Many priests and religious have abandoned their vocations, fewer young people are filling their ranks. Vatican II was a pastoral council and the pastoral scene has changed.

The "communitarians" reply that much good has come from Vatican II already and it is understandable that so many radical switches in the catholic position have resulted in many being confused and upset. If there is disenchantment among many youth, they say, it is not structural reform causing it but conservative bishops blocking reforms. Most participation given to laity is given as concessions, not as rights, many of these have been given to "stooges" of the hierarchy, not laity who are representative of the majority of catholics.

Not all catholics remain in such clearly delineated camps. The reaction to the evils of the secular world has, of course, been compounded by many "liberal" christians who have denied the transcendental God or heaven or hell or sin or all of them: "There you are" say the neo-Augustinians, "that is what happens if you start opening out to the world. Christianity or Catholicism is totally eroded." The neo-Augustinian is, of course, a firm adherent of centralized control to impose his or her ideology in order to save the faithful from contamination and if this means more bureaucracy then he or she retorts that all the new commissions and endless meetings since Vatican II are another form of bureaucracy.

The fundamentalism of black or white mentality that many neo-Augustinians fall into as a defensive mechanism when they claim theirs is the only orthodox way is a religious phenomenon shared by the protestant fundamentalists who lacking an infallible papacy return to the literalism of an infallible Bible to give all the answers in a world dominated by the Evil One. Both need a support of laws for all occasions and circumstances. Both see outside their own orthodoxies evil and weak people who flounder in the mire of ignorance and sin to be sucked up finally in the vortex of hell.

Neo-Augustinianism has, of course, an honourable tradition within Christianity from the neo-platonist influences of the second century, strengthened in the West by Augustine's theology, and reinforced by monastic spirituality and the writings of Dionysius the Areopagite. One suspects as with platonism roots deeper than Christianity itself, human nature appealing to certain religious archetypes shared with many eastern religions where a spiritual/world dichotomy is needed as a religious or philosophical basis for belief.

Neo-Augustinian tradition is an honourable one and will probably always be with us. I do not think "neo-Augustinanism" and "Communitarianism" are necessarily opposite ends of the pole - a good pope or bishops could marry them. However, when one, in this case neo-Augustinianism, now appears to be in power in the Catholic Church with little toleration for deviates as one concludes from its silencing of many reputable teachers, from its appointment of bishops sympathetic to its same stance, as well as its public utterances, then one can sense danger as well as history repeating itself.

With the insertion of really representative laity on theological commissions and a greater delegation of centralized authority to regional and diocesan authorities, a lot of this anger could abate. Especially when one reflects on the unity in diversity principle applying to all groups in the Church, left or right, who do not go against the essential Tradition of the Church. Uniformity must not be confused with unity. Why cannot latin mass catholics exist side by side with vernacular mass adherents in the same church?

It is obvious too that if laity were involved in the selection and election of bishops that a different type of bishop who was felt to be a real leader of his people would emerge.

The second point of ferment was the danger of many bishops being selected by Rome because of their "safety" and their ability to be loyal to the centre rather than put their peoples' interests in the pursuit of faith first. If laity were consulted about their leaders as in the early Church, a stronger, more caring man arising from his people yet teaching the Jesus the Apostles taught and trying to image it in his own life would be their choice. In most cases, once the laity have seen a priest in action, heard him preach and conversed with him, they have a fairly uncanny sense of who and what this priest really is. A different type of bishop, closer to and chosen by his people would be a step forward in this time of ferment.

The third manifestation of this impasse as mentioned in chapter one was the Church's increasing lack of credibility among her own members. O'Sullivan remarked in chapter one on the powerlessness arising from no one who really listens to one, to what is said and the inability to effect change. With lay people in positions of power sharing that situation could be modified. To inject a personal note here, I used to say as a parish priest to a newly elected parish council:- "If I go into a meeting with my own ideas and you with yours and at the conclusion, all of us leave with our ideas unchanged, it has been a bad meeting." The idea that I can be an active member of a Church which listens to me and makes therefore credible statements which I can see even if I disagree with them does make a difference as regard credibility.

The same carries over to the fourth point of credibility mentioned in chapter one – credibility to outsiders. If they see a Church which has a unity of agreement about essentials but a variety of opinions about the less essential things, they can see signs of hope for ecumenism. Instead they often see a church where the hierarchy says one thing and many of the members are living an entirely different life. They see themselves denied the reception of the Eucharist because of lacking agreement on catholic doctrine or morals or both, yet they witness Catholics who disagree heartily with some official Church doctrine or morals going to Communion side by side with other Catholics. In both cases of credibility, lay people in sharing power with Apostolic Authority can alter much of the present Church's attitudes.

The fifth point of ferment was mentioned as Conscience. This could be helped by lay feed-back and truthfulness about how often conscience is used as a reason for the non-observance of the Church's rules and regulations to make Authority aware of the frequency where laws are more honoured in the breach than the observance. Lay help in this area could be a blessing for Authority to understand the real situation.

This can certainly apply to the sixth point made about the distance many feel between themselves and Authority on sexuality. We have seen the basis of the Church's teaching on sexuality and the shadow of Augustine still hovering above its theology. Lay people can bring a wealth of experience to celibate males to make them realize some of the sufferings people have regarding their own sexuality. It was said by several participants that in the first commission advising Pope Paul VI on contraception that Patty Crowley's reading of letters from women who had suffered because of the Church's teaching had a lot to do with changing the minds of several of the commission's members. This true interchange when laity have positions of power within the appropriate bodies could help the situation greatly.

The seventh point in chapter one where there seemed to be an impasse was on gender. Again with power sharing with women and men, Apostolic Authority can see and hear women's accounts of their oppression whether in secular, commercial or ecclesiastical society and in having to answer them face to face a learning and a healing process can take place.

What I think all this ferment is suggesting accompanied by the feeling of impasse is that Authority at present in its centralized, bureaucratic form needs a more balanced and modified approach. History shows there will always be a certain amount of ferment going on in the Church. What is troubling is when many can see much of it need not be contentious. As said above, crusades for this or that change could produce some positive result. But why not try underlying all these suggested attempts by restoration of the rights of the laity as exercised in the early Church? They could effect a more modified and balanced approach than at present which could take away much of the bitterness and polarization existing in the Church today as well as making it a more credible witness to the Gospel of Jesus Christ which is its very purpose for existing.

One would like to see the lay balance restored immediately. Like all changes it will probably take time. So often the Church resists change until things start collapsing and it implements them under duress. It seems never to have learnt this lesson. Beginnings could be made by letting bishops be elected by representative laity and clergy with endorsements by other bishops in the region with roman intervention only in the case of proven heresy as was the case in many catholic kingdoms in the post-reformation period. Lay representation could be introduced or strengthened on all commissions within the Church with their vote having a recognizable significance in ultimate decisions. They should be elected with views endorsed by a majority of active laity. After all we are entering an age where the laity have had more formal education, often in theology, than in the preceding nineteen centuries. As is catholic teaching, they would recognize that Apostolic Authority has the right of ultimate decision making whereas now it has the sole right. Gradually Apostolic Authority must get used to shared authority retaining its ultimate right of teaching Jesus the Apostles taught, but recognizing the right of all disciples to share in decision making and exercising their right also to be involved in Apostolicity.

One suspects that a lot of the channelling of Vatican II's opening up to the laity's position into keeping a control mechanism as in canon law and the catechism is a fear that laity might take over internal governance and theological decisions. Decisions could then be made by democratic voting and the Church turned into a modern democracy with large minorities or simple majorities determining Apostolic teaching. The reply to that by the present administration ignoring the lessons of the early Church, is that the Church is not a democracy and hands are upheld in horror at this happening.

In the sense of one person, one vote, the Church is not that kind of democracy. On the other hand one asks the question did Christ intend the Church to be a total dictatorship, an autocracy as it is now expressed by a self perpetuating oligarchy? Catholics believe there are grounds in the Gospel and history for an ultimate authority that is responsible to a democratic assembly preferably coming to a consensus after discussion but being put to a majority vote if agreement cannot be reached. Here I return to the argument at the beginning of the book. Surely we can get as far as possible into the minds and intentions of Jesus and the apostles by discerning very carefully the churches they set up and left behind. Modern historical and scriptural studies have enabled us to do this more accurately than in the past. The structures they set up were established by men who knew the mind of Christ and had a far greater exemplary character and balance necessarily than those that developed from them.

The danger of the present set up where authority is not answerable to any other corrective or balancing system can be that one school of theology claiming to be the only catholic interpretation can hold unquestioned power. Rahner puts it well when he noted this point: "There is undoubtedly a dogmatic positivism current today. It confines dogmatic theology within the limits of assembling and systemizing official Church teachings.

"Possibly an attempt is made to place the teaching in the perspective of its historical development, but it uses exclusively the concepts and models of teaching itself and stays entirely within its problematic and its conceptual framework. Nor does dogmatic theology break out of the positivism by working with the concept and within the framework of an academic and academically comfortable neo-scholastic philosophy that is, by cultivating a certain rational and conceptual technical apparatus .. .. .. the positivism fails to recognize the historical nature of the concepts employed even in official church statements. It absolutizes these concepts by considering them as "natural", intelligible to everyone, and adequate to express the dogma for all times." (4)

Perhaps the underlying assumption of catholic theology and particularly ecclesiology is that because an idea developed in a particular way and often answered a particular need at a particular time it should be kept as truly developed teaching until it is shown to be counter productive, rather than it being questioned from time to time as to whether it remains true development or not. As we shall see in the final chapter, the Hierarchy of Truths gives the Church an opportunity to do just that. It would then free up the constriction to which the present Church policies seem to be leading.

There is always a danger with centralized bureaucracy dominated by a particular ideology or school of theology to over-legislate and over-define. Putting teachings in the context of a Hierarchy of Truths gives a sense of proportion to what is being taught.

Gregory Baum, the eminent scholar from Toronto, puts his finger on this tendency:- "The word magisterium has acquired an ambiguous meaning today. Over many centuries the Catholic hierarchy has regarded the magisterium as part of their jurisdictional power and hence have affirmed doctrinal positions with the same frequency and the same ease as they made laws. Magisterium was understood in accordance with a legal model. This misunderstanding of the Church's teaching authority has led to an over-extension of the magisterium. Popes and bishops have over-reached themselves in their teaching. They have spoken with certainty on many matters about which no certainty was available. Today the vast body of official teaching is being questioned in many areas, whether it be the interpretation of Scriptures, the understanding of councils, the role of the papacy in the Church or the norms of moral life. Since so many official positions have been transcended or corrected by recent developments, it is the special task of the magisterium today to withdraw from fields where in the past it has claimed competence. If the magisterium wants to reaffirm its authoritative role in the Church; it must first learn to step back from the exaggerated claims, even if this causes confusion among many people." (5)

✿ ✿

Of course the fear will still persist in the minds of the present officials exercising Apostolic Authority that somehow the Tradition they are set in place to preserve will be weakened by letting the laity into their domain. I would like to suggest in the chapter twelve how this Tradition could be preserved even more accurately than at present with the balance of lay shared authority. It is enshrined in a teaching of Vatican II that has barely been implemented, certainly `at a practical level – the Hierarchy of Truths. This too can be reinforced by a study of the early Church's functions. In these two suggested reforms – the restoration of the laity's balance and the preservation of the Tradition by the Hierarchy of Truths, I would see the beginning of the Church's entering that third era that Rahner so confidently predicted (p. 16) when the Church will become truly catholic.

1. See J A Coriden, T J Green and D E Heintschel. The Code of Canon Law. Mahwah, Paulist. p. 15
2. Valadier, P. S.J. "Universal Catechism published in French". London, Tablet 21 November 1992. pp. 1480-1481
3. Dulles, A. Article in Jossua J.P. and Komonchak J.A., (Ed. Alberigo, G.). The Reception of Vatican II. Washington DC, Catholic University of America Press. 1987. pp. 353-355
4. Rahner, K. "Philosophy and philosophising in theology" in Theology Digest. Sesquicentennial Issue. 1968. p. 19
5. Baum, G. New Horizon, Theology Essays. New York, Paulist Press. 1972 p. 150

CHAPTER TWELVE

The Hierarchy of Truths as a preservation of Tradition

When the Catholic Church was confronted at the beginning of the Protestant Reformation with the challenge:- "Scripture (the Bible) alone. Faith alone", it had to reply that what Jesus had revealed was not just in Scripture, but in Tradition (unwritten handing down) also. It gave rise to the "Two Sources of Revelation" theory which was included in most catholic theology books until Vatican II.

Tradition had always been an important word to the early christian writers and continued to be so to the subsequent theologians. It was not difficult to point this out in the polemics of the Reformation. What of course muddied the waters was the confusion even among catholic theologians and at times Apostolic Authority between Tradition (with a capital "T"), the original essential deposit of Faith left by the apostles, and traditions (with a small "t") of teachings going back a long way but not in the original deposit even though at times many thought so. These traditions included many of the philosophical greek ideas used to speculate on christian Tradition. They included "parasite" ideas as we have seen that translated the Tradition into another cultural milieu and often in time became as important as the idea they were attempting to explain. Unfortunately they included too forgeries and their influence especially on the sensus fidelium (or belief of the Faithful) such as the Donation of Constantine and the False Decretals on the status of the papacy. They were often believed as Tradition at a certain time. For instance the literal interpretation of Scripture; of the sun rising and setting around the centre of the universe, the earth, used to condemn Galileo.

The trouble has always been there is no one big book (containing all the Tradition) to consult if necessary. The Church is loath to do so, because of getting it wrong at times in the past. Pope John Paul II has apologised for Galileo four hundred years later or Paul VI to Constantinople nine hundred years later. Attempts to make a list can be quite difficult to agree on. Congar points out that attempts to define Tradition at the Council of Trent (1545-63) resulted in different lists from different theologians. Congar cites some of the beliefs they listed belonging to the Tradition which include:- praying towards the east: the fire of purgatory: praying standing on Sunday: the triple immersion at baptism: fasting on Wednesdays and Fridays and many more. Most of these, today's theologians would say would not be of the essence of Tradition. We saw earlier where the threefold use of ministry (bishop, priest and deacon) taught as of divine institution was changed to a threefold ministry from ancient times at Vatican II.

Modern scriptural and historical research as in so many other areas was able to show the Tridentine declaration of threefold ministry not of divine origin even though ministry was. (cf p. 20) Often what was considered vitally important at a certain time such as interest on money or limbo just slip out of the back door and now receive no mention.

I remember how the Sisters at school stressed with us the necessity of having children baptized as soon as possible. Otherwise these babies could go to limbo if they died. I still meet grandmothers of my generation who go around secretly baptizing their grandchildren while babysitting for their sons or daughters who have refused to have their children baptized. Limbo is not even mentioned in the new catechism.

While all bishops and theologians could draw up a list of mutual agreement on what is Tradition and agree there is certainly a Tradition, as the list gets longer the shadier the boundaries between Tradition and traditions get. This grey area which could hundreds of years from now be declared infallible Tradition is the area often of theological dispute.

When the preparatory commissions of Vatican II were presented with the "Two Sources of Revelation" theory, they rejected it and the bishops at the Council agreeing with them stated in the final document:- "Sacred Tradition and sacred Scripture form <u>one</u> sacred deposit of the word of God, which is committed to the Church. Holding fast to this deposit, the entire holy people united with their shepherds remain always steadfast in the teaching of the apostles, in the common life, in the breaking of the bread, and in prayers (Acts 2, 42) so that in holding to, practising and professing the heritage of the faith, there results on the part of the bishops and faithful a remarkable common effort". I see in this a marvellous commendation of what this book is attempting to present. The document goes on to speak of the teaching office (Apostolic Authority) adding:- "This teaching office is not above the word of God, but serves it, teaching only what has been handed on, listening to it devoutly, guarding it scrupulously, and explaining it faithfully by divine commission and with the help of the Holy Spirit: it draws from this one deposit of faith everything which it presents for belief as divinely revealed." (1)

This lack of strict delineation between Tradition and traditions has been both a strength and a weakness – a strength because it allows a certain flexibility at the lower ends of Tradition but a weakness in that from time to time the Church has confused the grey area as pointed out above marking off the Tradition from traditions. It has also allowed a rather subtle ideology to creep in with canon law and the catechism by placing all teaching on a level playing field and giving the impression all should be followed and obeyed. While highlighting the remarks of Vatican II about the laity it has given an impression of:- "We are the institutional ministers, Apostolic Authority. We form you laity to go out as apostles to the world and to assist us to a degree in the institution, but don't try and tell us what to do about doctrine or controlling the institution. That is our business."

If I were to put my finger on what is causing the impasse mentioned in chapter one, it would be this basic attitude. In the previous chapter mention has been made of bringing in the laity to balance out a lot of this intransigence which one suspects is often about preserving traditions rather than Tradition. For Tradition is important. Richard Rohr puts it appositely when he says: "That is why the tradition of the Church is so important: We stand on the shoulders of all the wise persons and saints of the past. This is the true Tradition. Some historical accidents have been facilely passed on as universal tradition, yet are not the consistent coherent pattern. So we need the Body to keep us beyond cultural arrogance and tied to *all* the ancestors. We can't each start from zero" (2)

One can see that the fear of those in office is that if you bring lay people into the running of the Church and even in helping form doctrine, then the Tradition could be impaired by democratic voting or lack of theological acumen. This fear is not unfounded; but the greater truth is found in the apostles and early christians seeing the need of the whole community to share in a synodal way in what was believed and in trusting it to elect Apostolic Authority. We would then have the faith to do so. If ideologies are used to block the erosion of what is seen as the power of the Apostolic Authority to be the sole authority and make it only the ultimate authority then the Holy Spirit will use the "signs of the times" to show big cracks in the foundation. This is happening with the sex scandals and cover ups by some bishops who have become so institutional that they became blind to the Gospel values of protecting the poor and the victims of abuse and so on for many of the other points mentioned in today's ferment. This searching for answers is met by the impasse created by an intransigence of one school of theology from which there is no appeal. Laity need to be brought in to share their experience of real life, common sense and God given gifts. But how to protect the Tradition? I find in an almost practically neglected teaching of Vatican II an answer to this – the Hierarchy of Truths.

This book has followed the path of these two millennia and tried to show the reasons how the recognized ultimate appraisers of the Tradition became the sole appraisers. While the correction of this anomaly will not inevitably solve all the difficulties that confront the Church, it will help to give more balance and shared authority as existed among the early Christians. But how to go about this great change in structures that are centuries old?

I think the Church has within its grasp an attempted beginning to the solution in an idea expressed by Vatican II. Pope John XXIII had given a lead to this idea in his opening speech at the Council when he said:- "the substance of the ancient doctrine of the deposit of faith is one thing and the way it is presented is another. And it is the latter that must be taken into great consideration with patience if necessary, everything being measured in the forms and proportions of a magisterium which is predominantly pastoral in character." (3) Echoing Pope John's assertion the Decree of Ecumenism of the same Council stated: "When comparing doctrines they should remember that in Catholic teaching there exists an order or 'hierarchy' of truths, since they vary in their relationship to the foundation of the Christian Faith." (4)

The first reason for adoption of the Hierarchy of Truths stems from a realization that some system must be devised in the Church that takes account both of its faithfulness to Tradition and its witness to the contemporary world. The resultant tension can be a healthy one, because it prevents the present and possibly future polarization between blind traditionalism and a change to suit the fads of a given age. Setting in place a Hierarchy of Truths to be reviewed at given periods of time will be to meditate on and plumb the depths of the Tradition corrected by contemporary scholarship and relate it to the needs of the time. This in turn contextualizes right and left wing extremes preventing the kind of mindless zealotry we so often see at this time because some people think Tradition exists in vacuum needing no scholarly criticisms and on the other hand modernity can often be a new disguise for the old fashioned vices and habitual evils that have plagued humans from their beginning on earth. Such a healthy tension and contextualization is badly needed and can be supplied by the Hierarchy of Truths.

The autocratic system now in the Church does need modification. Perhaps nothing has proved this more than the recent shocks in the Catholic world of sexual abuse by some clergy and religious. More disturbing for many Catholics have been Episcopal cover-ups, lack of understanding of addictive paedophilia, apparent lack of compassion for victims whose lives could be ruined for the sake of institutional silence as well as the huge economic drain on the Church when challenged. It has brought home to catholics that the same cover-ups which occur in any autocracy and bureaucracy, whether it be secular or ecclesiastical, not to admit mistakes in order to prove the authoritative power is always right, is especially needed when the cloak of creeping infallibility is thrown over all the actions of the centralized bureaucracy. It makes catholics ask the question: "Does Christ's Body have to be manifested in this particular, autocratic form or do I have some say in how it is run and how my resources which I gift are used?" The Hierarchy of Truths helps to restore, as in the early Church, that surety and participation, because the hierarchy's regular review of what is more important based on both Tradition and what is needed now, could open the way to more shared democracy as in the early Church. A leading theologian has commented: "A religious community must constantly reflect on its original purposes, the values of its founder, the convictions about God and human life which originally set the community apart. It must take care that each of its institutional forms and patterns of behaviour facilitates rather than impedes those basic purposes. The challenge to a religious community that would remain faithful to its original charisma is not to find ways to deinstitutionalize itself but to reinstitutionalize itself according to its abiding faith. A religious community without any institutional forms at all, on the other hand is a religious community which no longer exists, or is on the verge of extinction. By their very nature, charisms die out unless they are somehow routinized, i.e., unless they find adequate institutional expression." (5)

The second reason for the Hierarchy of Truths is that while history cannot be reversed it can be placed in proportion as Pope John XXIII so wisely recommends, by taking into account criteria that are formed from historical experience. These criteria can be grounded on the experience of those who either knew Jesus or his apostles and how they functioned at the dawn of christianity. I have set out the arguments in the first chapters calling them the undergirding principles. They were and still are Koinonia or community which functioned in a special way with every gift of every member listened to, used and supervised by Apostolic Authority elected by all the members with that authority having the ultimate say, unity rather than uniformity in essentials but the allowance of diversity to an agreed point and the Scriptures in which the community is soaked and lives in its everyday life. Later as we saw these were hardened and narrowed by the experience of the second century into Irenaeus' three building blocks of "catholic" christianity.

The Koinonia was centred in and on one man, the bishop, who still supervised all the gifts given to each of the members, was elected by them and referred to them in all important decisions giving ultimate but not sole approval. The unity in diversity was expressed more negatively by Creeds which delineated more sharply how far one could go in diversity without breaking the unity. Irenaeus' third building block was the Canon of Scriptures necessitated by so many false Scriptures flourishing in the second century but the community still grounded on the authentic Scriptures.

The undergirding principles can be used as criteria or litmus paper for the developing doctrines and teachings of the Church and as points of reference. You cannot change history; but the Hierarchy of Truths enables one to correct some of its distortions.

The third point is that such a Hierarchy acts as a guide to the consciences of catholics to discern the more important teachings of the Church from the less important. Part of the present impasse is that all is presented as binding and the reaction to such intransigence popping out of roman chanceries every few months is just to shrug one's shoulders if disagreeing and "follow ones conscience". Common sense or experience is often not enough, rather one's conscience needs to be carefully reinforced.

The fourth point is that the present impasse can be tackled especially the ideology of placing all teaching on a level playing field which has caused a significant part of the problem. The other part of the ideology to keep the laity in their place in the world spreading the Gospel has been shown to not hold credibility by I hope the argument of the book. With lay involvement at all levels, still allowing for the ultimate Apostolic Authority, a new balance is brought into decision making without one school of Theology holding sway.

The fifth point is that all Tradition and traditions are respected without having to slip teachings out the back door when they obviously become obsolete.

Much of that apprehension among other Christians could be dissipated by the obvious picture of a Church that has a sense of priorities, as O'Sullivan has put it, and one that consults its own members widely as well taking into account well proven contemporary study. Many non-Catholic churches have been weakened by a laissez-faire liberalism that seems to cut out all definite teaching and long for a Church that has a definite model respecting its Tradition but open to the "signs of the times". A hierarchy of Truths could give such an image.

One of the "signs of the times" is the present generation's search for spirituality and a decreasing interest in institutional religion. Many reasons could be adduced for this phenomenon; but often given are the petty legalisms and exclusive theologies of religion in alienating so many particularly of the young. A Hierarchy of Truths would give more benign and less absolutist face to the Catholic Church's teaching and would show the Church was prepared to take on board some modern ideas without surrendering her essential Truth. It would allow her to concentrate more on her mystical Tradition which can match any other religion's experience and history of spirituality.

As noted above, the realization that the ultimate Authority is not the sole Authority in the Church becomes very clear when one has to appraise the

Hierarchy of Truths which require many charisms to discern how important are the truths particularly those that will come directly after the central truth of our beliefs – one God, Jesus Christ, the Trinity, Love of God and Neighbour. It cannot be left entirely to theologians or bureaucrats to decide in the name of the magisterium again narrowed down to the pope, curia and bishops appointed by them to become the sole articulators of the magisterium when there is an older theory of the magisterium (cf St. Thomas Aquinas p. 115) and when the early Church used all charisms to build up the Body of Christ. Even when the custom of one bishop for each diocese evolved, the understanding was an ultimate appraiser sharing Apostolic Authority who was elected by the presbyters and faithful of a particular church. Cyprian stated the Church consulted its people on every important decision. (p. 59)

A wider context for judging even official teachings in their historical context (as Rahner assesses) as well as how representative they are of the whole Church, how they have been "received" by the whole Church and other criteria would have to be assessed by experts and would constitute the Hierarchy of Truths. These experts would consist of theologians from different schools, historians, anthropologists, psychologists, sociologists and experts in the behavioural sciences and very importantly the "prophets" in today's Church, such as Mother Teresa, Abbé Pierre and many others. To this would be added representative laity chosen by their contemporaries, emotionally mature, married and single, people who can speak from their own experience as people.

One of the good points of the Hierarchy of Truths is that without discounting any of the Tradition or for that matter the traditions it gives a badly needed sense of perspective to this whole area when Authority can if it wishes cloud the boundaries between Tradition and traditions and use its authority to enforce the latter without the consent of most schools of theology. The Hierarchy of Truths obviates this situation by restoring a sense of proportion to what seems to have been Authority's fear and intransigence over the last decades.

When people can see the relative importance on the scale of teaching, they have a help in making decisions conscientiously. They can also more directly influence these decisions through being consulted particularly from their own experience and through their elected bishops. A balance is achieved not only between Tradition and traditions but decisions that arise from the whole community participating as in the early Church with the Apostolic Authority still making the ultimate decision.

Perhaps as Baum suggests (p. 177) less directives may proceed from the chanceries of power which can at times arise from lack of reality, a reality that the grass roots could have taught them.

Gregory Baum goes on to say: "The gospel revealed in Jesus Christ needs periodic re-interpretation. We cannot be faithful to this gospel simply by repeating the Bible or the ecclesiastical tradition. Because men's questions change in every age and the demonic takes on new forms, the central thrust and message of the self-same gospel must also change. Unless the gospel is re-focused in a new age, we cannot proclaim it in fidelity to the original gift. This re-focusing takes place through Christian experience, through a new listening to God's Word, through reading the Scriptures and engaging in dialogue with no questions in mind, through a process involving Christians committed to wrestling with the evil of their culture, but ultimately, this is my position, it is the task of the collegial magisterium to spell out the core meaning of the gospel for the age. This is exercise of charismatic authority. For this pre-supposes that Pope and bishops are in touch with the various parts of the Catholic Church, represent in dialogue and possibly in conflict, the various convictions of people and eventually seek to spell out the gospel. The unity and the universality of the movement depends on this exercise." (6) I feel in an oblique way Baum is really stating what a Hierarchy of Truths could fulfil.

Rahner has already pointed out above the danger of "doing" theology in one way. The Hierarchy of Truths is a way of restoring history to its corrective charism in placing Theology or more correctly theologies in their true perspective judged by the extended magisterium outlined above. In a further paper on the "Historical Dimension in Theology" Rahner summarizes the issue pertinently:- "Theology's possibility of error is intellectually, not just as the passive object of a change of mind, but as a subject in a free decision. This kind of change and development is at once the most difficult, the most bitter, and the most blessed. Hence, at a time when we hope for increased dialogue between Christian theology and modern science we would do well to ponder this historical dimension in theology. In so doing we shall be considering one of its most important aspects. Our considerations here will inevitably be fragmentary and incomplete. For behind this problem of the relationship between truth and history lies what has really been the whole problematic of the metaphysics of knowledge from its beginning up to the present time. The compatibility of the absoluteness of .. .. .. what we shall try to do quite simply is to show from theological considerations the fact that theology must take its historical nature into account and the practical consequences which follow from this for the Christian who is a scholar." (7)

No system of course will ever be perfect. Each of the undergirding principles by itself can become unbalanced. With the first, the whole episkope of the people of God, each person with his or her charism or special gift, bound together in the koinonia (community) as the Body of

Christ and led by an episkopos (bishop, leader) who has the charism of leadership and teaches the same Jesus the apostles taught chosen from and by that particular community can have by itself severe disadvantages. The community can develop into a legalistic, inward looking religious group if it is not leavened by the diverse charisms with which it is gifted just as creeds taken in their literal sense are capable of several interpretations as we saw in the case of Stephen I and Cyprian. They create a balance of contrasts and challenges. It too must always be steeped in the Gospels which keep the community alive. Tradition passed down through and with a community with those three undergirding principles is the best vehicle for ascertaining the Hierarchy of Truths for its time and place.

The actual relativity such a Hierarchy of Truths would establish by using strong historical arguments would create the true relationship between truth and history that Rahner mentions above. History is the best antidote to Theology over-absolutizing or claiming too much.

The Hierarchy of Truths is not going to solve the Church's problems: but it could well begin the process of implementing the wider vision of the Church begun in Vatican II and leading to a Vatican III Council. The democracy envisaged by and implemented in the early Church was not the one person one vote situation of the present Western democracies. Nor was it what has become the autocracy of the present Catholic Church. The democratic elements from our earliest history as christians, retained to a degree by the orthodox churches and revived by most mainstream protestant churches, is that the local community or Church has a certain paramountcy electing its own leader or leaders. (The earlier monoepiscopal debate becomes important). That leader or those leaders should give guidance and leadership based on the Gospels and Faith in Our Lord Jesus Christ and the Jesus the apostles taught, not the Jesus of the Middle Ages or the Jesus of the modern liberals necessarily.

This universal Church need not be a centralized body. By the principle of subsidiarity it should direct and act in all those areas where the local churches are unable to act for themselves. United in love by the bishop of Rome all local churches should have the freedom and dignity to work out their own theologies and liturgies and forms of commitment. The Pauline teaching of each gift given by God should be listened to and sifted upwards within the local church and in turn be sifted upwards within the Universal Church. Let us abandon "the Church is not a democracy therefore only autocracy will work as has been done for half the Catholic Church's life" for "let us use democracy wisely in our Church and according to our real Tradition rooted in the first christian centuries so that no charisms or Gifts of the Spirit are lost to the Church". This means that we will have to live more dangerously as adults not children, replacing authoritarianism with the mature authority the Gospel demands as the early christians lived and catholicism at its best respected. This democracy should not deny Apostolic Authority's right as a last court of appeal - but hopefully an Apostolic Authority elected by the presbyters and people based on the right criteria not an Apostolic Authority appointed by one party entrenched in a self-perpetuating oligarchy fast becoming a gerontocracy.

After Vatican II one of the great protestant theologians, Oscar Cullman, went so far as to call the Hierarchy of Truths the most revolutionary passage of the entire Council. (8) In an interesting article written on the same subject later, he attributes diversity and pluralism to the very work of the Holy Spirit and actually asserts that "uniformity is a sin against the Holy Spirit." On the basis of the Scriptures and early creeds, Cullman feels that "Consensus about nonnegotiable fundamentals is already within the grasp of the Churches...the Protestant spirit can guard against spurious and superfluous doctrinal developments, but needs to be challenged to recognise the importance of truths only implicitly taught in the Scriptures. The Catholic spirit can guard against a reduction of the faith to only one of its truths or aspects, but needs to be monitored with regards to its proclivity towards syncretism. Isolation of truths is what leads to heresy." (9)

Even though W. Henn in his scholarly work The Hierarchy of Truths according to Yves Congar O.P. takes a quite different view from mine, his analysis of Congar's ideas on the Hierarchy show distinct points of convergence with what I have been endeavouring to say. He quotes Congar as saying that each baptized person has a unique charism in the Church: "some in order to pronounce, ultimately in an infallible way, a regulating judgement of the ecclesial faith: all in order to live, in a way which itself ultimately is infallible, the life of the faith which includes therefore also an aspect of Christian thought." The Spirit of Truth guides and assists the Church to live in the truth in order "to locate the 'magisterium', especially the papal magisterium within the totality of the people of God which represents the plenitude of spiritual gifts. This is what we must honour in the Orthodox theology of 'sobornost'." (10) In the Catholic Church we call 'sobornost' the "consensus fidelium" or assent and agreement of all the baptized to the truths taught to them in their thoughts, spirituality and lives. This is ideally the process before a doctrine is really accepted by the whole Church.

The Commission itself would be merely advisory but must not be ignored by the leadership charism and it could draw up a list of more important and less important truths in ascending order. Quite apart from what I have suggested above with Love and Forgiveness of God and neighbour being on top of the list - and how wholesome it would be for churches to highlight these as their most important teachings above all other doctrines.

The Commission appointed above to advise the Apostolic Authority on the Hierarchy of Truths could be guided well by the three undergirding principles we have seen arise from what has been discussed in this book, particularly:

(a) Those truths that from antiquity have been believed by the people of God rooted in Scripture, rooted in Tradition and consented to by the whole 'episkope' or synodal principle and expressing an agreed upon unity that has not crushed diverse schools of theology which are basically in agreement. These truths would come highest on the list.

It is against the backdrop of this total sharing of any teaching promulgated by the ultimate Apostolic Authority that criteria for judging all decrees and pronouncements can be made. This was always implicit in the Western Church for the first five centuries by the fact of the ordained ministry and people electing their own bishops who, in turn, like Cyprian who at times seemingly autocratic, always discussed things with his people (p. 59). It would seem then that when decisions are unilateral with no prior or very little consultation of the whole people then it takes a lower place on the hierarchical scale. When, say in the Roman Catholic Church, bishops are consulted, weight is given to the official decree that emanates from papal teaching and fewer points are lost than a purely unilateral decision. However, there are degrees of consultation. When the whole body of bishops is consulted and they are genuine products of their local churches, hopefully elected by their priests and people whose beliefs they represent and can discuss freely without physical or moral coercion of any sort, this is a much better scenario and loses less points than bishops whose agenda is set and whose meeting is controlled or bishops being consulted in writing who have to write back expected answers. The Church is certainly not a democracy in the sense of one person one vote, but neither is it an autocracy where the ordained ministry alone initiates as well as promulgates doctrines.

(b) When a truth has been supported by Scripture in its literal or allegorical sense which has now changed or been amplified with better exegetical understanding, then such a doctrine slips further down the scale of a Hierarchy of Truths.

(c) When documents, especially non-scriptural documents, are shown to have had a disproportionate effect on Tradition then the truths which rested on them should go further down the list. Arguably if Joly's thesis about Ignatius of Antioch (p. 24 & footnote 11 pp. 36-37) was accepted by the scholarly world and what we know of the lack of mono-episcopacy in Clement of Rome and the Didache were accepted then mono-episcopacy may slip down the list of the Hierarchy of Truths in importance. Mono-episcopacy (not Apostolic Authority or episkope which is always there) composed of bishops nominated from outside the local community or in opposition to the local community could slide even further down the scale, because they become less appraisers by virtue of not arising from the local church.

(d) Obviously doctrines emanating or partly emanating from forgeries would go a few notches down. Much interest has arisen from a younger Ratzinger's comment on the difference between the papacy prior to the break with the Eastern Churches and the reformed papacy afterwards. "Would the Eastern Churches," he asks, "have to accept the Papal developments since the break?" (11).

This can be steadily endorsed by estimating the effects of the post-Damascus documents (pp. 72 sq) the Donation of Constantine (pp. 83 sq) and the False Decretals (p. 85). Such documents and the theology and the parts of canon law based on them even though normative for centuries, would assume a lower place on the scale.

In that regard also J.M.R. Tillard remarks how, in the Papacy, the roles of the patriarch of the West and head of the Church are capable of overlapping and at times the origin of diverse rights can get confused (12). One questions whether Gregory VII's reformed Papacy's "reception" by all the Church which, after 1054, was confined to the Western patriarchate only was facilitated by that fact, because the Eastern churches would certainly not have "received" it. Even in the Western patriarchate that fairly unilateral decision was not happily or universally "received" for many a long year. It could well be that "Papacy pre 1054" could be higher on the hierarchical scale than "Papacy post 1054."

One can see how a younger Hildebrand (Gregory VII) brooding over the forged documents in the roman chancery as well as the genuine ones, often taken out of context when he served in the curia as counsellor, for several "reform" popes, would have been convinced of their genuineness. When he became pope, as Gregory VII, he pronounced a very new concept of papacy mixed of course with older ideas. Was this quantum leap in development from "a presidency and last court of appeal" type of papacy to a "centralized monarchy" type of papacy proclaimed unilaterally really true development given Gregory's conviction that all the curial documents were normative? The real damage done by these documents is difficult to assess, but their ongoing effects should be subject to criteria.

(e) "Reception" comes in here - that a teaching or Tradition arises from the whole Church and is filtered through and accepted by the whole Church. The Eastern churches would certainly not have accepted the reformed papacy's claims made by Gregory VII given their previous 1000 years history, attitudes and Tradition. It gives much more credibility to their conviction that there can be no more Ecumenical or General Councils until the whole "Catholic" Church sits together in Council. Therefore the Eastern churches have had none since the break of 1054 and even though many of their leaders joined in Lyons (1274) and Florence (1438) the bishops, clergy and laity, completely disavowed those Councils on the participants' homecoming. Can there be a genuine Ecumenical Council before East and West re-unite? In any case, like the papacy, a General Council in the West after 1054 may come lower on the list than a General Council pre 1054.

That is why in a theology coming from the synodal principle, the "reception" by the whole body of the Faithful is so important. Unfortunately, in the Western Church in the thousand years preceding Newman, the teaching had become a passive "reception" with the laity touching their forelocks to the pope/bishops' decisions unquestioningly. It had continuity more strongly in the Eastern churches often called by its Russian name 'sobornost.' The whole body of the Faithful must be caught up in the decision making and "receive" it actively in their lives and spirituality once it is defined. And only then can it be said to be doctrine properly so called. If this process is lacking in some way or another, the teaching suffers and goes further down the hierarchical scale.

But there would still remain ultimate or Apostolic Authority properly constituted and there for the final sifting of truth. John Henry Newman earned for himself official opprobrium for the next two decades when he wrote On Consulting the Faithful on Matters of Doctrine in 1859 (13). He was merely reminding a very authoritarian and clerical Church that it was not that Body's sole authority but its ultimate one. That the laity too, as part of the royal and priestly people (1 Peter 2,9) of the new dispensation, share some of its priestly authority not only as recipients of the ordained ministers' teaching but helping in its framing. At times, Newman went on to claim that when the bishops spoke variously against each other in dealing with arianism in the 4th century which obscured the true meaning of the Council of Nicea, it was often the laity who maintained and asserted it.

(f) Again where physical and moral pressure has been brought to bear on any Council of the Church or its representation "rigged" to suit those in power, it does not necessarily negate the decisions from such a Council; but it does by defect push such a Council further down the scale of hierarchical truths. Much debate and discussion has centred around Vatican I as mentioned earlier (pp. 147-148 sq) and the debate still goes on. What has been said above would place it and its definitions lower on the scale than many other Councils.

(g) The same applies to the "parasite" ideas so helpful to the Church at certain stages of its developments. Thinking then moves on from the time these ideas were absolutized or almost so. Transubstantiation would be one of these ideas and the dependence on the Natural Law Theory as presently espoused by Rome based too much on Aristotalian Natural Law Theory taught by St Thomas when so many of the modern insights into human relationships, sexuality, psychological and sociological principles have shown a need to widen the original Natural Law Theory. All these factors would need to be weighed in grading a truth's place on the scale of hierarchical truth. A skilled commission could assess the degree of "parasite" influence accordingly.

(h) Much was made at Vatican II of the "signs of the times" - the good contemporary things happening in the world that the Church can learn from and the really evil things it can teach its people to avoid. These "signs of the times" should never be forgotten in any assessment. A deep faith can see in them the Holy Spirit working in the world and bringing good from the human condition. These "signs" can often be a clue to the Church on its way as they have often been in the past.

That is the beauty of the Hierarchy of Truths, no one is asked to reject any doctrine or tradition.

It would simply be assumed a doctrine has come down from the Gospel, developed organically with little or no pressure (notice I say, 'pressure' not necessarily 'influence') and has arrived at this point of time as a true culmination of the original Gospel truth or "deposit of Faith" as many western theologians have called it. Where defects in this transmission have been detected, then this is taken into account in the re-appraisal of Tradition and goes to a lower place on the hierarchical scale.

But there are several alert signals for "reception": that a commission of the nature suggested would have to watch out for. The first is that the "receiving" community must ideally be soaked in the Scriptures as the early christians were. This is the main way the attitudes and life of Jesus can be carried on by the Body of Christ. The main danger of any religious community, christian or not, not exposed to the whole range of Christ's life and attitudes can have a narrowing effect as tragedies like Jonestown and Waco have testified. In the case of Waco especially an ideology can take over its own purposes and ignore the lives and experiences of millions who have gone before it and which have formed the constant Tradition. Such a community could well lack the fullness of a living Christian community aware of Christ's attitudes. Religion is a powerful force in a christian's life, but he or she must be always aware of how it can take over Gospel values and distort them in the name of piety or legalism or ritual purity negating some of the main thrusts of the Gospel.

Some historians of the Middle Ages lack such an awareness so that, despite that period's religious fervour, it can also be interpreted as religiosity and some would even say superstition. I would tend to think such accusations extravagant as even the most illiterate of those medieval people, often bereft of regular preaching, had the Gospel and living Scripture explained to them in their stained glass windows, passion and morality plays and devotions to Jesus and Mary. However, a commission could assess that such an age could lack certain points as "receivers" of the teaching. Mention has been made already of a "receiving" community formed by certain "parasite" ideas mixed with the true Gospel and Tradition. History has shown often how "prophets" or small minorities can still spring up to oppose a non-Gospel direction. These factors too have to be taken into consideration in forming criteria for judging. A genuine Gospel community while respecting and revering the Tradition passed down should also have an orientation to the "signs of the times" which can, after all, be the Holy Spirit speaking to it through the positive strengths of a given age.

There is a great danger with the relentless and often ruthless snowballing effects of Tradition and traditions that there exist no criteria for evaluating what is passed down and hence people's reaction "we can give up none of them". A selection and assessment such as the Hierarchy of Truths can free people to judge which truths are of greater importance than others. In the theory I have tried to enunciate such a categorisation can be made with no traditions being rejected. More, an ordering of important truths can be attempted which will ultimately improve ecumenical dialogue.

There should be no reason why all christian churches should not place on the top of their Hierarchies of Truths the positive teachings of christianity - Jesus as Saviour, the triune God, the Ten Commandments, to love one's neighbour, to forgive one's enemies; but once teachings that are debatable among such churches start appearing on the hierarchical list it would be good if the individual churches had the humility to accept the commission, appointed by their own church, in its objective ordering of their list of truths. Then it becomes possible for churches in unity negotiations to say: "We agree on the top twenty or thirty truths on the hierarchical list, it is time to admit each other to communion."

While I would not rule out corporate reunion, I think we live in an age of pluralism where ecumenism would seem to be more and more an agreement on essentials yet retaining one's traditions. It also fits well into the undergirding Unity and diversity principle. This is precisely what the method examined in this book attempts to do once two churches have agreed to union on the basis of the top twenty or thirty truths held in common then the degree of intercommunion, sharing of buildings, ministerial swapping and training will depend on each church's decisions as well as each church's independence of the other.

This returns us to the questions raised in the earlier chapters. For those who have specialist knowledge the Roman Catholic Church does have a sort of Hierarchy of Truths. Obviously what its mainstream theologian and church leaders agree on as infallible teaching must be the core of catholic belief. In the non-infallible area there are gradations (or used to be in the older text books) of a teaching "close to the Faith" "commonly held" and so on down a fairly rarefied scale plus teachings that just disappeared when they were so obviously outdated, such as usury, but never officially came off the books by public apology or by rescinding in official declarations from roman papal congregations. Canonists often graded documents by some fourteen or so degrees of importance depending on wording, by whom they were signed from which congregation they emanated and so on. It took a specialist to fathom the distinctions and was lost on the average catholic followed then by a resigned reaction among many to follow one's conscience.

Perhaps one of the unforeseen consequences of a neo-Augustinian control of the papal curia and presenting all catholic teaching, great and small, as necessary for catholic belief is the scepticism and reservation of many if not most catholics to roman decrees. Despite the many good features of the new catechism, there has been a constantly informed criticism that to present all catholic doctrine on a level playing field as necessary for belief has been one of the deterrents to widespread catholic acceptance, an argument developed in this book. It continues and aggravates a polarization already in the Church instead of the appeal a Hierarchy of Truths would have to people reflecting on the seriousness certain truths have in their lives and the commitment they would share when they found millions of others having the same conviction around truths at the top of such an Hierarchy. (14)

Ecumenism is also possible still allowing for pluriformities of Tradition and belief to exist among those who already have agreement at the top level of the Hierarchy.

A further and more disastrous consequence of the neo-Augustinian control allowing for no deviates is not just the already increased polarizations that have and are occurring but a search by church members for smaller communities either within or sometimes outside the official Church. The same phenomenon is taking place within the mainstream protestant churches and, of course, is helping the proliferation of many fundamentalist church fringe groups. The very thing the present regime in power in Rome wants is the continuation of the Church. By its intransigence it is not only hastening the possible disintegration of the institutional Church, and creating grassroots who disagree with it in large numbers, but by its inability to deal with the pluriformity of ecumenism it is encouraging, at least indirectly, the same reaction within the protestant mainstream churches weakened by the disunity among themselves and needing the strength a roman unity could give all of them but not in the present model Rome has helped to create.

Perhaps it is the intention of the Holy Spirit that the 21st century Church should be predominantly a unity of hundreds of thousands of smaller christian communities; but history still tells us Christ's prayer for unity is more than just a combined meeting of christian or religious orientated collectives. It is a unity arising from a universal agreement about Christ and his mission despite the pluriformity of approaches and theologies.

The criteria I have presented in this book are merely suggestions: but I feel deeply a kickstart must be given again to theological ecumenism. There is today among all Christians an unbearable thirst for communion. It would be wonderful if that great teaching of the Second Vatican Council, the Hierarchy of Truths, could be enlisted to help assuage that thirst. I would see it as a permanent adjusting mechanism for the imbalances of the past - a corrective without having to deny the past or prove it necessarily wrong.

I have written this book to enable catholics to look again at their Church and see what are the essential structures and what are the non-essentials. These latter may not need change; but the reformers must be free to see the possibilities if the "signs of the times" necessitate change. He or she will be able to see how much can change, how much cannot. Instead of having Tradition thrown in his or her face, but never defined exactly, he or she can assess Tradition's importance by its hierarchy on the scale of Truth.

Richard McBrien puts his finger pertinently on the changes and the need for re-evaluation when he says: - "In the years before the beginning of the second christian millennium and before the pontificate of Gregory VII in particular, popes functioned largely in the role of mediator, resolving disputes and conflicts over belief and discipline "by common consent" (John Paul II, Ut Unum Sint N. 95). They did not claim for themselves alone the title Vicar of Christ. They did not appoint Bishops (except in neighbouring Dioceses or in Missionary Dioceses founded by the Roman Church). They did not govern through a Roman curia. They did not impose or enforce clerical celibacy. They did not write encyclicals or authorize catechisms for the universal Church. They did not retain for themselves alone the power of canonization of saints. As a rule, they did not convene or preside over ecumenical councils - and certainly not the major doctrinal councils of Nicea (325) Constantinople (381) Ephesus (381) and Chalcedon (451). The papacy of the third christian millennium will more probably resemble the papacy of the first millennium than of the second, but it will surely be different from both as the Church faces new and currently unforeseen pastoral circumstances, challenges, and opportunities in the decades and centuries to come." (15)

How will the laity be restored to their rightful place in decision making? It will of course be a long process in an institution as old as the Church. Before embarking on systems, one has first to clear the ground. The Hierarchy of Truths in which lay people have a say and are listened to as of right is one way of clearing the ground. The other is a credible way of electing the bishops by the clergy and laity of a given diocese. If these two processes were put in motion many things would gradually present themselves in the way the twenty first century is moving just as Nicholas of Cusa was suggesting in the fifteenth century (pp. 121-122). Less things are set in concrete than many Catholics especially still emerging from a pre-Vatican II Church think.

Suggested ways of electing bishops without establishing what is the tradition and its legitimate alterations may only lead to factionalism and even trying to solve what is teaching and Tradition on a one person/one vote basis which need not be a true or valid solution. No, establish the flexible tradition (Hierarchy of Truths). Concomitant with electing bishops and the possibility becomes present of the balance of laity now restoring itself in a Church left unsteady after a too rigid interpretation of what magisterium really is with a too inflexible appointment of the magisterium. The bishops, the pope all have an authentic place in Christ's Church but need a re-assessment only a proper Hierarchy of Truths can give.

We have looked at how the Church developed from the time of Jesus and the apostles and, although more loosely than many roman catholic theologians postulate, there were certain underlying principles that were always there even if at those early stages they were implicit rather than explicit. In following these principles through we saw how the Tradition developed and how, at times, traditions, thought to be more genuinely original than they were, became confused with what we know, at least now, was the real Tradition. The appraisal of this Tradition as it grew were appraisers who at times were not as representative of the wider community as they should have been. A re-appraisal seems necessary of the whole Tradition in order that the Tradition become more respected.

I have written this book in the hope that a re-appraisal of our own deeper Tradition can give us a tool for forging ahead in the future. It is necessary to restore a balance that was there originally; but often time and distance have distorted it in the eyes of many catholics and christians. Congar put it well when he said: "At the present time, we live in a period of rediscovery in breadth and depth of our own heritage. And this is due above all to the active investigation of the permanent sources: scripture, tradition, the Fathers, the liturgy. This return to the sources has already begun to emphasize the necessity of a certain rediscovery of the two religious realities by reference to which authority must find out the truth about itself. They are the living God active among us through His grace and the holy community and brotherhood (sic, written in 1964) of the faithful. It is by setting authority in an authentic relationship with these two christian realities that we shall be able to go beyond legalism which consists of seeing the formal validity of phenomena without penetrating to their meaning. Since we are returning to a pre-Constantinian situation in a pagan world, since we are aware that we are in a minority and that it is our task to preach Jesus Christ, we are doubtless approaching a period in which, while we shall lose nothing of value acquired in the course of history, we shall recover wholly evangelical ways of exercising authority in the new world in which God calls us to serve him." (16)

1. Abbott, W M S.J. (Ed). Documents of Vatican II <u>Revelation.</u> pp. 117-118
2. Rohr, R. <u>Radical Grace</u> (Ed. J. Feister). Cincinnati, St Anthony Messenger Press. 1995. p. 318
3. Ibid p. 715
4. Ibid p. 715
5. McBrien, R. <u>Catholicism.</u> San Francisco, Harper. 1994. p. 367
6. Baum, G. <u>New Horizon, Theology essays.</u> New York, Paulist Press. 1972. pp. 150-151
7. Rahner, K. <u>"The historical dimension in theology"</u> in Theology Digest Sesquicentennial Issue. 1968. p. 31
8. Henn, William. "Hierarchy of truths twenty years later." <u>Theological Studies</u> 48. 1987. p. 440
9. Ibid., pp. 464-465
10. Henn, William. <u>Hierarchy of Truths according to Yves Congar O.P.</u> Rome, Gregorian University, 1987. p. 188. William Henn in the same book observes that in his year of writing two books and thirty articles had appeared on the subject. Many after 1987 are named in the bibliography of this book; but the authors seem to be groping for answers.
11. Ibid, XI.
12. Tillard, J M R. <u>The Bishop of Rome</u> (transl. J. de Satge). London, SPCK. 1983. pp. 49-50.
13. Newman, J H. <u>On Consulting the Faithful on matters of Doctrine,</u> (ed. J. Coulson). London, Geoffrey Chapman. 1961.
14. Marthaler, B, notes how prior to the final draft of what is now the catechism of the Catholic Church, a provisional draft was sent to the Bishops of the world for their criticism and suggestions. "One of the main concerns expressed by the American critics was that the catechism did not respect the principle of hierarchy of truths that the General Catechetical Directory said should take into account 'on all levels" Marthaler B "Does the Catechism reflect a Hierarchy of Truths?" in <u>Introducing the Catechism of the Catholic Church: Traditional Themes and Contemporary Issues</u>. New York, Paulist Press. 1994. p. 43. This was re-echoed by many theologians throughout the world before and after the catechism's publication.
15. McBrien, R. <u>Lives of the Popes.</u> San Francisco, Harper, 1997. pp. 400-401.
16. Congar Yves O.P. <u>Power and Poverty in the Church</u>. London, Geoffrey Chapman. 1964. pp. 78-79.

SELECTED BIBLIOGRAPHY

Abbott, W, S.J. (Ed.). The Documents of Vatican II. London-Dublin, Geoffrey Chapman. 1966.

Ancient Christian Writers, newly translated and annotated by James A Kleist, S.J. Westminster MD, The Newman Bookshop,. Vol. 1, The Epistles of St Clement of Rome and St Ignatius of Antioch. 1946.

Arbuckle, G. Refounding the Church. Homebush, St Paul Publications. 1993.

Attwater, D. A Dictionary of the Popes. London, The Catholic Book Club. 1939.

Avis, Paul. The Church in the Theology of the Reformers. Atlanta, J Knox. 1981.

Banks, Robert J. Paul's Idea of Community. Grand Rapids. W. B. Endmans. 1980; Exeter. Paternoster Press. 1981.

Baum, Gregory. The Credibility of the Church Today. New York, Herder & Herder. 1968.
—— New Horizon. New York, Paulist Press. 1972.
—— Religion and Alienation. New York/Paramus/Toronto, Paulist Press. 1975.

Bausch, William J. Traditions, Tensions, Transitions in Ministry. Mystic, CT, Twenty-Third Publications. 1982

Bermejo, Luis. Towards Christian Reunion. Anand, India, Gujarat Sahitya Prakash. 1984.
—— Church, Conciliarity and Communion, Anand, India, Gujarat Sahitya Prakash. 1990.

Biemer, Gunter. <u>Newman on Tradition. London,</u> Freiburg, Herder-Burns & Oates. 1967

Black, Antony. <u>Council and Commune: The Conciliar Movement and the Fifteenth Century Heritage.</u> London, Burns & Oates, Shepherdstown, Patmos Press, 1979.

Boff, Leonardo. <u>God's Witnesses in the Heart of the World</u>. Chicago, Claret Center for Resources in Spirituality. 1981.

Bokenkotter, T. <u>A Concise History of the Catholic Church.</u> Garden City, NY, Image Books, Doubleday & Co. 1979.

Boudens, R. <u>Alfred Plummer</u> <u>Conversations with Dr Dollinger</u> 1870-1890. Leuven, Leuven University Press. 1985.

Bouyer, L<u>. The Church of God: Body of Christ and Temple of the Holy Spirit</u>. Chicago, Franciscan Herald. 1982.

Brown, P. <u>Augustine of Hippo,</u> London, Faber & Faber. 1967.

Brown, Raymond E. <u>Priest and Bishop,</u> Biblical Reflections. London/Dublin, Geoffrey Chapman. 1970.
—— <u>Biblical Reflections on Crises Facing the Church</u>. New York, Paulist. 1975. London, Darton, Longman & Todd. 1975.
—— <u>The Community of the Beloved Disciple.</u> London, Geoffrey Chapman. 1979.
—— <u>The Critical Meaning of the Bible.</u> New York, Paulist. 1981.
—— <u>The Churches the Apostles left behind</u>. New York, Paulist. 1984.

Brown, R E & Meier, J P. <u>Antioch and Rome</u>. Ramsey, NY, Paulist Press. 1983.

Brown, Raymond E, Donfried, Karl P, and Reumann, John, eds<u>. Peter in the New Testament</u>. Minneapolis, Augsburg, New York, Paulist. 1973.

Bühlmann, W. <u>The Coming of the Third Church</u>. Maryknoll, New York. 1977.

Butler, Christopher. <u>The Theology of Vatican II</u>. Revised edition. Westminster, MD, Christian Classics. 1981.

Butler, Cuthbert. The Vatican Council. Reissue. Westminster, MD. Newman. 1962.

Calvez, Jean Yves. The Social Thought of John XXIII, Chicago, Henry Regnery Co. 1964.

Caraman, Philip, S.J. University of the Nations, New York/Ramsey, Paulist Press. 1981.

Cayré, F, A.A. Manual of Patrology, transl. H Housitt AA, Paris Desclee, Vol. I, 1935, Vol. II, 1940.

Chadwick, H. The Early Church, Pelican History of the Church, Vol. I, Harmondsworth, 1967

Chadwick O. The Reformation, Pelican History of the Church, Vol. III, Harmondsworth, reprint with revision. 1972.
—— From Bossuet to Newman. Cambridge, University Press. 1987.

Chirico, Peter. Infallibility: Crossroads of Doctrine. Kansas City, Andrews & McMeel, 1977. (Reprinted with new introduction Wilmington. Del 1983).

Congar, Yves M. Lay People in the Church. Westminster, MD, Newman. 1957.
—— Power and Poverty in the Church, transl. by J Nicholson, London, Geoffrey Chapman. 1964.
—— Traditions and Traditions. New York. Macmillan. 1966.
—— I believe in the Holy Spirit. 3 Vols. New York. Seabury. 1983.

Congregation of the Doctrine of the Faith. Mysterium Ecclesiae. Acta Apostolicae Sedis 65 (1973) 396-408.

Cooke, Bernard. Ministry to Word and Sacraments. Philadelphia, Fortress. 1976.

Coriden, James A. An Introduction to Canon Law, Mahwah, NJ. Paulist Press. 1991.

Coriden, J, Green, T J, Heintschel, D E (ED). The Code of Canon Law commissioned by the Canon Law Society of America. Mahwah, NJ, Paulist Press. 1985.

Cornwell, Peter. On the River's Edge. London, Darton, Longman & Todd. 1988.

Cragg, Gerald R. The Church and the Age of Reason 1648-1789. Pelican History of the Church, Vol. IV, Harmondsworth, reprint with revisions. 1966.

Curran, Charles E. and Dyer, George J. (eds). Shared Responsibility in the Local Church. Chicago, Chicago Studies. 1970.

Cuskelly, E J, No Cowards in the Kingdom. Melbourne, Spectrum Publications. 1969.

Cwiekowski, F J. The Beginnings of the Church. Mahwah, Paulist Press. 1987.

Davis, Charles. The Temptations of Religion. London, Hodder & Stoughton. 1973.

Dawson, C. Religion and the Rise of Western Culture. Garden City, NY, Image Books, Doubleday & Co. 1958.
—— Religion and World History, Garden City, NY, Image Books, Doubleday & Co. 1975.

de Broucker, José. The Suenens Dossier - the Case for Collegiality. Dublin, Gill and Macmillan, 1970.

de Rosa, Peter. The Dark Side of the Papacy. London, Corgi Books. 1989.

de Satgé, John. Peter and the Single Church. London, SPCK, 1981.

de Vries, Wilhelm. Orient et Occident: Les structures ecclésiales vues dans l'histore des sept premiers conciles oecumeniques. Paris, Cerf. 1974.

Denzinger, H. Enchirdion Symbolorum, Editio 30. Friburg, Herder, 1955.

Dionne, J Robert. The Papacy and the Church. New York, Philosophical Library. 1987.

Dominian, Jack. Authority, London, Darton, Longman and Todd. 1981.
—— Proposals for a New Sexual Ethic, Longman and Todd. 1979

Doohan, Leonard. The Lay-Centred Church: Theology and Spirituality. Minneapolis, Winston. 1984.

Doyle, Phyllis. A History of Political Thought. London, Jonathan Cape, 1963.

Dulles, A. The Dimensions of the Church. Westminster, MD, Newman. 1967.
—— Models of the Church. Garden City, New York, Doubleday. 1974.
—— The Resilient Church. Garden City, New York, Doubleday, 1977.
—— A Church to Believe in. New York, Crossroad, 1982.

Dunn, James D G. Unity and Diversity in the New Testament. London, SCM Press. 1977.

Duquoc, Christian. Provisional Churches, transl. John Bowden. London, SCM Press. 1986.

Dvornick, F. Byzantium and the Roman Primacy. New York, Fordham University Press. 1979.

Eliade, Mircea. The Sacred and the Profane. New York, 1951

Empie, Paul C & T Austin Murphy Ed, Papal Primacy and the Universal Church, Lutherans and Catholics in Dialogue V. Minneapolis, Augsburg Publishing House. 1974.

Eno, Robert B. Teaching Authority in the Early Church. Wilmington, Michael Glazier, 1984
—— The Rise of the Papacy. Wilmington, Michael Glazier, 1990

Eusebius, "The History of the Church", transl. G A Williamson. Harmondsworth, Penguin Classics, 1965

Evans, L, OP Ed. Light on the Natural Law. London, Compass Books, Burns & Oates. 1965.

Evans, Robert F. One and Holy: The Church in Latin Patristic Thought. SPCK. 1972.

Femiano, S D. Infallibility of the Laity. New York, Herder & Herder. 1967.

Fox, Matthew. <u>On Becoming a Musical, Mystical Bear.</u> New York/Paramus Paulist Press/Deus Book, 1972.

Gager, John G. <u>Kingdom and Community: The Social World of Early Christianity</u>. Englewood Cliffs, NJ, Prentice-Hall, 1975.

Galbraith, John Kenneth, <u>The Anatomy of Power</u>. London, Corgi Books. 1985.

Garraty, J A & Gay, P Ed. <u>The Columbia History of the World</u>, NY, Harper & Row, 1972.

Grabowski, S J. <u>The Church: An Introduction to the Theology of St Augustine</u>. St Louis. Herder. 1957.

Granfield, Patrick. <u>Ecclesial Cybernetics: A Study of Democracy in the Church.</u> New York, Macmillan. 1973.
—— <u>The Papacy in Transition.</u> Dublin, Gill and Macmillan. 1981.

Grant, Michael. <u>History of Rome</u>. London, Weidenfeld and Nicholson. 1981.

Grant, Robert. <u>The Apostolic Fathers</u>, Vol. IV. London, Nelson & Sons. 1966.

Gratsch, Edward J. <u>Where Peter is: A survey of Ecclesiology</u>. Staten Island, New York. Alba House. 1975.

Gryson, Roger. <u>The Ministry of Women in the Early Church</u>. Collegeville, Minn. Liturgical, 1976.

Harrington, Daniel J. <u>God's People in Christ: New Testament Perspectives on the Church and Judaism</u>. Philadelphia, Fortress. 1980.

Harris, P, Hastings, A, Horgan, J, Keane L & Nowell, R. <u>On Human Life - An Examination of 'Humanae Vitae'</u>. London, Burns & Oates Ltd. 1968.

Hasler, August Bernhard. <u>How the Pope Became Infallible</u>, Intro by Hans Kung, transl. by Peter Heinegg. Garden City, NY, Doubleday & Co. 1981.

Hastings, Adrian. Church and Ministry. Kampala, Gaba. 1972.

Hazard, Paul. The European Mind 1680-1715. Harmondsworth, Penguin, 1964.

Hebblethwaite, Peter. The Runaway Church: Post-Conciliar Growth or Decline. New York, Seabury. 1975.

Hellwig, Monika. What are the Theologians Saying?, Cincinnati, Ohio, Pflaum/Standard. 1970.

Henn, W, OFM CAP. The Hierarchy of Truths According to Yves Congar OP. Rome, Gregorian University. 1987.

Holmes, J D & Bickers, B W. A Short History of the Catholic Church. Tunbridge Wells, Burns & Oates. 1983.

Holmberg, Bengt. Paul and Power: The Structure of Authority and Power in the Primitive Church as Reflected in the Pauline Epistles. Philadelphia, Fortress, 1980.

Hughes, G. God of Surprises. London, Darton, Longman and Todd. 1996. (2nd Ed).

Husslein, J. Social Wellsprings Vol. II. Milwaukee, Bruce, 1942.

Illich, I. The Church: Change and Development. Chicago, Urban Training Center. 1970.

James, William. The Varieties of Religious Experience. London, Collins Fontana. 1971.

Jay, Eric G. The Church, Vol. I. London, SPCK, 1977; Vol. II, London, SPCK, 1978.

Jedin, H. Ecumenical Councils of the Catholic Church. Glen Rock, Paulist Press. 1961.

Joly, R. Le Dossier d'Ignace d'Antioche. Bruxelles, editions de l'Universite de Bruxelles. 1979.

Jungmann, Josef A, SJ. The Early Liturgy to the time of Gregory the Great. London, Darton, Longman & Todd. 1960.

Käsemann, Ernst. New Testament Questions for Today. Philadelphia, Fortress. 1963; London, SCM. 1969.

Kelber, Werner H. The Oral and Written Gospel. Philadelphia, Fortress, 1983.

Kelly, J N D. Early Christian Creeds. Harlow, Essex, Longman. 1981.

Ker, Ian. John Henry Newman. Oxford, New York, Oxford University Press. 1988.

Knowles, David. What is Mysticism? London, Burns & Oates. 1967.

Komonchak, Joseph A, Jossua, JP, Alberigo, G Ed. Transl by M J O'Donnell. The Reception of Vatican II. Washington DC, Catholic University of America Press. 1987.

Kung, Hans. Structures of the Church. London, Burns & Oates. 1965.
—— The Church. London, Burns & Oates. 1968.
—— Infallible?, transl. by Eric Mosbacher. London, Collins. 1971.
—— Infallible? An Inquiry. Garden City, New York, Doubleday. 1971.
—— Christianity, transl by John Bowden. London, SCM Press. 1995.

Lash, Nicholas. Change in Focus. London, Sheed & Ward. 1973.
—— Voices of Authority. London, Sheed & Ward. 1976.

Latourelle, R. Christ and the Church: Signs of Salvation. Staten Island, New York. Alba House. 1972.

Lemaire, André. Les ministères aux origines de l'Église - Naissance de la triple hierarchie: êveques, presbyteres, diacres. Paris, Cerf. 1971.

Lohse, Eduard. The First Christians: Their Beginnings, Writings, and Beliefs. Philadelphia, Fortress. 1983.

McBrien, Richard P. Do we need the Church? New York, Harper and Row. 1969.
—— Catholicism. San Francisco, Harper 1994.
—— Lives of the Popes. San Francisco, Harper. 1997.

McKelvey, R J. The New Temple: The Church in the New Testament. London, Oxford, 1969.

McKenzie, John L. Authority in the Church. London/ Dublin/Melbourne, Geoffrey Chapman. 1966.
—— Dictionary of the Bible. Geoffrey Chapman, London/ Dublin. 1965.

Mackey, J P. Tradition and Change in the Church. Dublin & Sydney, Logos Books, Gill & Son. 1968.

Mahoney, J. The Making of Moral Theology. Oxford University Press. 1987.

Metz, J B. The Emergent Church. New York, Crossroad. 1981.

Meyendorff, J. Catholicity and the Church. Crestwood, New York, St Vladimir. 1983.

Meyer, Harding and Vischer, Lukas, eds. Growth in Agreement: Reports and Agreed Statements of Ecumenical Conversations on a World Level. Ecumenical Documents II. New York, Paulist, Geneva, World Council of Churches. 1984.

Minus, Paul. The Catholic Rediscovery of Protestantism: A History of Roman Catholic Ecumenical Pioneering. New York, Paulist. 1976.

Mirgeler, A. Mutations of Western Christianity. London, Compass, Burns & Oates. 1964.

Mobbs, F. Beyond its Authority? Alexandria, NSW, E. J. Dwyer. 1997.

Moran, G. Theology of Revelation. London, Burns & Oates. 1967.

Moss, H St L B. The Birth of the Middle Ages 395-814. Oxford University Press. 1963.

Muller, Alois. Obedience in the Church. London, Compass Books, Burns & Oates. 1966.

Murphy, John L. The General Councils of the Church. Milwaukee, Bruce Publishing Co. 1960.

Neill, S. A History of Christian Missions. Harmondsworth, Pelican History of the Church, Vol. VI. 1964.

Newman, J H. An Essay on the Development of Christian Doctrine. Garden City, NY, Image Books, Doubleday & Co. 1960.
—— On Consulting the Faithful in Matters of Doctrine, Ed & Intro. by John Coulson. London, Geoffrey Chapman. 1961.

O'Meara, T F, OP. Theology of Ministry. New York, Paulist Press. 1983.

O'Sullivan, Owen O.F.M. Cap. The Silent Schism. Dublin, Gill & MacMillan. 1997.

Oakley, F. Council over Pope? Towards a Provisional Ecclesiology. New York, Herder and Herder. 1969.
—— The Western Church in the Later Middle Ages. Ithaca, New York, Cornell University Press. 1979.

Pagels, Elaine. The Gnostic Gospels. Harmondsworth, Penguin. 1982.

Pannenberg, W. The Church. Philadelphia, Westminster Press, 1983.

Philips, Gérard. L'Eglise et son mystère au IIe Concile du Vatican, 2 Vols. Paris, Desclée. 1967.

Plummer, Alfred. Conversations with Dr Dollinger 1870-1890, Ed Robrecht Boudens, Leuven, University Press, 1985.

Pope Paul VI. Encyclical Letter on the Regulation of Birth Humanae Vitae. Acta Apostolicae Sedis LX (1968) 481-503

Rahner, K. The Shape of the Church to come. New York, Seabury. 1974.
—— Theological Investigations, Vol. XIV. transl. David Bourke. London, Darton, Longman & Todd. 1976.
—— Concern for the Church, Vol. 20, Theological Investigations, transl. Edward Quinn. London, Darton, Longman & Todd. 1981.

Rokeah, M. The Open and Closed Mind. New York, Basic Books, 1960

Rohr, R. Radical Grace (Ed. J.B. Feister). Cincinnati, St Anthony Messenger Press. 1995.

Sanks, T Howland. Authority in the Church, a Study in Changing Paradigms, American Academy of Religion, Dissertation Series, Number two. Missoula, Mont. 1974.

Schillebeeckx, Edward. Ministry: Leadership in the Community of Jesus. New York, Crossroad. 1981.
—— The Church with a Human Face. London, SCM Press. 1985.

Schlette, H R. Towards a Theology of Religions. New York, Herder & Herder. 1966.

Schnackenburg, Rudolf. The Church in the New Testament. New York, Herder & Herder. 1965.

Sewell, Brocard. The Vatican Oracle. London, Duckworth. 1970.

Shorter, Aylward. The Theology of Mission. Notre Dame, Ind. Fides. 1972.

Smart, Ninian. The Philosophy of Religion. New York, Random House. 1970.

Southern, R W. Western Society and the Church in the Middle Ages. Pelican History of the Church, Vol. II, Harmondsworth, reprint. 1976.

Stanley, David M. The Apostolic Church in the New Testament. Westminster, MD, Newman. 1965.

Stevenson J. Ed, A New Eusebius - Documents illustrating the History of the Church to AD 337. New Edition revised by W H C Frend. London, SPCK. 1987.

Stransky Thomas F, and Sheerin, John B., eds. Doing Truth in Charity. Statements of Pope Paul VI, Popes John Paul I, John Paul II and the Secretariat for Promoting Christian Unity 1964-1980 Ecumenical Documents I. New York, Paulist. 1982.

Suenens, Cardinal. Coresponsibility in the Church, transl. F Martin. London, Burns & Oates. 1968.

Sullivan, Francis A. Magisterium: Teaching Office in the Catholic Church. New York, Paulist. 1983.

—— Creative Fidelity. New York/Mahwah, Paulist Press, 1996.
—— From Apostles To Bishops. Mahwah, Paulist. 2001.

Tarnas, Richard. The Passion of the Western Mind. New York, Ballantine Books. 1993.

Tavard, G H. The Quest for Catholicity: A Study in Anglicanism. New York, Herder & Herder. 1964.

Tierney, B. The Crisis of Church and State 1050-1300. Englewood Cliffs, NJ, Prentice-Hall. 1964.
—— Foundations of the Conciliar Theory. Cambridge University Press. 1955. Reprint 1968.
—— The Origins of Papal Infallibility (1150-1350). Leiden. Brills. 1973.

Tillard, J M R, OP. The Bishop of Rome, transl. by John de Satge. London, SPCK, 1983.

Torrance, T F. Kingdom and Church: A Study in the Theology of the Reformation. Edinburgh, Oliver and Boyd. 1956.

Torres Sergio and Eagleson, John eds. The Challenge of Basic Christian Communities. Maryknoll, New York, Orbis. 1981.

Tracy, D. (Ed.) with Hans Kung & Johann B. Metz. Toward Vatican III. Dublin, Gill and Macmillan. 1978.

Trevor, M. Prophets and Guardians. London, Hollis & Carter. 1969.

Tyson, Joseph B. A Study of Early Christianity. New York, The Macmillan Company. 1973

Ullman, W. The Growth of Papal Government in the Middle Ages. London, Methuen. 1955.
—— A Short History of the Papacy in the Middle Ages. London, Methuen & Co. 1974.

Von Campenhausen, Hans. Ecclesiastical Authority and Spiritual Power in the Church of the First Three Centuries. London, A & C Black. 1969.

Vidler, A R. The Church in an Age of Revolution. Pelican History of the Church, Vol. V, Harmondsworth, reprint with revisions. 1974.

Walgrave, J H. <u>Newman, The Theologian.</u> London, Geoffrey Chapman. 1960.

Walker, John Baptist. <u>Christianity, an End to Magic.</u> London, Darton, Longman & Todd. 1972.

Walsh, Michael and Davies, Brian Ed. <u>Proclaiming Justice and Peace.</u> Mystic, CT, Twenty Third Publications. 1991.

Ware, Timothy. <u>The Orthodox Church.</u> Harmondsworth, Penguin, reprinted with revision. 1969.

Wilken, Robert L. <u>The Myth of Christian Beginnings</u>. London, SCM Press. 1979.

ARTICLES

Alberigo, Giuseppe. "The Christian Situation after Vatican II", <u>in The Reception of Vatican II</u>, Ed by Giuseppe Alberigo, J P Jossua and Joseph A Komonchak. Washington DC, The Catholic University of America Press. 1987. pp. 1-24

Bickerman, E J & Morton Smith. "The Later Roman Empire" in <u>The Columbia History of the World</u>, Ed J A Garraty & P Gay. NY, Harper & Row. 1972. pp. 221-236

Black, Antony. "The Council of Basle and the Second Vatican Council" in <u>Studies in Church History.</u> Cambridge University Press. 1971. Vol. 7, pp. 229-234

Brown, Raymond. "Episkope and Episkopos: the New Testament Evidence" in <u>Theological Studies,</u> Vol. 41, No. 2. June 1980. pp. 322-338

Cardman, Francine. "Cyprian and Rome: The Controversy over Baptism" in <u>Concilium Religion in the Eighties,</u> Ed Hans Kung and Jurgen Moltmann. Edinburgh, J & T Clark Ltd, New York, The Seabury Press, October 1982. pp. 33-39

Daley, Brian E, S.J. "Structures of Charity: Bishops' Gatherings and the See of Rome in the Early Church", in <u>Episcopal Conferences,</u> Ed Thomas J Reese SF. Washington DC, Georgetown University Press. 1989. pp. 25sq

Delooz, Pierre. "Has popular religion in the West come to an end?" in <u>Pro Mundi Vita Studies</u>, No. 6. November 1988. pp. 41-44

Duggan, Paul E. "The Hierarchy of Truths" <u>Priest.</u> June 1994. pp. 12-18

Dulles, Avery, S.J. "The Reception of Vatican II at the Extraordinary Synod of 1985", pp. 349-363, appendix in <u>The Reception of Vatican II</u> edited by Komonchak, J A, Jossua J P, & Alberigo, G. Washington DC, Catholic University of America Press. 1987

Franzen, August. "The Council of Constance", <u>Concilium</u> No. 7. pp. 29-68. (Ed. R. Aubert). Glen Rock, NJ, Paulist. 1965

Fuhrmann, H. "False Decretals", <u>Catholic Encyclopedia</u>, Vol. 5, p. 820-824. New York, McGraw-Hill Book Co. 1967

Gerest, C. "Spiritual Authority in the 11th and 12th Centuries, <u>Concilium Theology in an Age of Renewal</u>. p. 87

Girault, Rene. "The Reception of Ecumenism" <u>in The Reception of Vatican II</u>, Ed by G Alberigo, J P Jossua and Joseph A Komonchak. Washington DC, Catholic University of America Press. 1987. pp. 137-167

Granfield, P. "The Church as Institution: A Reformulated Model", <u>Journal of Ecumenical Studies</u> 16. 1978. pp. 425-447

Henn, W. O.F.M. Cap. "The Hierarchy of Truths Twenty Years Later" in <u>Theological Studies</u> 48. 1987. pp. 439-471

Jay, Eric. "From Presbyter-Bishops to Bishops and Presbyters" in <u>Second Century</u>, Vol. 1, No. 3. Fall 1981. pp. 125-162

Marthaler, B.L. "Does the Catechism Reflect a Hierarchy of Truths?" in <u>Introducing the Catechism of the Catholic Church: Traditional Themes and Contemporary Issues</u>. New York, Paulist Press. 1994. pp. 43-55

Nedoncélle, M., Aubert R. Congar, Y.M., et al. "L'ecclesésiologie au XIXe siècle". <u>Unam Sanctam</u>, no, 34. Paris, Cerf. 1960.

Oakley, Francis. "The 'New Conciliarism' and its Implications: A Problem of History and Hermenentics". Journal of Ecumencial Studies, 8. 1971. pp. 815-840.

O'Donohoe, James A. "Tridentine Seminary Legislation – its Sources and its Formation". Louvain, Publications Universitaires de Louvain. 1957. (Biblio Ephemeridum Theologicarum Lovaniensium Vol IX)

Orsy, L. S.J. "Magisterium: Assent and Dissent" in Theological Studies 48. 1987. pp. 473-497.

Osiek, Carolyn. "The Second Century through the eyes of Hermas: continuity and Change" in Biblical Theology Bulletin, Vol. 20, No. 3. Fall 1990. pp. 116-122

Parker, Christian. "Popular Religion in Latin America" in Pro Mundi Vita Studies, No. 6. November 1988. pp. 18-28

Rahner, K. S.J. "Open Questions in Dogma considered by the Institutional Church as definitively answered" in Catholic Mind. March 1979 pp. 8-26.
—— "Hierarchy of Truths" in Theology Digest. Fall 1982. pp. 227-229
—— "Philosophy and Philosophizing in Theology" pp. 17-29 and "The Historical Dimension in Theology" pp. 30-42 in Theology Digest sesquicentennial issue. 1968

Remmers, Johannes. 'Apostolic Succession: an Attribute of the Whole Church' in Concilium, Vol. 4, No. 4. April 1968. pp. 20-27

Rutayisire, Paul. "Popular religiosity or the failure of the missionary churches?" in Pro Mundi Vita Studies, No. 6. November 1988. pp. 37-40

Sanders, James A. "Fundamentalism and the Church: Theological Crisis for Mainline Protestants" in Biblical Theology Bulletin, Vol. 18, No. 2. April 1988. pp. 43-49

Schnackenburg, Rudolf. "Community Co-operation in the New Testament" in Concilium, Vol. 7, No. 8, Burns & Oates. Sept. 1972. pp. 9-19

Sherwin-White, A. "The Roman Background of Early Christianity" in Concilium, Vol. 7, No. 3, Burns & Oates, pp. 5-9

Tierney, Brian. "The Idea of Representation in the Medieval Councils of the West" in <u>Concilium</u>, "The Ecumenical Council". NY, Seabury Press. 1983

Tracy, D. "Fragments and Forms: Universality and Particularity Today" in <u>Concilium, The Church in Fragments: Towards what kind of Unity?</u> 1997/3. pp. 122-129.

Valadier, P. S.J. "Universal Catechism Published In French", <u>London Tablet</u>, 21 November 1982. pp. 1480-1481

Van Iersel. "Who according to the New Testament has the say in the Church?", <u>Concilium</u>, V.148. pp. 11-17.

Vandervelde, George. "BEM and the Hierarchy of Truths: A Vatican Contribution to the Reception Process" in <u>Journal of Ecumenical Studies</u> 25. 1988. pp. 74-84.

Vooght, Paul de. "The Results of Recent Historical Research on Conciliarism". <u>Concilium</u> no. 64. <u>Papal Ministry in the Church</u>. (Ed. H. Kung) pp. 148-157. New York, Herder & Herder. 1971

Ward, Benedicta, "Monastic Spirituality, Monasticism" in <u>A Dictionary of Christian Spirituality</u>, Ed Gordon S Wakefield. London, SCM Press Ltd. 1983. pp. 267-269

Wright, David F. "Why were the Montanists condemned?" in <u>Themelios 2</u> 1976. pp. 15-22

Wilken, Robert L. "Diversity and Unity in Early Christianity" in <u>The Second Century</u>, Vol. 1, No. 2. Summer 1981. pp. 101-110

ABOUT THE AUTHOR

John Broadbent holds a doctorate in religious studies and history from Louvain University, Belgium. He has an honours degree in history from Victoria University, Wellington, New Zealand and a post-graduate degree in education. He was Rector of the Holy Cross College, Mosgiel, the diocesan seminary for New Zealand (1987 to 1991) and taught at Otago University as well as the Pacific Regional Seminary, University of the South Pacific, and the Pacific Theological College, Suva, Fiji. He was ordained in 1955 and has spent half the time since then in parish work.

Printed in the United States
1416600003B/67-306